AF580163

Nineteenth Century German Drawings from the Grand Duchy of Baden

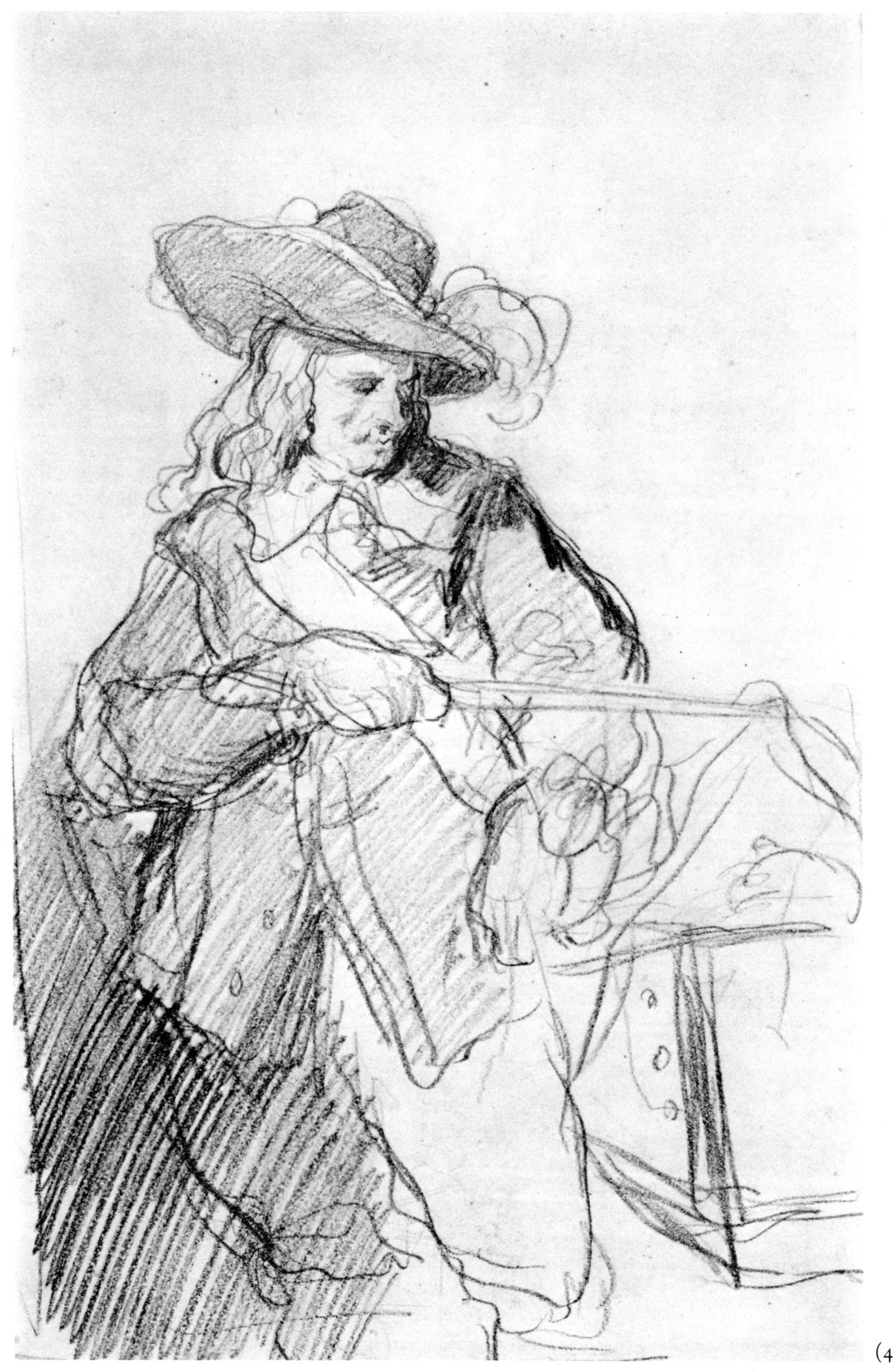

(4)

Cincinnati Art Museum
1983

Nineteenth Century German Drawings from the Grand Duchy of Baden

Lent by the
Staatliche Kunsthalle Karlsruhe

Introduction and Catalogue by
Rudolf Theilmann

Translated by
Robert E. Lewis

Contents

Exhibition dates: June 25 to September 4, 1983.

Library of Congress Catalogue Card No. 83-071462.

Photography by Elvira Beick.
Typesetting by Craftsman Type Inc.
Offset lithography by Young and Klein, Inc.
Typography and design by Noel Martin.

The Cincinnati Art Museum gratefully acknowledges operational support from the Cincinnati Fine Arts Fund and the Ohio Arts Council.

Acknowledgments

This exhibition, *Nineteenth Century German Drawings from the Grand Duchy of Baden,* is generously lent to the Cincinnati Art Museum by the Staatliche Kunsthalle Karlsruhe in celebration of the Museum's Centennial. In 1980, the Museum lent from its holdings a group of drawings by Carl Friedrich Lessing to Karlsruhe on the occasion of the one-hundredth anniversary of the artist's death. This sharing of exhibitions between two art museums demonstrates a cultural exchange of the highest order. The work of some of the romantic period's most impressive, but little known, draftsmen is placed before the public, and the two catalogues record for posterity the scholarship directed towards these artists and their graphic works. And, lastly, not only does this loan of Karlsruhe drawings complete the two-part exchange, but it salutes in 1983 the German-American Tricentennial Jubilee that commemorates the first German settlers to arrive in this country.

Many individuals contributed to this catalogue and exhibition, and all of them deserve the Cincinnati Art Museum's gratitude. We would like to thank Dr. Horst Vey, Director of the Staatliche Kunsthalle, and his staff for their many contributions and the cordial spirit of sharing that made this exhibition possible. We are particularly grateful to Dr. Rudolf Theilmann, Curator of Prints and Drawings at the Staatliche Kunsthalle, who not only selected the drawings but also wrote the catalogue.

We are deeply indebted to Robert E. Lewis for his expert translation of the catalogue's German manuscript and to Jonathan Z. Kamholtz, Associate Professor of English and Comparative Literature at the University of Cincinnati, for his careful editing of the text and catalogue entries.

Members of the Museum staff played indispensable and varied roles. Kristin L. Spangenberg, Curator of Prints, Drawings and Photographs, edited the footnotes, exhibition and bibliographical references. Elisabeth Batchelor, the Museum's Conservator, offered invaluable suggestions on the translation of technical references. Lucy Woodworth expertly typed the final manuscript, and Noel Martin provided the excellent catalogue design. Kristin Spangenberg skillfully coordinated the production of the catalogue and exhibition arrangements with the help of the Curatorial Assistant, Dennis Kiel.

Millard F. Rogers, Jr., Director
Cincinnati Art Museum

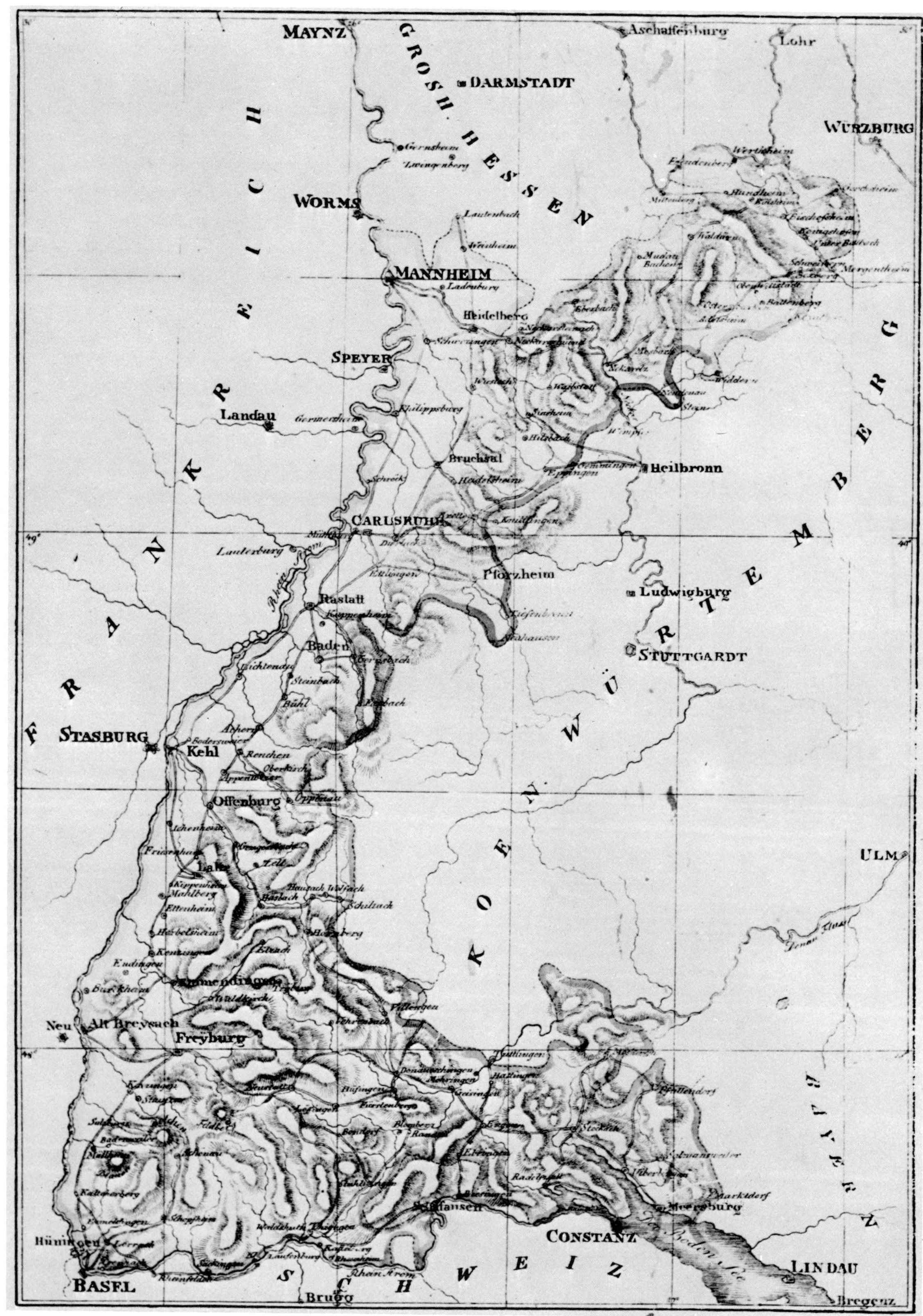

Map of Baden, 1812, Badisches Generallandesarchiv, Karlsruhe.

Foreword

We would like to express our gratitude to the Cincinnati Art Museum for its generous assistance to us in 1980, enabling us to commemorate the hundredth anniversary of the death of Carl Friedrich Lessing (1808-1880), the historical and landscape painter from Düsseldorf and former Director of our museum. Seventy-five of his best drawings from the Cincinnati collection were made accessible to the German public for the first time since they disappeared from Karlsruhe in 1880. Just how Lessing's drawings happened to come to Cincinnati is explained by Director Millard F. Rogers, Jr. in the preface to our exhibition catalogue, *Carl Friedrich Lessing 1808-1880*.

This exhibition of drawings and watercolors from the former Grand Duchy of Baden covering the years 1825-1880 is our grateful response to Cincinnati's loan. It is our gift to all art lovers of Ohio in honor of the Centennial of the Cincinnati Art Museum celebrated in 1981. We hope that the selection we have made will delight all viewers and win many new friends for Baden and its landscape.

German art was especially prized in Cincinnati even during the lifetime of the artists represented. In the 1867 spring issue of the *Kunstchronik*, a widely read journal in Germany, correspondent G. W. N. reported from Cincinnati:

> *Even though a public exhibition of American art has never taken place in Cincinnati, there is certainly no other city west of the Alleghenies in which such a sound and lively concern for the cultivation of the fine arts exists as it does here. In addition to the splendid architecture of commercial edifices, there are private painting collections of great value . . . . One of the peculiar aspects of these collections is the fact that the Germans, especially the Düsseldorf artists, are more strongly represented than other artists. Even though this may surprise our readers, it is definitely true that, with the possible exception of the capitals of German states, Cincinnati has a greater number of German works of art than any other city in the world. This fact is related in one respect to the large number of Germans residing in our city, but more so to the efforts of one or two art connoisseurs and to the influence of Mr. Whittredge and other artists who have spent some time in Europe and who have been instrumental in bringing these paintings here.*[1]

Another tie between these artworks and the Cincinnati audience stems from the fact that some visitors to this exhibition may have ancestors who emigrated to America from the Grand Duchy of Baden at the same time that these works were being created. These emigrants were nearly always forced to leave for economic or political reasons, having experienced the effects of a world much more disturbing than the one depicted in these generally optimistic drawings; the magical aura of the works in this exhibition is only part of the reality of that disturbing era. The dark side, however, was not portrayed by the artists represented here. Even if it had been, would the ensuing works have been acquired by the Grand Ducal Print Room? Those persons interested in a fuller understanding of the period are invited to consult the historical archives in Karlsruhe, where they will find a wealth of information concerning these turbulent years of the nineteenth century.

Our American viewers will surely wish to know something concerning the history and the character of the Karlsruhe collections: Like so many public art collections in Germany today, the Staatliche Kunsthalle Karlsruhe (known as the Großherzogliche Kunsthalle between 1846 and 1919 and the Badische Kunsthalle between 1919 and 1933) was formed around the princely private art collection of the Margraves (later the Grand Dukes) of Baden. The present collection thus reflects the personal tastes of the rulers of Baden as well as historical and dynastic developments. Many paintings, prints and drawings in the collection can be traced back to the princes of the seventeenth century; among the holdings in the Print Room, those early-acquired works include Hans Baldung Grien's silverpoint sketch book, the thousand-odd designs for stained glass panels from Switzerland and the upper Rhine, Albrecht Dürer's prints, and German sixteenth century drawings. Many works can also be traced to the interests of the women who married into the ruling family. Indeed, the most enthusiastic collector of the House of Baden was the versatile and intellectually gifted Princess Caroline Louise of Hesse-Darmstadt (1723-83), who married Margrave Karl Friedrich (1728-1811) in 1751. Despite her own drawing abilities, she did not collect drawings and prints but rather concentrated on Dutch and French painting.

When, around 1800, Napoleon rearranged the countless territories which made up the Holy Roman Empire, the margravate of Baden was expanded to cover three and a half times its former territory and its political significance grew in proportion. In 1806 Margrave Karl Friedrich received the title of Grand Duke. Until 1918, when the German Empire became a republic, he and his successors ruled a long, narrow land which stretched from Lake Constance in the south to

Mannheim in the north, and which extended to the northeast almost as far as Würzburg. At its narrowest, the territory was only about eleven miles wide; there, Fort Rastatt was situated, where the hopes of the 1849 republican revolutionaries of Baden lie buried.

The city of Karlsruhe was founded in 1715 by Karl Friedrich's grandfather in the midst of a forest. The residence of the rulers of Baden, it became increasingly important during the nineteenth century. In 1786 Karl Friedrich had erected in the vicinity of his palace a drawing academy which provided models for young artists to copy selected from among the numerous engravings, woodcuts, drawings, paintings, and plaster casts in the possession of the ruling family. We still retain in our collection a number of carefully executed drawings by these young eighteenth century students. The court painter Philipp Jakob Becker (1759-1829) was the director of the academy as well as overseer of the margrave's art treasurers, which, with the special permission of the margrave, he was able to show to occasional visitors. In 1830 the overseer, the landscape painter and engraver Carl Ludwig Frommel (nos. 12-13), who had been given the title of "gallery director," energetically set about organizing the museum rooms in the academy, above all putting the collection of prints and drawings in order. In 1836 the first catalogue of engravings was completed. The elegant print cabinets which were built at that time are still in use today.

More and more visitors appeared on those days when the collections were open to the general public. With each year the rooms seemed less adequate and it became clear that it was time to build a new, independent museum. Between 1836 and 1846 the first wing was constructed, situated at right angles to the drawing academy. Grand Duke Leopold had the various collections of his family transferred to the new museum so that he might encourage "the education and enrichment of the people" as much as possible in the future. The detailed catalogues of the mid 1800's enable one to reconstruct the contents of the individual rooms and the manner of their display: the numerous plaster casts of classical and renaissance sculpture, antique vases, terra-cotta pieces, bronzes and marbles, the "antiquities of the fatherland" (i.e., medieval works of all types, most of which had fallen to the collections of the Grand Dukes as a result of the secularization of Church properties in 1803), the paintings of various European schools (Dutch, French, German, and Italian), the cartoons of German neo-classical fresco artists (a particularly rare and prized aspect of our holdings), and finally the cabinets containing drawings and prints of every kind.

Interestingly, the new building was not called a "museum." Rather, it was given a German name which had been proposed around 1800 as a translation of the original Greek: "Kunsthalle," or "hall of the arts." The parliament of Baden voted unanimously to provide funds for its erection, making this the first public German museum constructed under the auspices of a parliament, rather than by personal order of a monarch. In 1845 the graphic collections were installed in both of the upstairs corridors. There the works were "exhibited in sliding frames which facilitated the changing of displays and thus were made accessible to the public." However, the installation of the graphic collections was not as satisfactory as that of the other works of art and was changed several times even during Frommel's directorship. Furthermore, because of financial difficulties, the construction of the entire museum, which was to have consisted of four wings surrounding a central courtyard, was halted after the first wing had been built. The second wing was finally constructed during 1894-96 and the third in 1908-09. The old drawing academy, which was to be replaced by the new fourth wing, remained standing until 1944, when it was destroyed during an air raid. We hope to complete the museum within the next few years.

Even though the construction of the museum came to a temporary standstill in 1846, Grand Duke Friedrich I nevertheless established, in 1854, a new art academy in Karlsruhe in order to provide his residential city with a fitting artistic center. The first director of the Karlsruhe Academy, the landscape artist Johann Wilhelm Schirmer (nos. 37-43), was not from Baden but rather from Düsseldorf. After Frommel's retirement in 1858, Schirmer persuaded his old Düsseldorf friend Lessing to come to Karlsruhe to assume the directorship of the Kunsthalle. One of the early students enrolled at the Academy from 1867 to 1868 was Laudon Rives Longworth of Cincinnati whose father Joseph Longworth (1813-1883) purchased Lessing's artistic estate in 1880 and gave it to the Cincinnati Art Museum in 1882.

From the outset, the directors of the museum not only viewed themselves as preservers of older works of art, but turned their attention to contemporary matters as well. In the very first catalogue of paintings, which appeared in 1833, Frommel pointed out that "the people's participation in and their love for art is especially heightened by the continuing acquisition of works by our national artists." Frommel's openness towards his contemporaries was also beneficial to the drawing collection. To be sure the emphasis was similar to that placed on the painting collection: preference was given to works by "artists of the fatherland," which meant artists of the region, the Grand Duchy of Baden. Occasionally one recognized the German "neighbors"—the principalities of Württemberg, Bavaria, the Palatinate, and Hesse. The only "distant" art center to be noticed was Düsseldorf on the lower Rhine. As "archenemies" of the German people, the French were of course totally ignored—both the academic painters as well as the moderns such as Eugène Delacroix, Gustave Courbet, and the Barbizon painters.

Thus, the catalogue of our collection of nineteenth century drawings, which was published in 1978 and lists as many as 8,400 individual works and 127 sketchbooks with 5,500 additional sheets, represents almost exclusively artists from Baden. Even though this compendium appears to be exhaustive and complete, deeper analysis will reveal that no attempt at all was made to achieve comprehensive representation even of local artists. How could an attempt have been made under the circumstances? At first, Frommel had to do his work alone; only later was he assisted by the young court painter Ernst Richard (1819-1899). Frommel had the support of an acquisitions committee and enjoyed the continual, vivid interest of the Grand Duke, but being responsible for the day-to-day operation of the entire museum, Frommel was simply unable to follow artistic developments throughout the Duchy and to collect drawings in a systematic way. Lessing faced similar working conditions, but in contrast to Frommel he viewed his post at the museum as a sinecure and left much of the day-to-day business to the competence of Ernst Richard. The estates of Baden artists were acquired—but not Lessing's. The conservative taste of the era had of course a significant influence on the nineteenth century painter-directors; but are not art historians also children of their times? In 1863 a portfolio of drawings by Carl Philipp Fohr, an important early romantic artist of the Heidelberg school, was not acquired because it was "considered to have no merit," a decision we still regret today. Works by the Berlin artist Adolf Menzel, considered by many today to be the foremost German draftsman of the nineteenth century, were not acquired until 1928. Despite the close family ties between the ruling families of both Baden and Prussia, the residents of Karlsruhe seem to have known nothing about art in Berlin. During his long rule between 1852 and 1907, Grand Duke Friedrich I received five albums containing watercolors and drawings by contemporary artists, but the artists represented in these albums were almost exclusively from Baden. Such albums were favorite gifts of that time. Selections from the "Heidelberger Friedrich—Luisen—Album" of 1856 and "Friedrich I Album" of 1877 are included in this exhibition.

This regional narrowness was not overcome until 1920, when the last of the Museum's painter-directors, Hans Thoma (nos. 57-63), was succeeded by an art historian. In the past sixty years the acquisition efforts of the Print Room have been extended to include other regions and artistic centers of Germany as well as France. However, the emphasis which arose during the previous century, the concentration on works from the territory of Baden, works such as those contained in this exhibition, will surely remain unchanged. And why not? A collection as old as that of the Kunsthalle is entitled to have its particular features. Are not such nice particularities precisely those which lend character to an art collection, which make it unique and attractive?

The visitors to this exhibition and the readers of this catalogue owe a debt of gratitude to one person from our side of the Atlantic, our colleague Dr. Rudolf Theilmann. For over a decade he has devoted himself to the acquisition of expertise in the field of the art of Baden. With his accustomed energy and thoroughness he set about choosing the drawings for this exhibition, writing the catalogue, and organizing all the details.

Horst Vey, Director,
Staatliche Kunsthalle Karlsruhe

1. *Kunstchronik* II, 1867, pp. 152-53.

Introduction

The seventy-one graphic works from the Grand Duchy of Baden in this exhibition range in style from late romanticism to realism. The works selected date from the years 1825 to 1880, a period deliberately chosen to correspond to the active career of Carl Friedrich Lessing (1808-1880), the landscape and historical painter whose extensive graphic oeuvre is preserved in the Cincinnati Art Museum. In 1980 the Staatliche Kunsthalle Karlsruhe held a survey exhibition of Lessing's drawings. The present exhibition contains examples of the creative works of thirty-three of Lessing's contemporaries, many of whom were personally acquainted with Lessing, some of whom were his close friends. All of the artists chosen were either born in Baden and produced a majority of their work in the province which Lessing chose as his home, or else they resided in Baden at a time when their artistic development was profoundly affected, when they were students or instructors at the Karlsruhe Academy.

The influential Academies of Munich and Düsseldorf dominated the German artistic world in the nineteenth century and for a number of years determined the styles and values of German art. In the extreme southwestern part of the country, however, especially during the first half of the century, artistic matters proceeded quietly and without spectacular developments. The cause of this tranquillity did not lie in the scarcity of talent to be found in those artists working in Baden; rather it was due to the absence of an appropriate educational institution. It was not until the Karlsruhe Academy opened in 1854 that the situation was fundamentally changed. Johann Wilhelm Schirmer (nos. 37-43), then professor at the Düsseldorf Academy and an influential landscape painter in his own right, was named the first director of the new institution. The Karlsruhe Academy promptly acquired a reputation as an institution striving for the same high goals as the Düsseldorf Academy. Soon Karlsruhe began to play an important and respected role among Germany's leading artistic centers. Art critics had high expectations of the Academy, and works produced by students and instructors alike were noted and reviewed in contemporary journals. Founded by Regent, later Grand Duke, Friedrich I and in the succeeding years supported and encouraged by this art-loving monarch, the Academy developed rapidly under the leadership of Schirmer, who was well-known as an educator and as a landscape artist outside of Germany (especially in Switzerland, Scandanavia, and the United States). It was he who provided the solid basis for the school's development in the following years. By the end of the century critics proclaimed that "the artistic production of Karlsruhe [was] along with that of Munich the freshest and most vigorous in all of Germany."[1] The reputation of Karlsruhe was closely bound to the achievements of Gustav Schönleber (nos. 47-48). After he assumed the directorship of the Academy in 1880, Karlsruhe became known as a leading center of landscape painting, one from which "a multitude of excellent young artists emerged."[2]

It was primarily landscape artists who carried the Academy's reputation far beyond the borders of Baden. One example was the Norwegian painter Hans Frederik Gude, Schirmer's successor and Schönleber's predecessor, who for sixteen years taught the landscape class in Karlsruhe. During the first half of the century, Carl Kuntz and Carl Ludwig Frommel (nos. 12-13) called critical attention to the artistic production of their Baden homeland. Although figure and portrait painting, and to a lesser extent historical painting, were practiced in the area, landscapes constituted the preponderance of artwork produced in the Grand Duchy. Even after the Academy was established, there was no instructor of portrait or historical painting who had anything other than a local reputation; thus landscape painting continued to dominate.

This situation is strongly reflected in the paintings and drawings of the era as well. With the exception of Josef Durm (nos. 5-6), Friedrich Eisenlohr (nos. 8-9), and Heinrich Hübsch (no. 17), all of whom were leading architects, the artists represented in this exhibition devoted themselves primarily to painting, to carefully composed and executed watercolors (nos. 7, 12, 16, 37, 38, 65-66) or large and complex drawings (nos. 40-42). In many cases, however, the drawings and watercolors were not conceived in advance as autonomous works of art, but rather served to formulate the concept of a picture or fixed one stage in the development of a composition in another medium. A solid foundation in drawing, however, was a *sine qua non* of the contemporary academic curriculum and a rigid prerequisite for admission to the advanced classes in painting. In his "Statutes of the Art School of Karlsruhe" ("Statuten der Großherzoglich Badischen Kunst-Schule in Carlsruhe") dated July 12, 1856, Schirmer prescribed a highly regulated course of instruction:

> § *4: In the elementary classes students are taught how to copy other drawings. This is the preliminary study which leads to the following class in the antique study collection. In the*

antique study collection they practice drawing after models: ancient and modern busts, statues, and individual parts of the body.

§ 5: Drawing is the common basis for the study of art, especially drawing after antique models, for no student of the Academy is permitted to enter a class in a specialty area before having completed the course in the antique study collection. The only students excepted from this rule are those who have presented a portfolio demonstrating that they have acquired elsewhere the knowledge and skills which are taught in the antique collection.

§ 6: During the winter months all students are to participate in group exercises in drawing from live models; these sessions will take place in the evening under artificial lights. Special attention is to be paid to these exercises, and it will be required that all students of the Academy, with the exception of those in the elementary classes, shall take part in them. . . .

§ 8: In order to proceed from the preparatory painting class into the advanced class, a student is required to prepare a portfolio of painted studies of busts and nudes taken from life and one completely finished drawing of original composition. A student is accepted into the advanced class only if this portfolio demonstrates clearly that he has a talent suited for an artistic career.

§ 9: For those students . . . who wish to devote themselves to landscape painting, classes will also be taught in the application of their nature studies to drawings and to small pictures . . . .[3]

The graphic medium served primarily as a means of familiarizing the beginning artist with his trade, and particularly as the medium through which the student learned human anatomy and human proportion. Nor were the numerous landscape drawings created in Düsseldorf after the 1830's when Lessing and Schirmer began to teach there considered to be independent, finished works of art; their only purpose was to serve the artist as readily accessible sources for ambitious works. In preparing complicated compositions, the artist referred to these drawings and to the descriptive notes that accompanied them. Landscape artists in particular collected a horde of suitable motifs during their periodic travels noted in the catalogue, and these motifs were used when the situation called for them. Soon no traveling artist was to be found without his sketch book.

The absorption with landscape which is so evident in this exhibition is found in the entire German-speaking world of 1830-1900 and is typical of Karlsruhe and the upper Rhine. Even before Schirmer was called to be the director of the new Academy, several painters and draftsmen of the region had begun to concentrate on the representation of their native countryside. Most notable among them was the influential painter and Gemäldegalerie director Carl Ludwig Frommel. Although Frommel's oeuvre as a painter is not particularly extensive, he executed a number of drawings and watercolors which are regarded as some of the most outstanding examples of Baden's artistic production in the first half of the nineteenth century. Like the great majority of his contemporaries, Frommel accepted the basic structures and followed the compositional models of classical landscape without question. At the same time, however, his idealistically formulated watercolors of Baden's fortresses and castles go beyond this formulaic academic canon. His self-imposed goal of systematically recording all of the important medieval structures of the Grand Duchy forced him to abandon familiar, idealized landscape compositions and to adopt a more objective stance towards his subject matter. This project, which required him to note accurately both the buildings and their sites, led Frommel to adopt a style which was closely related to the objective reproduction of his subject matter, although he did not commit himself to a rigorous and consistent realism. On the whole, his works suggest a romanticized reflection about these monuments standing as witnesses to the history of his homeland.

By the time Schirmer and Lessing, the two most prominent landscape artists in the Düsseldorf Academy, came to Karlsruhe, they had already devoted themselves with passionate intensity to the study of botany and geology. This type of scientific knowledge was indispensable to the development of their artistic work. While they paid much attention to the accurate reproduction of the various components of their landscapes, the oil paintings based on their preliminary drawings seldom contained topographically accurate representations of particular sites. Instead, they reflected artistically sublimated concepts of these sites. This combination of both realistic and idealistic compositional principles is characteristic of the landscape school of the Düsseldorf Academy as well as of the Karlsruhe Academy.

As the director of the Academy and as the supervisor of the landscape class, Johann Wilhelm Schirmer continued the tradition of landscape art embraced by Frommel and brought it to its first stage of brilliance. He too oscillated between idealism and a type of realism which, although dominated by an artistic formalism nonetheless had a direct relationship with nature. After his trip to Italy (1839-40), Schirmer painted large and thematically complex landscapes. In the 1850's he created a series of landscapes with Biblical motifs. Both of these types of paintings consistently incorporate conventional models of ideal and historical landscape representation (nos. 39, 41-42). At the same time, Schirmer executed a more modest, rapidly and confidently type of nature study (no. 43), although this type of study remained for him merely a tool which might later be used as part of his larger, more formal compositions. Among his later works, Schirmer considered the large, idealistic landscapes which he carefully executed in charcoal to be as important as his oil paintings. He may have intentionally dispensed with the sensuality of color in his religious paintings in order to stress their serious philosophy. The human truths of the foreground are made to harmonize with the implied philosophical content of an idealized landscape in the background.

Among Schirmer's pupils it was Emil Lugo who most clearly absorbed the predominant stylistic traits of his teacher and then adapted and expanded them to suit his own purposes. None of Schirmer's other students pursued the idiom of heroic landscape with the same amount of enthusiasm, passion, and intellectual devotion. Lugo's drawings from the 1860's are rigidly composed and free of any decorative frills (no. 28). This method of drawing, reduced mainly to contrasts between black and white, stands in direct contrast with his painted works. Lugo's oils were influenced by Arnold Böcklin and they reveal a far more lyrical approach to nature. During his studies in Karlsruhe, Lugo devoted himself to painstakingly executed detail studies, but in later years he denounced his earlier attempts to capture "the reality of nature." On February 15, 1870, he expressed his reformed views in a letter to Susette Hauptmann, the wife of Moritz Hauptmann, the organist of the church of St. Thomas in Leipzig and a musical theorist and composer of some note:

> *Nature is . . . not the goal, not the Queen of art, rather she is the servant of art . . . . Thus I find the current infatuation of modern artists for so-called "nature studies" to be senseless and ridiculous. What good do they do anyway? They should be doing* art *studies. If the study of art is at all alive in them, then the Spirit of Art will be alive, and this Spirit will find within itself, with little need of external assistance, the means of creating works that live . . . .*[4]

Lugo's ideas are further clarified by a comment he once made about Phillip Röth, another of Schirmer's students:

> *I think R. is a decent, sensitive landscape artist, but he sees nature as being both picturesque and as just being "everyday." For me nature is a festival, a holiday, and I want it to lift me up out of the drudgery of everyday life.*[5]

For Phillip Röth (nos. 34-36), whose everyday, banal themes were criticized by Lugo, the subject matter of a painting served merely as a vehicle for his subtly orchestrated coloring. As a twenty-year-old student he made a dramatic debut with outstanding examples of his impressive graphic talents. After moving to Munich in 1871, he was quickly accepted into the circles of the most important representatives of the Munich landscape school, among them Eduard Schleich, Adolf Lier, Carl Ebert, Dietrich Langko, and Josef Wenglein. These artists represented a type of landscape art which had been initiated by the Barbizon painters, one which rejected the models and themes which had been common since the baroque in favor of a more intimate landscape. These artists no longer took the superiority of the classical-heroic Italian countryside for granted. Many artists, including Röth, began to discover that their own local countryside sufficed and, often using a small format, began to paint their surroundings with a heightened artistic sensitivity. Very early in his artistic career, Röth had trained his eye by studying the precursors of French Impressionism such as Rousseau, Daubigny, Corot and Troyon. In addition he had concentrated on the Dutch landscape artists of the seventeenth century including Ruisdael, Hobbema, and van Goyen, systematically copying these artists' works using chalk, watercolor, and gouache. Röth had absolutely no desire to visit Italy, the traditional paradise of landscape painters; for him the subject matter of a painting was of little consequence. Instead he concentrated chiefly on solving purely artistic problems posed by painting and drawing. In the final analysis this commitment to art for art's sake went hand-in-hand with a rejection of the importance of subject matter. Until now, landscape painting had consisted largely of a skillful combination of various elements. Röth, however, was content to depict what he found at hand. Eugen Bracht, a fellow-student and an old friend of Röth's, characterized the latter's method of painting with ironic finesse:

> *Röth's art and style was based on "the perfect motif" – one that nature preserves intact for you. All you have to do is find it. Once you've found it, you're safe.*[6]

This preference for simple and unaffected themes taken

directly from immediate surroundings is clearly seen in the early works of Hans Thoma, executed until around 1870 (no. 58). Along with Röth, Bracht, and Lugo, Thoma was one of the most significant of Schirmer's students, and quickly proved himself to be a talented draftsman with an interest in both landscape and figure drawing. In his early years he systematically recorded the vicinity of his home town of Bernau in the southern Black Forest, making meticulous studies of trees, grasses, rocks, tranquil forest paths, and the peaks which characterized this nearly untouched mountain wilderness. He drew his familiar surroundings with an astoundingly secure sense of line and a firm grasp of both proportion and organization of the picture surface. No object was beneath his dignity. By faithfully drawing every detail, he made himself examine it carefully with a high sense of objectivity. Thoma approached portraiture with the same kind of intensity, using as models primarily his mother (no. 60), his sister Agathe, or his wife Cella (no. 63), but also other relatives, acquaintances, or fellow artists (no. 57). He was able to portray persons whom he knew well with a great deal of psychological insight and without resorting to flattering corrections.

The uncompromising realism of this phase of Thoma's artistic development put him on a collision course with the official policies of contemporary art. In 1869 an exhibition of his paintings in the Karlsruhe Kunstverein was strongly criticized by the members of this artistic association. The board of trustees, of which Lessing was a member, denounced "this new development of Thoma's," thus echoing an opinion "which had often been expressed to the artist by professors at the Academy."[7] While his drawings received critical praise and acceptance (in March 1870 he sold five works to the Kunstverein and to Grand Duchess Luise for a total of 100 guilders), his paintings continued for some time to receive devastating condemnation. He was mocked as "a mere imitator of Courbet and his crowd,"[8] and the critics assigned him to the circle of "those artists who worship Absolute Realism" and who produced "works which, totally disregarding anything other than 'truth to nature,' portrayed nothing but revolting eyesores."[9]

At first Thoma made precise drawings in pencil, but after the late 1860's he turned more and more to softer pastels or to the more delicate medium of brush and ink. This change of media corresponded to his striving for painterly expression—a tendency which is reflected in his frequent choice of colored papers. Toward the middle of the 1870's, Thoma began to distance himself somewhat in style and content from the realism of his early years and the vehemence of the criticism began gradually to abate. His paintings and drawings, and later his prints, reflected themes taken from Germanic mythology and from his personal philosophy based on Christian principles. The increase of literary content in his works corresponded to a decrease in their formal aesthetic qualities. But when his work became more abstract and idealized, Thoma—apparently without realizing it—lost touch with the real, external world, which was essential to his art.

The appointment of Gustav Schönleber as Director of the Academy in 1880, succeeding the Norwegian landscape artist Hans Frederik Gude, provided the ideal conditions for the development of realistic landscape art at the Karlsruhe Academy. During the thirty-odd years that he held this position, Schönleber spread Karlsruhe's reputation as a center for realistic landscape painting far beyond the borders of the German-speaking world. Scores of students from England, Austria, Switzerland, America, and the Scandinavian countries, testify to the tremendous attraction of Schönleber's name. The appeal of his instructional technique must have elicited the envy and disdain of many of the students in the other art classes. Members of the portraiture class of the historical painter Ferdinand Keller viewed the landscape students with increasing dismay, fearing "the advance of Naturalism against the idealistic constructs taken from Fantasy and History which until then had dominated the Fine Arts."[10] Their contempt was expressed in the *bon mot:* "I'm giving up art for good; I've decided to paint landscapes."[11] For them the term "'landscape artist' was so insulting an epithet that it simply could not be uttered."[12] Since this exhibition ends with the year 1880, Schönleber is represented by only two early drawings (nos. 47-48). Even though they were executed before his studies in Munich, they indicate clearly the first stages of an approach which later would blossom into a completely realistic style. His drawings of the old section of Eßlingen with its partially decayed half-timbered houses point to his later works, in which architectural motifs provide the impetus for the artistic composition. The early series of views from Eßlingen is impressive because of the extremely secure, even masterful control of line and wash. Even though these works are primarily objective and documentary, Schönleber achieves a pleasant mood of intimacy by the effective addition of a few strokes of wash.

Far removed from the realistic developments of Thoma and Schönleber and totally separated from the heated debates concerning contemporary art, a few artists retained an older, traditional approach to landscape composition. Among these were Wilhelm Klose (nos. 22-23), who was strongly influenced by Carl Rottmann, and Ernst Schweinfurth (no. 53), who was devoted to the classical landscape of Italy. Despite their highly accomplished refinements in the technique of monochrome, Theodor Verhas' views of the Heidelberg Castle also still adhere to the conventional rules of idealistic compositions (nos. 65-66).

Through his acutely perceptive architectural compositions, Karl Weysser made a unique contribution to the art of the time. His three thousand drawings of buildings in southwestern Germany, in Hesse, and in Alsace are of inestimable archival value in today's efforts towards historical conservation and restoration. Numerous reconstruction and restoration projects have been based on his absolutely reliable records. His early study of the facade of Heidelberg Castle (no. 67), despite its hesitancy and a few technical deficiencies, gives an indication of his later drawing style—one which strives for absolute faithfulness without wasting effort on fussy details.

All of the various aspects of nineteenth century landscape art can easily be documented by superb examples in the collection of the Kunsthalle, but neither portraits nor figure studies—whether individual studies, genre scenes, or historical composition—can be found in such quantity nor with such quality. The reasons for this scarcity have already been mentioned: first, there was no indigenous tradition cultivated by leading artists which could have been developed during the course of the century; second, the Academy was rather late in hiring an accomplished and well-known artist to take over this aspect of instruction.

In 1809 the "patriotic-religious" reform movement of the Nazarenes was organized to oppose classicism. The spirit and mood of this movement, consciously devoted to the style of the old masters, are most clearly to be found in the portraits of Marie Ellenrieder (nos. 10-11), an accomplished artist who had, however, no direct followers in Baden. The angelic innocence of her figures, free of all earthly and human imperfections, testifies to her deeply felt religious convictions. Her portraits show idealized figures with little trace of individuality. The gestures of her figures express an internal, naive piety totally divorced from both animated ecstasy and from intellectual reflection. These images are characterized by a modesty and quiet grace far removed from everyday reality.

The portraits of Friedrich Mosbrugger are completely different. They show tangible personalities taken directly from life itself and presented in surprising and unconventional poses or postures. In one of our examples, the artist depicts himself while suffering a toothache, calling his viewers' attention to the state of his health and seeking to gain their sympathy for his misery (no. 30). In another, he takes the perspective of a voyeur to peek in upon his brother in a relaxed pose within his sparely furnished study (no. 29). Whatever the subject matter, one notices Mosbrugger's attempts to communicate feelings and actions by simple artistic means. Mosbrugger's art has nothing at all in common with the missionary fervor of the orthodox Nazarenes. His themes are taken from the world of tangible reality, and demonstrate his admiration for the Dutch genre painters of the seventeenth century.

Portraiture during the Biedermeier years is represented in this exhibition by four outstanding examples: the brush and ink drawings of Franz Xaver Winterhalter (nos. 68-70) and the technically brilliant watercolor by Johann Grund (no. 15). Winterhalter's later, large portraits were commissioned by the aristocracy and established his reputation throughout Europe. The portraits in this exhibition are surprising in their intimacy; the naturalness of representation shows clearly that Winterhalter had no need to satisfy the vanity of his subjects, although one does notice that he was keenly interested in fashionable accessories, such as the puffed sleeves or the striking hairdo of the young lady (no. 69). Winterhalter chose brush and ink to facilitate lithographic reproduction of his work, a medium he used to portray numerous members of the ruling family of the Grand Duchy.

Executed at almost the same time as Winterhalter's portraits, Grund's watercolor of his young wife (no. 15) is a fascinating *tour de force*. This picture acquires its extraordinary aesthetic intensity primarily from the contrast between the broad, loose execution of the woman's dress and the painstakingly and delicately modeled face which, leaning slightly to the left from the central axis, seems to open softly upwards like a flower emerging from the dark surface of the bodice. Recalling the perfection of miniature painting, Grund's brush technique lends magical charm to the lady's youthful beauty. This work was surely conceived from the outset as a finished, autonomous work of art, not just as a study or a sketch for a larger painting.

With the exception of Jakob Goetzenburger's impressive cartoon designs for the murals in the festival hall of the University of Bonn, there are few noteworthy examples of historical paintings in the Grand Duchy of Baden. The ruling family rarely handed out official commissions for public buildings. As a result, conditions in Baden were hardly conducive to a steady development of this type of art, although it had been cultivated at Germany's other academies, especially in Düsseldorf and Munich, during the first half of the nineteenth century. For a while it seemed as if Moritz von Schwind would be able to overcome these difficulties and to develop this neglected art form; after all, he received the commission to execute the murals in the grand entrance hall of the newly-erected Gemäldegalerie (the first wing of the current Kunsthalle) in 1838, and a few years later undertook a cycle of figure compositions in the former Ständehaus, the parliament building. But this independently-minded artist, bitterly disappointed at losing his bid to decorate the Baden-Baden Trinkhalle to his competitor Jakob Goetzenburger, left Karlsruhe after spending only four years in the city he once had highly praised. Schwind's compositions are infused with an abundance of creative fantasy, but every now and then one is unpleasantly jarred by the dry, conventional style of some of his drawings (no. 54). Schwind's finished pictures lack the playful *élan* evident in his quickly improvised pen and ink sketches. But one should also take into consideration the accurate caricatures he executed in Karlsruhe; these drawings use sharp wit and biting irony to attack human weaknesses without ever seriously injuring the dignity of the persons represented (no. 56).

In the early 1850's, Heinrich Hübsch succeeded in attracting Rudolf Gleichauf to Karlsruhe and finally gave the Academy a well-known figure painter. Gleichauf subsequently decorated with frescoes several public buildings in Karlsruhe designed by Hübsch and Durm. He represents the link between Schwind and Ferdinand Keller, the influential and renowned historical artist of the Bismark era. Gleichauf himself was not a significant draftsman; his oeuvre is almost totally restricted to figure studies for frescoes and pictures of peasants in costume. His autonomous compositions in a style like the one included in this exhibition (no. 14) are very rare. Here one sees the type of line prevalent in works by the late Nazarenes and finds indications that Gleichauf was influenced by the circle of Heinrich Maria von Hess, Julius Schnorr von Carolsfeld, and Edward von Steinle.

Adolf Schrödter, who for some time was active in Düsseldorf and Frankfurt am Main, joined Lessing and Schirmer in giving the artistic life of Baden a fresh impetus in the late 1850's. Both his home and that of Lessing, who had a suite of rooms in the north wing of the Gemäldegalerie, became the center of Karlsruhe's social life. A few Academy students including Thoma had access to this circle of painters, musicians (Johannes Brahms, Clara Schumann, Ferdinand Hiller), poets (Turgenev, Berthold Auerbach, Gustav Freytag), actors (Eduard Devrient), and scientists (Rudolf Redtenbacher). With the exception of a few portraits (nos. 49-50) and some literary subjects, Schrödter followed Barthel Beham in drawing mainly fantastic arabesques and several series of figurative allegories, mostly variations on the themes of his joys in wine, fellowship, and conviviality (no. 51).

Schrödter and nearly all the other figure painters and portraitists in the Grand Duchy held themselves aloof from any kind of artistic confrontation with contemporary social or political issues. The great majority of the artists included in this exhibition consciously avoided any direct, unfiltered representation of the real, physical, everyday, commonplace world. Neither the artists' view of their roles as artists nor the public's perceptions of the basic problems of the day had undergone a shift, leaving their artistic realism bereft of social context. Their intentions and goals had little to do with programmatic realism. However, in contrast to the finished oil paintings of the day, the drawings of these artists, whether they followed a basically idealistic or a fundamentally realistic theory of art, allow us to look discretely over their shoulders and to become acquainted with a variety of individual styles and working methods. A series of related sketches can often give precise information concerning the development of a complex composition, or it can show the stages that an artist went through in arriving at the definitive formulation of his subject.

The unpretentious and intimate nature of a drawing is part of its charm. Free as it is from constraints of fashion or economic taste, a drawing is the prime witness to artistic thought. When a creative act finds its first expression, when for the first time it takes on tangible form, it does so on paper.

Rudolf Theilmann

1. Paul Schultze-Naumburg, "Karlsruher Kunstleben," in *Kunst für Alle* IX (1894), p. 135.
2. Ibid.
3. Theilmann, 1971, pp. 288-89.
4. Beringer, 1925, p. 42.
5. Beringer, 1912, p. 85.
6. Theilmann, 1973, p. 42.
7. Minutes of the Vorstand (board of trustees) of the Karlsruhe Kunstverein, October 8, 1869.
8. *Kunstchronik* VII (1872), column 131.
9. *Dioskuren* XVII (1872), p. 238.
10. Franz Hein, *Willie und Weg: Lebenserinnerungen eines deutschen Malers*, Leipzig, 1924, p. 73.
11. Ibid., p. 75.
12. Ibid.

Explanatory Notes

Catalogue Order: Artists are arranged alphabetically followed by entries listed chronologically by date.

Titles: German titles are preceded by the English translation. Long descriptive titles have been shortened.

Dates: Dates without brackets appear on the work. Assigned dates appear in brackets. *Ca.* (circa) precedes uncertain dates.

Medium: Materials are individually described wherever feasible. The support is described along with its color and current condition where pertinent. Watermarks are recorded as they appear.

Measurements: Dimensions are listed in centimeters, height preceding width. Measurements represent the paper support unless otherwise specified.

Signatures and Inscriptions: Signatures and inscriptions have been transcribed as accurately as possible regardless of incorrect spelling and grammar. Virgules designate the beginning of another line.

Inventory Number: Those numbers preceded by P. K. were formerly in the Grand Ducal collection. Works acquired prior to 1935 usually have four numbers preceded by Roman numerals. Works acquired since 1935 have the year as part of the number. For example, 1964-14 would be the fourteenth object acquired in 1964.

Provenance: The source of the work appears first followed by previous owners. Collector's marks recorded in Frits Lugt's *Les Marques de collections de dessins et d'estampes* and the *Supplément* (see bibliography) are abbreviated respectively as *Lugt* and *Lugt S.*

Exhibitions: Exhibitions are listed by city and are in the Federal Republic of Germany unless otherwise specified. English spelling is used for foreign cities unless the city forms part of an institution's name. Where exhibitions are repeatedly mentioned, the abbreviated reference of city followed by date is fully cited in the bibliography. Exhibitions are listed chronologically.

Bibliography: Published references to the work with the exception of exhibition catalogues are listed chronologically. Where a reference is mentioned repeatedly, the abbreviated reference of author followed by date is fully cited in the bibliography.

Catalogue

August von Bayer

Rorschach 1803 – Karlsruhe 1875

Bayer was born on May 3, 1803, in the Swiss village of Rorschach on Lake Constance. In 1818 he began to study architecture in Zurich under Julius Stadler. After completing his professional examinations, he gained further experience during the early 1820's under Friedrich Weinbrenner in Karlsruhe. To continue his studies he moved to Munich, where he also studied figure drawing under Peter Cornelius. From Munich he made several trips into the Bavarian Alps and to Paris. Beginning in 1828 he devoted himself exclusively to architectural painting, in which he was particularly successful.

In 1839 he returned to Baden. On April 21 of that year he married Josefa Lamey, the sister of August Lamey, a high official of the Grand Duchy. Under the sponsorship of Grand Duke Leopold, he established in 1844 the Alterthumsverein für das Großherzogthum Baden, a historical preservation society, and became its first director. In 1852 he was appointed a court painter and on March 3, 1853, was named curator of the Grand Duchy, having responsibility for all its artistic treasures, whereupon he settled in Karlsruhe. In 1859 he became the director of the newly-established Altertumshalle, a historical museum. He died in Karlsruhe on February 2, 1875.

During his tenure as curator of the Grand Duchy, Bayer was responsible for the preservation and restoration of numerous buildings and sites: the Roman baths of Baden-Baden, the minster of Breisach, the monastery church in Allerheiligen, the town hall of Überlingen, and the churches on the island of Reichenau. But it is for his architectural painting that he is best known today. Bayer, whom Wilhelm Kaulen called "the last epigone of the Romantic School of German painting,"[1] produced an oeuvre whose themes are derived from pious Catholicism and from the romantic enthusiasm for medieval subjects. His works show primarily the interiors of churches, monasteries, cloisters and chapels, which he usually populated with monks or nuns. They do not reproduce actual buildings but instead are architectural fantasies which he derived from his knowledge of romanesque and gothic edifices. He achieved early fame, predominantly because of his keen interest in the multiplicity of architectural forms, which he worked out in great detail and with a fine sense of sculpturing in his use of alternating light and shadow. In the words of a contemporary critic, Bayer "achieved in architectural painting charming effects which had previously remained unobserved."[2]

1. Wilhelm Kaulen, *Freud' und Leid im Leben deutscher Künstler,* Frankfurt am Main, 1878, p. 144.
2. *Kunstblatt,* No. 6 (1836), p. 24.

1. Mournful Nun in a Cloister Garden

[*"Alles keimt und sproßt und blühet": Trauernde Nonne im Klostergarten*], 1870.

Pen and grayish-brown ink over pencil and watercolor on ivory cardboard, 30.5 x 23.3 cm.
Signed and dated in gray wash below left on the stairway: *AB/v/1870.* The following verses lower center in blue wash: *"Alles keimt und sproßt und blühet,/nur meine Welt ist todt."* (Everything is sprouting and budding and flourishing,/only my world is dead).

Provenance: Acquired 1873. Inv. no. VIII 1090.
Exhibition: Städtische Kunsthalle, Recklinghausen, *Der Einzelne und die Masse: Kunstwerke des 19. und 20. Jahrhunderts,* 1975, no. 11.
Bibliography: Theilmann and Ammann, 1978, I, p. 40, no. 145, illus. II, p. 101.

In his middle and later years, Bayer's central theme became the representation of monastic and cloistral life. This was a popular and often varied group of motifs used during the romantic period – see for example Caspar David Friedrich's *Klosterfriedhof im Schnee (Monastery Graveyard in Snow),* Carl Blechen's *Mönch in einer Felsengrotte (Monk in a Rock Grotto),* or Carl Friedrich Lessing's *Klosterhof im Schnee (Cloister Court in the Snow).* But Bayer's retreat into a quiet solitude far from the everyday world led to tormented doubts concerning his self-imposed isolation. In this drawing, these doubts are projected onto the nun who bemoans the loneliness of her uneventful life in the cloister. The fatalistic verses underscore her dissatisfaction with the way of life she has chosen. Her unspoken longings for worldly pleasures remain unfulfilled.

Eugen Bracht

Morges 1842 – Darmstadt 1921

Bracht was born on June 3, 1842, in Morges, a Swiss village on Lake Geneva. In 1850 he moved with his parents to Darmstadt, where he took drawing lessons from the court painter Friedrich Frisch. At the same time he became acquainted with August Lucas and Karl Ludwig Seeger, both of whom introduced him to landscape painting. In the summer of 1858 he and Philipp Röth (nos. 34-36) made a study trip to Heidelberg. During the next two years he studied at the Karlsruhe Academy under Johann Wilhelm Schirmer (nos. 37-43) and became a close friend of Hans Thoma (nos. 57-63). In 1861 he went on a study tour to Schwanheim and then moved to Düsseldorf. During the following year he traveled to Switzerland. In 1864, he abandoned painting and went to Verviers in Belgium to receive business training. In 1870 he moved from Belgium to Berlin, where he founded his own textile firm, "Eugen Bracht & Co." Five years later he returned to the Karlsruhe Academy and renewed his study of art, this time under Hans Frederik Gude. During the succeeding years he traveled to the Lüneburger Heide (1876, 1878), the Baltic Sea and the island of Rügen (1877), to Hoher Venn and the area of Malmedy (1879). In 1880 he undertook his first trip to the Near East, visiting the Dead Sea, the Red Sea, and the Sinai Peninsula. He returned to Karlsruhe in 1881 and a year later was appointed to succeed Christian Wilberg at

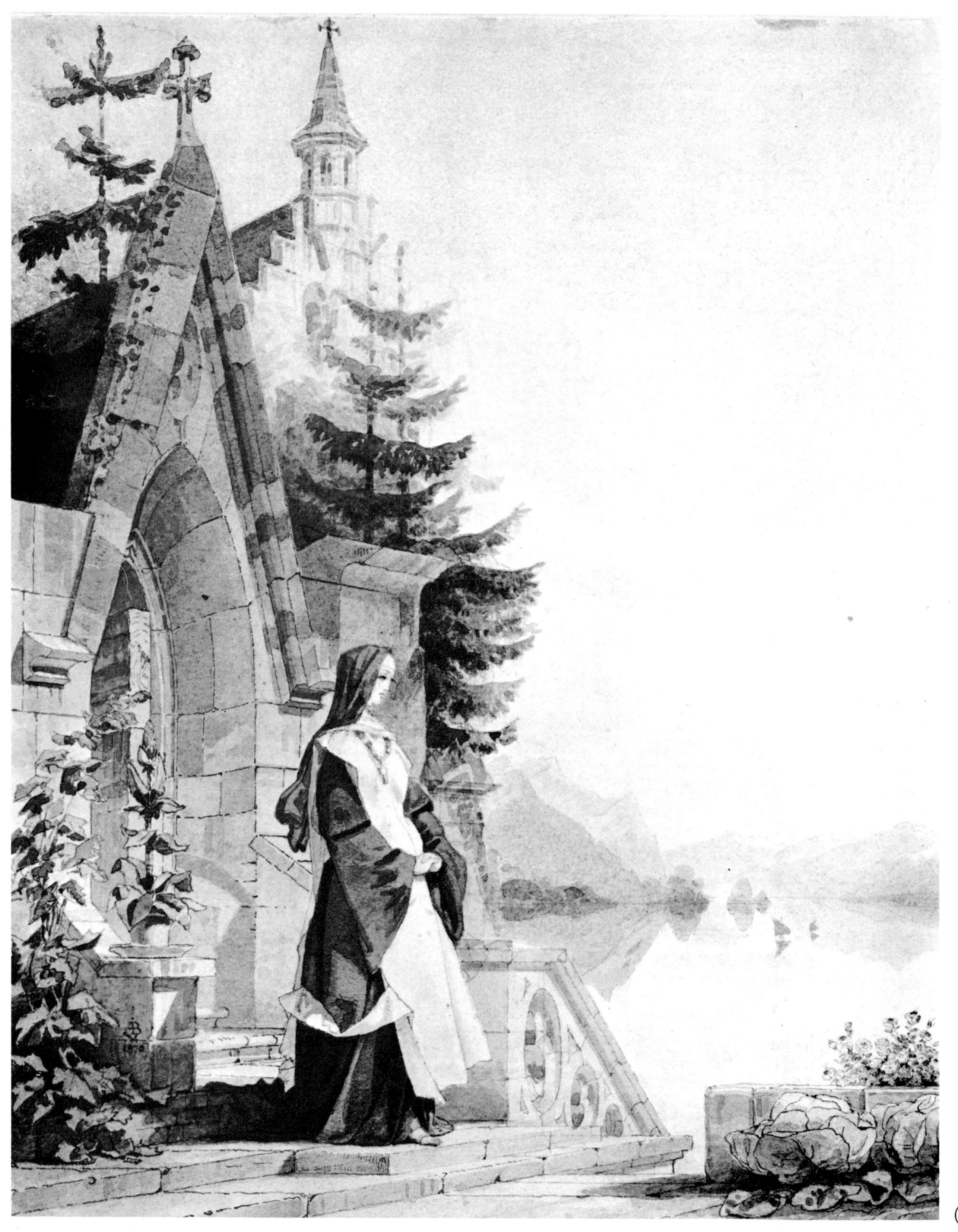

(1)

the Berlin Academy. In the following years he visited the United States (1885) and Switzerland (1887). His second trip to the Near East came in 1891; two years later he visited the Italian Riviera. In 1902 he left Berlin to become the director of the master studio of landscape painting at the Dresden Academy. On the occasion of his seventieth birthday in 1912, two large exhibitions were held in his honor, one in Dresden and the other in Darmstadt. Bracht spent some time in Holland in 1913. He retired from his position in Dresden in 1919 and moved to Darmstadt, where he died on November 15, 1921.

During his lifetime Bracht was considered one of the most significant German landscape painters, and as a teacher he was admired by his numerous students. He became especially well-known for the dramatic and skillfully composed landscapes which he executed in the 1880's and which were based on nature studies made during his first trip to the Near East. The exotic themes of these pictures appealed especially to the taste of Wilhelmian Germany. In the mid 1890's, Bracht's landscapes became increasingly realistic. After the turn of the century he developed a free, open style which he derived from the technique of the impressionists. Bracht also painted the industrialized landscape of the Ruhr, but he was more interested in the complex interplay of light from the furnaces and smoke from the chimneys than he was in the subject matter itself.

2. The Heidelberg Castle: The Hall under the Gallery of the Friedrich Wing

[*Das Heidelberger Schloß: Die Halle unter dem Altan des Friedrichsbaues*], [1859].
Pen and dark brown wash over pencil with highlights in white gouache on brownish paper (blindstamp: DE CANSON FRÉRES), 27.9 x 40.9 cm.

Provenance: Acquired in 1922, gift of Waldemar Bracht, Darmstadt, the artist's son. Inv. no. VIII 1150-12.
Bibliography: Schefold, 1971, II, no. 25262; Theilmann, 1971, pp. 171, 189, note 809, illus. no. 90; Theilmann, 1973, note 56; Theilmann and Ammann, 1978, I, p. 68, no. 365, illus. II, p. 244.

Bracht made this drawing in August 1859 during a stay in Heidelberg. A year earlier, in 1858, he and Philipp Röth had sketched the castle together. Schirmer happened to be at the castle at the same time, and was so impressed with their sketches that he urged them to come to Karlsruhe and study landscape painting under him. Bracht and Röth, however, waited a year before taking Schirmer's advice. A few weeks after the completion of this drawing, both of the young artists moved to Karlsruhe. A second version of this drawing with a somewhat more distant standpoint is dated August 10, 1859.[1] Philipp Röth made a similar drawing which is preserved in the Kurpfälzisches Museum Heidelberg.[2]

1. Theilmann and Ammann, 1978, I, p. 68, no. 364, illus. II, p. 244.
2. Kurpfälzisches Museum, Heidelberg, inv. no. Z 1367 B[2]; See Theilmann, 1971, illus. no. 135.

Hans Canon (Johann von Strašiřipka)

Vienna 1829 – Vienna 1885

Canon was born in Vienna on March 15, 1829. After attending the Piaristengymnasium in Krems and the Polytechnisches Institut in Vienna, he apparently remained at the Vienna Academy for only a semester before leaving to study privately with Ferdinand Georg Waldmüller for five months in 1847. He entered the Austrian Army in 1849. Between 1858 and 1860 he traveled to Paris, London, and the Near East. In 1862 he made his first brief visit to Karlsruhe and in 1863 moved there. After failing to secure an appointment as a professor at the Karlsruhe Academy, he moved to Stuttgart in 1869. In 1870 he spent some time in Rome and then extended his journey to include Africa. In 1875 he moved to Vienna and was awarded the Medal of the Archduke Karl Ludwig in 1877. During this time he was inundated with commissions for monumental wall paintings and ceiling frescoes, which he executed for the numerous public buildings being constructed in the Austro-Hungarian Empire. In 1882 he was awarded the *große goldene Staatsmedaille,* a prestigious national award. Canon died in Vienna on September 12, 1885.

A passionate opponent of naturalism, Canon was deeply influenced by the painting of the renaissance and the Flemish baroque. The painter Hans Ranzoni wrote of Canon: "His fanatic devotion to the old masters caused him to model all his later works after those of Titian, Rubens, Van Dyck – after those of old masters in general . . . ."[1] Canon's oeuvre consists primarily of mythological and historical themes, landscapes, genre scenes, and portraits.

Canon was a boisterous man with a strong military bearing. His first appearance in Karlsruhe was spectacular. As the story has it, he took only four hours to execute the portrait of the Director of the Academy, Johann Wilhelm Schirmer, which now hangs in the Staatliche Kunsthalle Karlsruhe. This electrifying event marked the beginning of a split in the Karlsruhe artistic community, one which became increasingly evident during the 1860's. Most of the younger painters gathered around Canon to form one camp. Another camp formed around the Norwegian landscape painter Hans Frederik Gude, who in 1864 succeeded Schirmer as Director of the Academy. In later years Gude characterized the sparkling personality of his former opponent as follows:

> *The historical artist Canon came to Karlsruhe, and his eloquence and his impressive self-confidence made its mark on everyone. He was an outstanding artist, . . . one who loved to gather a large crowd of admirers about his easel and lecture to them on how the "old masters" had painted and on how he had rediscovered their technique. He used a gray underpainting with complete modeling, which he then overlaid with brilliant colors. This was nothing new to us – we had done the same thing in Düsseldorf. But his way of doing it made a great deal of sense, and when I arrived at the Academy I found the place to be in a state of feverish excitement. In order to understand what a great impact he was able to make on*

the young artists and even some of the older ones, all you had to do was look at him. He was an imposing figure with a long beard and a shimmering velvet suit. As a former officer he spoke a great deal about weapons, and he proved himself to be an extremely accurate marksman. And then you would hear his marvelously glib conversation as well.

It was easy to figure out what he was after. He wanted first to get an appointment as professor and then to take over the entire Academy. He made studies of heads, attempting to demonstrate the correct technique of portraiture, but it was precisely this which caused us—Des Coudres and me—to oppose him. The color and the character of the faces had no similarity with nature; instead they resembled more closely the technique of this or that famous painter. It was our old respect for Nature, a respect which we had learned in Düsseldorf—our conviction that Nature is the most reliable, if not the only, source of art—which prevented us from allowing Canon to enter our Academy as a recognized and accepted teacher. As a result of our stand his influence on our students only increased, and over the years, he succeeded in winning over several of them . . . ."[2]

Wilhelm Trübner (no. 64), one of those who left the academy and followed Canon to Stuttgart in 1869-70, stated emphatically:

He had a complete and sound grasp of the old masters, had studied all the collections from St. Petersburg to Madrid, had a knowledge of anatomy equal to that of a surgeon and the ability to incorporate in his works all his knowledge and skill.[3]

Hans Thoma (nos. 57-63), one of the young artists who responded enthusiastically to Canon, described in his memoirs Canon's unusual technique:

His technique consisted of working up the forms and the lighting with white highlights on a dark background. The coloration was then achieved by glazes which surprised us with their shimmering enamel-like effects. At any rate, Canon inspired us to become acquainted with a wide range of painting techniques which if used intelligently could be turned to great advantage. At the same time Canon was the first to call our attention to the technique of the old masters. But a struggle broke out between the advocates of the more stylized glazing technique and those of the naturalistic impasto technique. This conflict, aggravated by certain personal animosities, soon took on a highly unpleasant character—the whole issue became charged with dogmatic controversy."[4]

1. Hans Razoni in *Kunst dem Volk* 12, No. 12 (1941), pp. 43-44; cited from Österreichische Galerie in Wien, Oberes Belvedere, Vienna, *Hans Canon: Skizzen-Entwürfe-Dokumente,* 1966, p. 14.
2. Hans Gude, *Karlsruher Künstlererinnerungen,* trans. Carèn Lessing, Karlsruhe, 1920, pp. 7-8.
3. Trübner, 1918, pp. 12-13.
4. Hans Thoma, *Im Herbst des Lebens,* Munich, 1909, p. 24.

3. Allegory of Steampower

[*Allegorie der Dampfkraft*], [ca. 1863].
Pencil and red chalk on beige paper, 38.7 x 50.5 cm.

Provenance: Acquired in 1903 from the painter Edmund Kanoldt, Karlsruhe. Inv. no. VIII 1206-7.
Bibliography: Schneider, 1935, p. 91; Gustav F. Hartlaub, "Dampfkraft und Telegraphie: Zwei technische Allegorien von Hans Canon," in *Die BASF* VII, Heft 1 (February 1975), pp. 33-35; Lauts and Zimmermann, 1971, p. 38, no. 1042; Schneider, 1968, p. 123; Theilmann and Ammann, 1978, I, p. 75, no. 416, illus. II, p. 105.

This drawing, a companion piece to *Allegorie der Telegraphie (Allegory of Telegraphy)* in the Staatliche Kunsthalle Karlsruhe, is a study for a painting no longer extant which was once in the waiting room of the old train station in Karlsruhe. Canon had received the commission from the Baden railway. In 1863 he painted an oil sketch after the preliminary drawing, so that he might plan the coloration.[2] The strong modeling which accentuates the bulging forms of the powerful muscles reveals the influence of Rubens.

1. Staatliche Kunsthalle, Karlsruhe, inv. no. VIII 1206-6; see Theilmann and Ammann, 1978, I, p. 75, no. 415, illus. II, p. 105.
2. Staatliche Kunsthalle, Karlsruhe, inv. no. 1041; see Lauts and Zimmermann, 1971, illus. p. 50.

4. Cromwell Lifting the Shroud from the Coffin of Charles I

[*Cromwell, von vorn gesehen, mit der Degenspitze das Leichentuch vom Sarg Karls I. hochhebend*], [ca. 1867].
Red chalk on thin yellow-beige cardboard, 31.8 x 19.8 cm.

Provenance: Acquired in 1903 from the painter Edmund Kanoldt, Karlsruhe. Inv. no. VIII 1206-19.
Bibliography: Theilmann and Ammann, 1978, I, p. 76, no. 418, illus. II, p. 248.

At the instigation of the Republican army, Charles I (1600-49), King of England, was brought to trial on charges of high treason. Cromwell himself was a member of this court which convicted Charles and sentenced him to death. After his execution on January 30, 1649, the body was enclosed in a coffin and removed from the scaffold. Wishing to see Charles once more, Cromwell opened the coffin and gazed intently at him. Before the coffin was set to rest at Windsor Castle, it remained on public display for seven days.

The drawing belongs to a series of preliminary studies for the figure of Cromwell in a painting entitled *Cromwell am Sarg Karls I. (Cromwell at Coffin of Charles I),* current location unknown. This painting, which was exhibited in the Karlsruhe Kunsthalle in 1867, practically overnight established Canon's reputation throughout Germany.[1] In all likelihood the theme was taken from a picture with a different composition by Paul Delaroche executed prior to 1831 and hanging in the Hamburger Kunsthalle.[2] Delaroche made a copy of this picture in 1849 now in the Hermitage, Leningrad. His composition was etched by Louis Pierre Henriquel-Dupont.

1. E. Ranzoni, in *Kunst für Alle* I (1886), p. 125.
2. Hamburger Kunsthalle, Hamburg, inv. no. 2665; see Eva Maria Krafft and Carl-Wolfgang Schümann, *Katalog der Meister des 19. Jahrhunderts in der Hamburger Kunsthalle*, Hamburg, 1969, p. 48, illus.

Josef Durm

Karlsruhe 1837 – Karlsruhe 1919

Durm was born in Karlsruhe on February 14, 1837. He studied architecture at the Karlsruhe Polytechnikum and completed his qualifying examinations in 1860. He visited Italy in 1866 with a travel stipend. Later he traveled extensively to Greece, Asia Minor, Palestine, Egypt, and Tunisia. In 1868 he was appointed a professor of architecture at the Karlsruhe Polytechnikum, and he taught there until shortly before his death in 1919. Durm turned down several offers of positions in Darmstadt, Munich, and Charlottenburg. He received several high government architectural appointments. In 1886 the city of Heidelberg made him an honorary citizen, and on the occasion of its five-hundredth anniversary the University of Heidelberg awarded him an honorary doctorate of philosophy. In 1902 he was given the title of Privy Counsel; in 1903 the Technische Hochschule Berlin awarded him an honorary doctorate of engineering. Rich in honors and awards, Durm died in Karlsruhe on April 3, 1919.

As an architectural historian, Durm was interested in the architecture of antiquity and the renaissance. He made extensive studies at the sites of many buildings,and he published the results of his studies in such large works as *Die Baukunst der Griechen (The Architecture of the Greeks), Die Baukunst der Etrusker und Römer (The Architecture of the Etruscans and the Romans)* and *Die Baukunst der Renaissance in Italien (The Architecture of Renaissance Italy)*. He also wrote numerous articles for scientific journals. His keen interest in architectural history led him to establish together with Franz Xaver Kraus and Ernst Wagner the ambitious series *Kunstdenkmäler im Großherzogtum Baden (Architectural Monuments in the Grand Duchy of Baden)*, for which he illustrated several volumes. For Durm the Italian renaissance represented the highest achievement of architecture, and the aesthetics of this period permeated all of his own designs. Throughout Baden there are numerous public and private buildings which stand as witnesses to the extensive accomplishments of this enormously active man.

Durm was a talented, driven and productive draftsman. His studies of buildings and details – the bulk of his drawings – were made with scientific exactitude. These are not just dry reproductions of the structures in question, but are often brilliant documentations in a secure and powerful style of draftsmanship – one which expresses the artist's sensualism and his passionate devotion to his subject matter.

5. St. Aposteln in Cologne

[*St. Aposteln in Köln*], [1857].
Black chalk, upper scrollwork in pencil, on light beige paper, 38.4 x 27.8 cm.
Signed in black chalk lower left: *D* (reversed); inscribed above on the scrolls in pencil: (left) ST APOSIII··, (right) COELN.

Provenance: Acquired in 1940, gift of R. Durm, Karlsruhe, the artist's son; formerly part of the artist's estate. Inv. no. 1940-230.
Bibliography: Theilmann and Ammann, 1978, I, p. 127, no. 725, illus. II, p. 279.

This view is from the southeast. The church was apparently built by Archbishop Heribert (999-1021) at the beginning of the eleventh century on the site of an earlier, less significant structure. After a fire in 1192 the building was expanded by the addition of the trifoliate choir at the east end. There is a lithograph by Durm entitled *St. Gereon in Cöln (The Cathedral of St. Gereon in Cologne)* and inscribed *Excursion Pfingsten 1857*. The subtle chalk technique suggests that this drawing was made as a study for a lithograph during the same trip to Cologne in 1857.

6. The Interior of the Cathedral in Limburg an der Lahn

[*Im Innern des Doms in Limburg an der Lahn*], [1862].
Pencil and brown wash on ivory paper, 39.6 x 24.6 cm.
Inscribed in pencil lower right: *Limburg a/d L.*

Provenance: Acquired in 1940, gift of R. Durm, Karlsruhe, the artist's son; formerly from the artist's estate. Inv. no. 1940-252.
Bibliography: Theilmann and Ammann, 1978, I, p. 127, no. 728, illus. II, p. 279.

The Cathedral of St. George was probably established by Count Heinrich von Isenburg. Construction was begun ca. 1215-20. It was consecrated in 1235 and completed around the middle of the thirteenth century. This view is taken from the crossing toward the north wall of the nave. This drawing was made during Durm's trip to Limburg an der Lahn in August and September of 1862. He made two other drawings of this late romanesque-early gothic edifice: a view from the northwest and a view from the east, both in the Staatliche Kunsthalle Karlsruhe.[1]

1. Staatliche Kunsthalle, Karlsruhe, inv. nos. 1940-253 and 1940-254; see Theilmann and Ammann, 1978, I, p. 127, nos. 726 and 727, illus. II, p. 279.

Georg Maria Eckert

Heidelberg 1828 – Karlsruhe 1901

Eckert was born in Heidelberg on September 17, 1828. In 1846 he began his studies at the Academy in Düsseldorf as a student of Johann Wilhelm Schirmer. Subsequently he went to Munich, where he lived during the early 1850's. From Munich he made study trips to southern Bavaria, Italy, and Switzerland. In 1858 he settled in Heidelberg, where he was active as a landscape painter and as a drawing instructor. After 1867 he devoted himself primarily to being an artist-photographer and published a series of landscape and architecture studies. For these he was awarded the *große Verdienstmedaille*, a medal of service, in 1873 and a gold medal in

1876. After experiencing some business difficulties he moved to Karlsruhe in 1877. He then began to execute a number of watercolor studies of landscapes and peasant costumes throughout Baden and to collect examples of Baden folk art. In addition he made a name for himself by constructing large models of complete farm houses and housing projects, as well as room interiors. His models were displayed in the collection of the Grand Duke, in the Germanisches Nationalmuseum in Nürnberg, and the Museum für Volkstrachten in Berlin. The extensive collection of folk art in the Badisches Landesmuseum in Karlsruhe is to a great extent due to his knowledgeable and enthusiastic collecting. Eckert died in Karlsruhe on January 22, 1901.

In addition to executing numerous scenes of the Black Forest, Eckert portrayed his home town of Heidelberg many times. These Heidelberg views, taken from several different points, are invariably marked by precise draftsmanship and a delight in the presentation of details. In his works he shows the city nestled within the hills of the Neckar valley, scenes which have come to epitomize the romantic concept of landscape.

7. View of Heidelberg and the Neckar Valley

[*Totalansicht von Heidelberg und dem Neckartal*], 1856.
Pencil and dark brown wash on beige paper, 31.3 x 41.5 cm.
Inscribed in pen and dark brown ink lower left: *GM Eckert. / Heidelberg im May 56* (*G* and *M* linked together).

Provenance: Formerly part of the Grand Ducal private collection. Inv. no. VIII 1302.
Bibliography: Theilmann and Ammann, 1978, I, pp. 138-39, no. 818, illus. II, p. 107.

This is sheet no. 31 of the "Heidelberger Friedrich — Luisen — Album," presented to Grand Duke Friedrich I and Princess Luise of Prussia on September 20, 1855, on the occasion of their marriage (see also nos. 14, 16, 27, 65-66).

This view is from the left bank of the Neckar facing up the valley near the Bergheimer mill, which was razed in 1905. To the left is the Heiligenberg, in the middle the city with the old bridge, the towers of the Jesuitenkirche and the Heiliggeistkirche, the castle and the Scheffelterrasse. To the right is the Molkenkur, and at the extreme right edge the tower of the Königstuhl.

At the request of the city of Heidelberg, Ludwig Kachel, director of the Karlsruhe mint, invited a group of Baden artists to participate in the compilation of the Heidelberg album. Eckert responded on January 15, 1856, that this was "a singular honor," and that he had already selected the subject for the work which he wished to contribute:

> *It is a comprehensive view of Heidelberg (i.e., one of the whole area) seen from the Rhine Valley. This is a view which has not been treated in other pictures and which combines and represents the city, the castle, the Molkenanstalt, the Königstuhl, the Heiligenberg, and the opening into the Neckar Valley. I made an oil sketch from this preparatory study last summer, and it has been well received in these parts. It will serve well as a companion piece to the work by Mr. Verhas in Munich* [see no. 65] *who, as I was informed by the art dealer Meder, has chosen a view of Heidelberg from the Molkenanstalt and has given a view of the city, the castle, and the Rhine Valley.*[1]

But Kachel discovered a few "deficient areas" in the work which Eckert sent him. Eckert, still at the beginning of his artistic career, promised in a letter dated July 13 to correct these portions "as best I possibly can," continuing that he had in the meantime finished a watercolor of the Stift Neuburg which he also wished to contribute to the Heidelberg album.[2] On July 23 he sent off both works with an accompanying letter in which he wrote:

> *I have corrected the view of Heidelberg as I saw fit and am convinced that you were right and that it is better now. I just wish that somewhat less had been removed from the right side at the Königstuhl and somewhat more instead from the Heiligenberg at the left side, since now both of the towers on the two hills seem equidistant from the sides. But it really doesn't matter.*

For the picture Eckert requested an honorarium of twenty-five guilders.[3]

1. Georg Maria Eckert letter to Ludwig Kachel, January 15, 1856, in the Badisches Generallandesarchiv, Karlsruhe (hereafter BGK), Abt. 69, N 9, no. 19.
2. Eckert to Kachel, July 13, 1856, in BGK, Abt. 69, N 9, no. 19.
3. Eckert to Kachel, August 5, 1856, in BGK, Abt. 69, N 9, no. 19.

Friedrich Eisenlohr

Lörrach 1805 — Karlsruhe 1854

Eisenlohr was born in Lörrach on November 23, 1805. Between 1822 and 1824 he studied architecture under Christian Arnold at the Polytechnisches Institut in Freiburg im Breisgau, and he then continued his studies at the Polytechnikum in Karlsruhe. He spent the years 1826-28 in Italy. Two years later in Karlsruhe he completed his state examinations in architecture with the accolade "extremely qualified." In 1832 he was appointed as an instructor at the school of architecture at the Polytechnikum in Karlsruhe, and in 1839 he received his appointment as professor. In 1853 he was named to the Baden architectural commission and was appointed to the board of directors of the school of architecture. He received many honors: in 1842 he became a corresponding member of the Royal Institute of British Architects and in 1843 an honorary member of the Swiss Society of Engineers and Architects. He was a recipient of the Prussian Order of the Red Eagle, Third Class. He died in Karlsruhe on February 27, 1854.

Eisenlohr is considered to be the founder of the romantic movement of Baden architecture. At the beginning of the 1840's the entire construction of the public buildings for the Baden railway was his responsibility. A law passed in 1838 had provided for the construction of a rail line between Mannheim and Basel, but the project was quite controversial, since it was generally felt to constitute a threat to nature. It was due to Eisenlohr's efforts that the various buildings were designed so that they would fit harmoniously into their natural settings.

Like many of his colleagues in the field of architecture (e.g., Weinbrenner, Hübsch [no. 17], Schinkel, Klenze, Gärtner), Eisenlohr was a highly gifted landscape draftsman. He received his first introduction to this field during his study years under Christian Meichelt, an engraver. Together with Meichelt's son Heinrich, Eisenlohr hiked throughout the valleys of the Black Forest and along Lake Constance, where he made numerous nature studies and several topographical studies of the type that were then quite popular. In these early years he was particularly interested in one outstanding architectural monument in Baden, the minster in Freiburg im Breisgau, which he drew several times. In 1820 he met the painter Georg Wilhelm Issel, who had a profound influence on his later drawing. That same year the two of them made a journey along the Rhine and executed many studies of medieval edifices. During the time he spent in Italy (1826-28), he met well-known draftsmen, among them Friedrich Mosbrugger (nos. 29-31), Ernst Fries, and Carl Oesterley. Many sketch books and individual studies survive from these years. Their clear stylistic development not only reveals the influence of Ernst Fries but also indicates the strong and immediate reaction to the landscape of Italy in response to which Eisenlohr's drawing becomes more subtle and his line relies more on nuance.

8. Mountain Crevasse

[*Felsschlucht*], [after 1828].
Pencil on off-white paper (watermark: PM), 48.4 x 37.3 cm.

Provenance: Acquired in 1968 from Anna Oehler, Karlsruhe, the artist's great-granddaughter. Inv. no. 1968-8.
Bibliography: Jahrbuch VI (1969), p. 261; Theilmann and Ammann, 1978, I, p. 143, no. 860, illus. II, p. 9.

The delicate, extremely varied execution of line and the strong development of the crystalline rocks indicate a date after his stay in Italy.

9. View through the South Cloister of the Monastery of Maulbronn

[*Blick durch den südlichen Kreuzgangflügel des Klosters Maulbronn*], [after 1828].
Pencil on ivory paper (watermark: J W [fragment]), 38.8 x 29.0 cm. Signed in pencil lower left: *F. Eisenlohr.* Inscribed in lower right margin: *Kloster Maulbronn/Würtemberg.*

Provenance: Acquired in 1954, gift of Mrs. M. L. Eisenlohr, Munich; formerly from the collection of Freiherr von Bergh. Inv. no. 1954-1.
Bibliography: Bernhard, 1973, I, illus. p. 230; Schefold, 1974, no. 5078a (incorrectly titled *Innenansicht des Paradieses);* Theilmann and Ammann, 1978, I, p. 144, no. 866, illus. II, p. 108.

The southern cloister of the monastery was built ca. 1220 by the so-called Paradiesmeister.

Eisenlohr planned to publish a large work in several fascicles which he entitled *Mittelalterliche Bauwerke im südwestlichen Deutschland und am Rhein (Medieval Architecture in South-Western Germany and along the Rhine).* The illustrations were to be perspective and picturesque views which he had executed during the previous twenty years. The corresponding geometric drawings were carried out during excursions by students of the school of architecture, of which Eisenlohr was a director. Due to Eisenlohr's untimely death, only the first four fascicles appeared with the title: "Zisterzienser-Kloster Maulbronn, Carlsruhe im März 1853" ("The Cistercian Monastery in Maulbronn"). The drawing in this exhibition was not used for this publication, which instead included three other scenes executed by Eisenlohr: *Vorhalle (Antechamber), Ansicht des Refectoriums (View of the Refectory),* and *Die Geißel-Kammer (The Flagellation Chamber).*

In the introduction to his publication Eisenlohr expressed a view which is characteristic of the artist and his work:

> *If* [*my drawings*] *were only to assist in a small way in the development of knowledge concerning the architecture of medieval Germany and in fostering a love for it, in providing for its rediscovery and restoration, then the purpose of their publication would have been attained.*

Marie Ellenrieder

Constance 1791 — Constance 1863

Marie Ellenrieder was born on March 20, 1791 in Constance. She received her earliest instruction from Joseph Einsle, a resident of Constance and a painter of miniatures. From 1813 to 1815 she attended the Academy in Munich and studied under Peter von Langer. Afterwards she was active in Constance, Zurich, and Freiburg im Breisgau. She lived in Rome for an extended time on two occasions, between 1822 and 1824, and from 1838 to 1840. During her first visit she was profoundly influenced by the group of Nazarenes which collected around Friedrich Overbeck and also by exposure to the works of Fra Angelico, Perugino, and Raphael. In 1829 she was named a court painter to the Grand Duchy. After 1842 she led a secluded life in Constance, where she died on June 5, 1863.

Of all Baden artists, Marie Ellenrieder was the one who incorporated the Nazarene ideals most purely and forcefully. The painter Louise Seidler, who was particularly attracted to Ellenrieder during her stay in Rome, introduced her deaf acquaintance to

> *the noble Germans, the Nazarenes . . . . As I suddenly recognized Truth and Beauty, my whole way of thinking began to change. I saw these pictures inundated with light, just like the sun. No matter*

how unsteady I was on my feet, now I knew that for the rest of my life I would be able to stand fast.[1]

With feeling and warmth Louise Seidler characterized her close friend and fellow artist:

> *Her pictures soon became well-known; they sprang from deep feeling, were full of transcendent charm and piety. In their poses and their expressions, her madonnas and figures of the Christ child had a genuinely spiritually uplifting effect. But what was more delightful in her works than any kind of artistic expertise was the pure, modest spirit which emanated from all of them.*[2]

Her delicately and sensitively modeled figures differ greatly from those of the highly ascetic drawings of the Nazarenes. Ellenrieder's works have a strong sense of color, which the Nazarenes avoided. Instead of spare, sharply defined pencil lines, she uses soft, flowing pastels — a technique which imparts a chaste allurement to the figures of women and children whom she so often portrayed, and which at the same time endows them with a heavenly grace and charm.

1. Marie Ellenrieder diary entry, April 15, 1823, quoted in Fischer and Blanckenhagen, 1963, p. 30.
2. Hermann Uhde, ed., *Erinnerungen der Malerin Louise Seidler*, Berlin, 1922, p. 134.

10. Portrait of a Young Girl

[Mädchenbildnis], 1834.
Black and colored chalk with highlights in white gouache on yellowish brown paper, 41.0 x 29.6 cm.
Inscribed in pencil lower right: *Studium nach der Natur von Marie Ellenrieder 1834.*

Provenance: Probably acquired in 1901 from Mrs. Metzger. Inv. no. VIII 1307.
Exhibition: Constance, 1963, no. 83, illus.
Bibliography: Siebert, 1915, p. 115 (erroneously dated 1835); Fischer and Blanckenhagen, 1963, p. 49, cat. no. 155, illus. no. 41; Theilmann and Ammann, 1978, I, p. 146, no. 876, illus. II, p. 109.

Apparently this is the pastel portrait of Nina Baumberger, governess in the household of Grand Duke Leopold of Baden, which was acquired by the museum on May 1, 1901. Referring to this work, Friedhelm Wilhelm Fischer writes:

> *Even though this portrait was made from a living model, it can still be categorized as an idealistic work . . . . Perhaps the artist was intending to use it later for a religious composition. The enchantment of the work lies primarily in the confrontation of reality and the ideal, in the inner relationship between nature and a higher purpose.*[1]

An altarpiece entitled "*Lasset die Kindlein zu mir kommen*" *(Suffer the Little Children to Come unto Me)* in the palace chapel of Kallenberg near Coburg completed by Ellenrieder between 1840 and 1842, contains a figure at the right edge which resembles this portrait, except that the head and glance are somewhat raised in the painting.[2]

1. Fischer and Blanckenhagen, 1963, p. 49, cat. no. 155, illus. no. 41.
2. Ibid., cat. no. 307, illus. no. 49.

11. John the Baptist as a Child

[*Johannes der Täufer als Knabe*], 1835.
Pastel over pencil with highlights in white and gold-bronze gouache on brown paper, 36.5 x 29.3 cm.
Signed and dated in pencil verso lower right: *Marie Ellenrieder 1835.*

Provenance: Part of the Grand Ducal private collection until 1915; acquired from a private collection in 1890 (?). Inv. no. VIII 1306.
Exhibition: Constance, 1963, no. 14.
Bibliography: Siebert, 1915, p. 115; Fischer and Blanckenhagen, 1963, cat. no. 352; Theilmann and Ammann, 1978, I, p. 146, no. 877, illus. II, p. 109.

A preliminary sketch for this work is in a private collection in Constance.[1]

1. Fischer and Blanckenhagen, 1963, cat. no. 352a.

Carl Ludwig Frommel

Birkenfeld an der Nahe 1789 — Ispringen 1863

Frommel was born in Birkenfeld an der Nahe on April 29, 1789. In 1799 his family moved to Karlsruhe, and between 1805 and 1809 he studied painting and engraving under Philipp Jakob Becker and Christian Haldenwang. In 1810 Frommel traveled to Paris and the following year journeyed with Friedrich Helmsdorf to Switzerland. He spent the years 1812-17 in Italy. In 1818 he was appointed to the board of directors of the newly-organized Badischer Kunstverein in Karlsruhe, and was given the rank of professor. He traveled to London in 1824 to familiarize himself with the new process of steel engraving. After his return to Karlsruhe in the same year, he established the first studio for steel engraving in Germany. In 1830 he was appointed director of the Großherzogliche Gemäldegalerie, the Grand Ducal art gallery in Karlsruhe. He returned to Italy in 1834. In 1858 he retired from his position as director of the Gemäldegalerie. He spent the remaining years of his life in Lichtental near Baden-Baden until 1862, and then in Ispringen near Pforzheim, where he died on February 6, 1863.

As a painter and a draftsman Frommel concerned himself primarily with the landscape of his homeland. Although rooted in the idealistic concept of landscape art as found in the works of Claude Lorrain, Frommel's style tended to develop towards a Biedermeier form of realism more acceptable to the middle class. This important step in his stylistic development took place in the 1820's and 1830's. It formed the basis for his outstanding achievement during this period — the depiction of all the important architectural monuments of Baden. During his mature years he executed watercolors of numerous significant castles, palaces, and churches in Baden. In these works, which are characterized by an objective representation of the subject matter, he paid equal attention to the structures and the landscape around them. But Frommel did not restrict himself to mechanical, dry reproductions; he used a controlled balance of light to add mood and atmosphere to his scenes.

In addition to his work as an artist, Frommel was responsible for the administration of the Gemäldegalerie. He served as director for over a quarter of a century, combining a strong sense of duty with a great deal of energy and action in the execution of his varied responsibilities. He was concerned with the preservation of the collection and with its expansion through new acquisitions. Above all he wished to inventory and register the works in the print collection and to provide for visitors a catalogue of those works displayed in the gallery. Frommel was one of the most prominent and respected individuals of the cultural scene in Karlsruhe. His home was the focus of an artistic and intellectual circle which included among others the architects Friedrich Eisenlohr (nos. 8-9) and Heinrich Hübsch (no. 17).

12. The Ruins of Ortenberg Castle with a View into the Kinzig Valley

[*Ruine des Schlosses Ortenberg mit Blick ins Kinzigtal*], *1832*.
Watercolor over pencil with touches of gum arabic on ivory paper (watermark: J W [fragment]), 40.2 x 55.2 cm.
Signed and dated in pen and ink lower right: *C. Frommel/1832*.

Provenance: Formerly part of the Grand Ducal private collection. Inv. no. P. K. I 553-1-2.
Exhibition: Karlsruhe 1966, no. 24.
Bibliography: Schefold, 1965, p. 121, color illus. no. 69; Schefold, 1971, I, color illus. no. 490, II, no. 31698; Franz Vollmer, *Burg Ortenberg und Bühlwegkapelle: Zwei Zeugen Ortenauer Vergangenheit*, Offenburg, 1976, pp. 66, note 226, 113, no. 17, and color illus. p. 71 (detail); Theilmann and Ammann, 1978, I, p. 198, no. 1140, illus. II, p. 33.

The work is a view from the northeast showing the castle ruins, the ancient floor of the river Kinzig, and the Bellenwald. The first fortification at the site was constructed by the Zähringer family in the eleventh or twelfth century at a strategically important location near the junction of the Rhine and Kinzig valleys southeast of Offenburg. This fortification was first mentioned in a document of the early thirteenth century. It was blown up in 1680 during the war with Louis XIV. Frommel's drawing shows the Ortenberg Castle in ruins after having been left to the elements. In 1837 the ruins were bought by a banker named Gabriel Leonhard von Berckholtz, who had the place rebuilt between 1838 and 1843 in neo-gothic style according to plans by Friedrich Eisenlohr. Together with another view of the castle taken from a more distant viewpoint,[1] Frommel presented this watercolor as a New Year's present in 1861 to Grand Duke Friedrich I of Baden. In an accompanying note, Frommel explained the purpose behind these pictures:

> *May the exalted love and enthusiasm which Your Royal Majesty has shown for art and science as well as for the therewith related history of our Fatherland in some fashion justify my most humble request that I might be allowed to place before Your Royal Highness' feet these two drawings of the Castle of Ortenberg which were made before its restoration. Should these works be added to the extensive collection which Your Majesty already possesses and which I previously had the great fortune to be able to draw for Your Majesty's Blessed Departed Father, then they will fulfill the purpose of their creation.*[2]

1. Staatliche Kunsthalle, Karlsruhe, inv. no. P. K. I 553-1-1; see Theilmann and Ammann, 1978, I, p. .199, no. 1141, illus. II, p. 124.
2. Carl Ludwig Frommel note to the Grand Duke Friedrich I, in Badisches Generallandesarchiv, Karlsruhe, Abt. 56 1265.

13. View of Merano

[*Blick auf Meran*], [1837].
Pencil on ivory paper; badly discolored (watermark: J WHATMAN) 29.6 x 39.4 cm.
Inscribed in pencil lower left: *Meran;* inscribed in pencil lower right by another hand: *Frommel.*

Provenance: Acquired from Auction 185, C. G. Boerner, Leipzig, 1934, no. 206 (incorrectly identified as a work by Karl Lindemann-Frommel); formerly part of the collection of Paul Arndt, Munich (Lugt. S. no. 2067 b). Inv. no. VIII 1875-1.
Bibliography: Theilmann and Ammann, 1978, I, p. 203, no. 1164, illus. II, p. 128.

This drawing, executed in the summer of 1837 during a visit to south Tyrol, shows the city from the east. In the middle of the town stands the church of St. Nikolaus, on the right edge the Passeiertor, above which the so-called Pulverturm, the inner fortification of the ruins of the castle of Ortenstein, stands on a promontory of the Kochelberg. Related to this work is a steel engraving, *Meran,* which appears in *Tyrol und seine nächsten Umgebungen (Tyrol and Vicinity).*[1] The engraving shows the city from a more southerly viewpoint.

1. *Tyrol und seine nächsten Umgebungen: Nach der Natur gemalt von C. Frommel,* Kunst-Verlag, 1842.

Rudolf Gleichauf

Hüfingen 1826 – Karlsruhe 1896

Gleichauf was born in Hüfingen near Donaueschingen on July 29, 1826. He received his first artistic instruction from the painter Lucian Reich and his brother Xaver Reich, a sculptor. From 1843 to 1846 he studied in the Munich Academy under Heinrich Maria von Hess and Julius Schnorr von Carolsfeld, leaving Munich to follow Carolsfeld to Dresden. In 1849 he went to the Städelsches Kunstinstitut in Frankfurt am Main, where he studied under Jakob Becker and Edward von Steinle. Gleichauf moved to Karlsruhe in 1852 after receiving a commission from Heinrich Hübsch (no. 17) to decorate the new court theater. He remained in Karlsruhe and in the following years he was given further commissions by Hübsch and by Josef Durm (nos. 5-6) for the decoration of public buildings. He died in Karlsruhe on October 15, 1896.

Gleichauf continued the tradition of monumental painting which had been established in Baden by Moritz von Schwind (nos. 54-56), although his compositions lacked the inventiveness and poetic charm of his famous predecessor. Gleichauf was a sensitive, educated artist, an intimate friend of the poet Joseph Victor von Scheffel and the painter Wilhelm Klose (nos. 22-23). Josef August Beringer characterized him as having

> *a harmoniously balanced artistic nature, which saw in its artistic calling the preservation of the purity of renaissance ideals and which remained steadfast despite all the changes and upheavals of art and life.*[1]

In addition to his murals for the public buildings of Karlsruhe and Baden-Baden, Gleichauf's series of thirty-nine watercolors portraying Baden peasant costumes, a series preserved in the Badisches Landesmuseum Karlsruhe, deserves special mention. Gleichauf planned to have these works printed in color and placed on sale, but because he could not get enough backing for this enterprise, the project was discontinued after only ten of the pictures had been printed.

1. Josef August Beringer, *Badische Malerei 1770-1920*, 2nd ed., Karlsruhe, 1922, p. 17.

14. Heidelberg and the Neckar Honoring Badenia

[*Die Stadt Heidelberg und der Neckar bringen der Badenia ihre Huldigung dar*], 1856.
Pencil on ivory paper, 35.1 x 46.4 cm (image with projecting arch 24.4/28.3 x 42.9 cm).
Dated in pencil on the tablet under the throne: *1856;* signed in pencil lower right under the borderline: *R. Gleichauf gez.*

Provenance: Formerly part of the Grand Ducal private collection. Inv. no. VIII 1475.
Bibliography: Theilmann and Ammann, 1978, I, pp. 215-16, no. 1239, illus. II, p. 134.

Responding in a letter on January 12, 1856, to the invitation to take part in the "Heidelberger Friedrich – Luisen – Album" (see nos. 7, 16, 27, 65-66), in which this work eventually became sheet no. 2, Gleichauf proposed three themes which he was willing to execute and then continued:

> *I would most of all like to be able to carry out my own idea, and I am sure that it would fit well with the whole project and at the same time give me an opportunity to create some beautiful forms and figures. It is as follows: Three allegorical figures in a group; in the middle the city of Heidelberg as an imposing matron, festively attired, holding two shields with the names or coats of arms of the Prince Regent and of Princess Louise. To one side would stand the Neckar as a youth holding in one hand a thyrsus staff with grapes, in the other an overflowing goblet. On the other side would be a young female figure representing the University and extending a wreath of laurel or of flowers toward the shield bearing the name of the royal bride. The whole thing would be done in watercolors and would make a fresh, festive impression. It could serve equally well as a dedicatory page or as the title page. If you are able to approve of this plan, then I am sure there will be no opposition to my undertaking it.*[1]

When Gleichauf sent the drawing off on August 28, he remarked in an accompanying letter:

> *With reference to the Heidelberg work, I must inform you that on the advice of my friends I have not added any color. Thus I am sending a pencil drawing which, I hope, will have its own role as a pale beauty among the others. The left figure, which represents the artistic city of Heidelberg, has a blank shield because I was simply unable to find a coat of arms for the city. If you know of any such insignia, please go ahead and draw in one with hard pencil or have it done in Heidelberg. – The middle figure is intended to represent Baden. – If you will, let me know what you think of the drawing. My colleagues here and also Hofbaumeister Diepold have praised it. As an honorarium I request the sum of one hundred guilders.*[2]

1. Rudolf Gleichauf letter to Ludwig Kachel, January 12, 1856, in the Badisches Generallandesarchiv, Karlsruhe (hereafter BGK), Abt. 69, N 9, no. 19.
2. Gleichauf to Kachel, August 28, 1856, in BGK, Abt. 69, N 9, no. 19.

Johann Grund

Vienna 1808 – Baden-Baden 1887

Grund was born in Vienna on May 19, 1808, and he attended the Vienna Academy. In 1831 he became a citizen of Baden; in 1839 he was named a court painter. He undertook extensive study trips to Munich, Vienna, Düsseldorf, and to Italy, where he lived for a total of nine months. After returning to Baden in 1843, he settled in Baden-Baden. In 1844 he made a trip to Hungary; in 1847 he spent three months in Paris. During the same year he received permission to remain abroad for two years. He died in Baden-Baden on August 4, 1887.

Grund primarily produced portraits, genre scenes and religious subjects. His portraits belong to the tradition of Biedermeier realism, but the sentimental coloring of his Biblical scenes reveals the influence of the later Nazarenes. The combination of emotionalism and idealism in his portraits of Italian peasant life indicates his acquaintance with the works of Léopold Robert. It is as a portraitist that Grund produced his best work.

15. Portrait of the Artist's First Wife

[*Bildnis der ersten Gattin des Künstlers*], 1831.
Watercolor and gouache with highlights in gold-bronze gouache on

smooth cream cardboard; slightly discolored, 13.9 x 11.1 cm. Signed and dated in pencil lower right: *C. Joh. Grund. 1831.*

Provenance: Acquired in 1939 from Mrs. M. Hofer, Hall in Tyrolia, the artist's granddaughter. Inv. no. 1939-6.
Exhibition: Karlsruhe, 1966, no. 26, illus. no. 15; Haus der Kunst, Munich, *Das Aquarell 1400-1950,* 1972-73, no. 111, illus. p. 102; Karlsruhe, 1978, p. 9.
Bibliography: Walter Koschatzky, *Das Aquarell: Entwicklung, Technik, Eigenart,* Vienna and Munich, 1969, p. 66, illus. no. 17; Theilmann and Ammann, 1978, I, p. 233, no. 1354, illus. II, p. 38.

Nothing is known about Grund's first wife who is depicted here with extraordinary aesthetic intensity. Recalling the perfection of miniature painting, Grund's brush technique lends magical charm to the lady's youthful beauty. This work was surely conceived from the outset as a finished, autonomous work of art, not just as a study or a sketch for a larger painting.

Louis Friedrich Hoffmeister

Karlsruhe 1814 – Karlsruhe 1869

Hoffmeister was born on July 20, 1814, in Karlsruhe. At first he studied under Carl Ludwig Frommel (nos. 12-13) and was trained as a steel engraver. Then he went to Munich, where he studied for an additional six years. Thereafter he traveled extensively, visiting London, Paris, Bremen, Hamburg, Berlin, Poland, Russia, Hungary, Dalmatia, northern Italy, Salzburg, and Vienna. In 1841 Grand Duke Leopold of Baden named him a court engraver. The Duke of Nassau bestowed on him the *goldene Verdienstmedaille,* a medal for service to art and science, and Friedrich Wilhelm IV of Prussia presented him with the Red Order of the Eagle, Fourth Class, for his portrayal of the general staff of the Prussian Army which in 1849 had crushed the republican uprising in Baden. In the mid-1850's Hoffmeister turned to photography. He died in Karlsruhe on July 15, 1869.

Hoffmeister worked primarily in watercolors, and his works show the clear influence of his teacher Frommel. Besides some individual portraits and a few group portraits, his work consists primarily of landscapes. Some of these are precise topographic representations of Freiburg im Breisgau, Schloß Eberstein, the island of Mainau, or the palace gardens of Karlsruhe; others suggest the general feeling of an area (e.g., southern Bavaria) but deliberately avoid identifiable details. Hoffmeister's technical background served him well in preparing his exacting works. His oeuvre is characterized not by wild fantasy nor by a strong sense of artistic individuality, but by a consistent dedication to his craftsmanship.

16. View of Freiburg

[*Blick auf Freiburg*], n.d.
Watercolor over pencil with touches of gum arabic on ivory paper, 19.3 x 29.4 cm.
Inscribed in brownish-red wash lower right: *L. Hoffmeister Carlsruhe.*

Provenance: Formerly part of the Grand Ducal private collection. Inv. no. P. K. I 675 3 30.
Bibliography: Schefold, 1971, II, nos. 23268 and 23275 (erroneously listed under both numbers); Theilmann and Ammann, 1978, I, p. 264, no. 1559, illus. II, p. 140.

This is sheet no. 30 of the "Heidelberger Friedrich – Luisen – Album" presented by German artists to Grand Duke Friedrich I and Princess Luise of Prussia on the occasion of their wedding on September 20, 1856 (see nos. 7, 14, 27, 65-66).

The view is taken from the Schloßberg, looking toward the northwest at the city and the cathedral. In the left foreground are the ruins of the old castle. In front of the choir of the cathedral is the archidiocisan Konvikt, a theological seminary. To the middle left is the Augustinian monastery and tower of the Martinstor, the medieval city gateway. To the center right is the Protestant Ludwigskirche, a building completed in 1839. It was designed by Heinrich Hübsch (no. 17) and constructed using the stones from the former monastery of Tennenbach. To the left of the church is the Karlskaserne, a garrison; in the background is the Rhine valley with the Kaiserstuhl.

Heinrich Hübsch

Weinheim an der Bergstraße 1795 – Karlsruhe 1863

Hübsch was born in Weinheim an der Bergstraße on February 9, 1795. In 1813 he began the study of philosophy and mathematics at the University in Heidelberg. Then in 1815 he moved to Karlsruhe in order to study architecture under Friedrich Weinbrenner. After three years' study he undertook trips to Italy, Greece and Constantinople. He successfully completed his qualifying examinations in 1821, and then spent some time in Rome. In 1824 he was appointed an instructor in the school of architecture of the Städelsches Institut in Frankfurt am Main, but he returned to Karlsruhe in 1827 to become the city's architectural supervisor. In 1829 he was appointed architectural counselor to the Grand Duchy and succeeded his mentor Weinbrenner as the highest ranking architect in the country. During the succeeding years, he traveled to Italy (1837, 1847, 1853, 1859), France (1840, 1853, 1859), London (1846), Berlin (1842), and Munich (1843, 1858). He died in Karlsruhe on April 3, 1863.

Hübsch was the designer of the Großherzogliche Gemäldegalerie (Grand Ducal Painting Gallery) in Karlsruhe (1838-46) and was, after Friedrich Weinbrenner, the most significant architect in Baden during the first half of the nineteenth century. Hübsch based his work on the architecture of early Christianity and of the Italian renaissance, and he made an independent and decisive mark on the historic-romantic architecture of his day. The most important aspects of his work were the technical soundness and the balanced proportions of his designs, his conscientious selection of materials suited to the form and beauty of his buildings, and his understated use of decoration. He published a number of theoretical treatises in which he expounded upon the bases for his aesthetic views on architecture, among them the following: *In welchem Style sollen wir bauen (What Style Should We Use for Our Buildings)*, 1828; *Die Architektur und ihr Verhältnis zur heutigen Malerei und Skulptur (Architecture and Its Relationship to Contemporary Painting and Sculpture)*, 1847; *Die Altchristlichen Kirchen nach den Baudenkmalen und älteren Beschreibungen und der Einfluß des altchristlichen Baustils auf den Kirchenbau aller späteren Perioden (Ancient Christian Churches in Earlier Descriptions and as They Survive Today, and the Influence of Ancient Christian Architecture on the Ecclesiastical Structures of All Later Epochs)*, 1862.

17. Façade of the Karlsruhe Theater

[*Die Hauptfassade des Karlsruher Hoftheaters*], [1850-52].
Watercolor over pencil on ivory paper (watermark: J WHATMAN / 1850), 40.0 x 61.8 cm.

Provenance: Acquired in 1963, by exchange with the Staatsgalerie, Stuttgart (Lugt 2323). Inv. no. 1963-53.
Bibliography: Theilmann and Ammann, 1978, I, pp. 271-72, no. 1612, illus. II, p. 42.

The old theater which Weinbrenner had designed was destroyed by fire on February 28, 1847. Quickly thereafter the Orangery on what is today Hans-Thoma-Straße, was modified to serve as a temporary theater. But the interior of this building was felt to be so unsatisfactory that it was soon decided to build a new theater, and Grand Duke Leopold gave Hübsch the commission for this building in May of the same year. After attempts were made to preserve the foundations of Weinbrenner's building and to salvage as much of the old materials as possible, construction began February, 1851. The façade shown in this drawing was started in June of 1852, and the theater was finally opened on May 17, 1853. The sculptures on the tympanum and the medallions on the pilasters were designed by Franz Xaver Reich. In his monograph on Hübsch, Arthur Valdenaire wrote:

> *Hübsch kept the façade relatively low so that it would not clash with the palace, attempting to identify the building as a theater by stressing both the raised portion over the stage and the rotunda above the auditorium.*[1]

Hübsch's theater was destroyed during World War II. Its site is now occupied by the Bundesverfassungsgericht, the highest court of constitutional law in the Federal Republic of Germany.

1. Arthur Valdenaire, *Heinrich Hübsch: Eine Studie zur Baukunst der Romantik*, Karlsruhe, 1926, pp. 71-72.

Johann Baptist Kirner

Furtwangen 1806 – Furtwangen 1866

Kirner was born on June 24, 1806, in Furtwangen in the Black Forest. In 1822, after a period of apprenticeship in Villingen and Freiburg im Breisgau, he entered the school of art in Augsburg, where he was trained in historical painting. He received a grant from the Grand Duchy to continue his studies at the Academy in Munich, where he took instruction from Clemens von Zimmermann and Peter von Cornelius from 1824 to 1829. In 1829 he traveled to Switzerland; from 1832 to 1837 he lived in Rome, except for the spring of 1833, which he spent in Naples. He stayed in Vienna in 1838, after which he took up residence in Munich, where with a few interruptions he remained until 1864. Kirner was named a court painter in 1840, but he lived in Karlsruhe only from 1842 to 1844. He died on November 19, 1866, in Furtwangen.

During his long stay in Rome, where he shared a studio with Franz Xaver Winterhalter (nos. 68-70), Kirner devoted himself to genre scenes portraying Italian peasant life without exaggerated pathos. A strong sense of color characterizes his work from this period, and his oil landscapes are marked by broad, bold brush strokes. The sketchiness of these works suggests that they were spontaneous renderings of the artist's direct and immediate experiences. Kirner's use of brilliant contrasts between bright and shaded surfaces reproduces convincingly the intensity of the southern light on the Italian countryside. After his return to Germany, Kirner used a darker palette to paint genre scenes portraying peasants of the Black Forest. These works were more anecdotal, concentrating on the humorous and idyllic aspects of rural life rather than on the harsh reality of peasants' existence.

18. Religious Procession in an Italian Mountain City

[*Prozession in einer italienischen Bergstadt*], [*1832-37*].
Oil on thin cream cardboard, 20.4 x 27.7 cm.

Provenance: Acquired in 1867, bequest of the artist. Inv. no. VIII 1776-147.
Exhibition: Furtwangen, 1967, no. 28.
Bibliography: Theilmann and Ammann, 1978, I, pp. 308-09, no. 1888, illus. II, p. 153.

19. Italian Landscape with Two Figures

[*Italienische Landschaft mit Eselreiter und Frau mit Kopflast*], [1832-37].
Oil on thin brown cardboard, 27.8 x 43.8 cm.

Provenance: Acquired in 1867, bequest of the artist. Inv. no. VIII 1776-21.
Exhibition: Furtwangen, 1967, no. 29.
Bibliography: Theilmann and Ammann, 1978, I, p. 309, no. 1889, illus. II, p. 153.

Both of these nature studies were executed during Kirner's stay in Italy between 1832 and 1837.

20. Wilhelm, Margrave of Baden

[*Markgraf Wilhelm von Baden, nach links gewendet*], [1841-42].
Oil over pencil on cream cardboard, 51.6 x 32.0 cm.

Provenance: Acquired in 1867, bequest of the artist. Inv. no. VIII 1776-12.
Bibliography: Theilmann and Ammann, 1978, I, pp. 312-13, no. 1925, illus. II, p. 351.

This is a preliminary study for an 1842 painting entitled *Eine Jagdpartie im Großherzoglichen Wildpark bei Karlsruhe (Hunting Party in the Grand Ducal Game Preserve near Karlsruhe),* which is currently part of the collection of His Royal Highness Margrave Max of Baden.[1] Wilhelm is the fifth figure from the left.

Wilhelm Ludwig August, Margrave of Baden, was born on April 8, 1792, the second son of Grand Duke Karl Friedrich and his second wife, Luise Freiin Geyer von Geyersberg. Wilhelm received the title of Graf von Hochberg (Count) in 1796. He became a lieutenant of the Royal Swedish Army while he was still quite young, and in 1805, when barely a teenager, he was named a major in the Royal Baden Army. In 1808 he was named a colonel and given the command of a front-line regiment. He served as a commander during the battle of Leipzig (October 16-19, 1813). In 1817 Wilhelm was elevated to the rank of prince and given the title Margrave of Baden. In 1819 he was named president of the upper chamber of the Baden parliament. Wilhelm was married to Duchess Elisabeth von Württemberg. He died on October 11, 1859, in Karlsruhe.

1. Badischer Kunstverein, Karlsruhe, *Romantiker und Realisten: Maler des 19. Jahrhunderts in Baden*, 1965, no. 65, illus.

21. Peasant Youth in Black Forest Costume

[*Nach links sitzender junger Bauer in Schwarzwälder Tracht, sich mit der Rechten an den Kopf greifend*], [1845-47].
Oil on beige cardboard, 46.5 x 30.7 cm.

Provenance: Acquired in 1867, bequest of the artist. Inv. no. VIII 1776-131.
Bibliography: Theilmann and Ammann, 1978, I, pp. 313-14, no. 1932, illus. II, p. 352.

This is a preliminary study for the young man seated at the narrow edge of the table in the 1847 painting *Die Kartenschlägerin (The Card Shark),* which previously hung in the Neue Pinakothek in Munich (current location unknown).[1]

1. Max Wingenroth, "Schwarzwälder Maler," *Vom Bodensee zum Main,* No. 19 (1922), illus. 44.

Wilhelm Klose

Karlsruhe 1830 – Karlsruhe 1914

Klose was born in Karlsruhe on November 18, 1830. From 1846 to 1851 he studied at the Academy in Munich; after his studies he undertook several trips, including excursions to the Alps, to Dalmatia (1851), and to Rome and its vicinity (1851-53). After a short stay in Karlsruhe he traveled to Sicily and Greece in 1867 and then spent some time in Egypt and Asia Minor. He continued to travel and spent several extended periods in Rome and Olevano (1869, 1872-74, 1877, 1878, 1892). Klose died in Karlsruhe on August 31, 1914.

The famous Italian and Greek landscapes which Carl Rottmann painted for Ludwig I of Bavaria profoundly influenced Klose. The inspiration he received from them during his student years was to affect his artistic production throughout his life. Klose totally ignored the stylistic revolution taking place about him, devoting himself instead to classical landscape in the heroic style. His broadly conceived subjects derive from sketches which he made during his numerous and extensive trips to Italy and Greece. These studies as well as the finished compositions are characterized by a masterful sense of balance; dispensing with human activity, the artist creates a mood of tranquillity in which he presents the landscape of a grandiose and ancient culture.

22. Etruscan Cliff Tombs in the Val d'Asso

[*Etrurische Felsengräber im Val d'Asso*], [1874].
Pen and ink over pencil on light beige paper (blindstamp: CARL SCHLEICHER & SCHÜLL), 41.1 x 51.9 cm.
Signed in pen and ink lower left: *W. Klose.*

Provenance: Acquired in 1942 from the estate of Medizinalrat Hoffmann; formerly part of the artist's estate. Inv. no. 1942-648.
Bibliography: Josef Durm. *Die Baustile: Historische und technische Entwicklung:* II, *Die Baukunst der Etrusker: Die Baukunst der Römer,* 2nd ed. Stuttgart, 1905, illus. following p. 16; Theilmann and Ammann, 1978, I, pp. 323-24, no. 2031, illus. II, p. 45.

This drawing, probably executed in 1874, is apparently the preliminary study for one of the fourteen frescoes in the Villa Klose (no longer extant) in Karlsruhe. The slightly curved upper margin of the picture is repeated in other views etched after the frescoes in the villa by Eugène Edouard Adler-Mesnard entitled *Cerveteri: Gräberstraße (Cerveteri: Row of Tombs)* and *Cerveteri: Etruskische Felsengräber (Cerveteri: Etruscan Rock Tombs)* in *Ansichten aus Griechenland und Italien (Views of Greece and Italy).*[1]

1. *Ansichten aus Griechenland und Italien: Vierzehn Blatt: Gemalt von Wilhelm Klose: Radirt* [sic] *von E. Adler-Mesnard,* Vienna: P. Kaeser, pls. XIII and XIV.

23. Classical Landscape: Corinth

[*Klassische Landschaft (Korinth)*], [by 1877].

Pen and ink over pencil on ivory paper, 17.9 x 30.4 cm.
Signed in pen and ink lower right: *W. Klose.*

Provenance: Formerly part of the Grand Ducal private collection. Inv. no. P. K. I 675-7-22.
Bibliography: Theilmann and Ammann, 1978, I, p. 325, no. 2042, illus. II, p. 45.

This is sheet no. 22 of the "Friedrich I Album" of 1877 presented by the artists of Baden to Grand Duke Friedrich on the occasion of the twenty-fifth anniversary of his reign on April 24, 1877.

The view is taken from the west towards the Acrocorinthus, the high rock fortress to the west of the ancient city. In the middle are the seven remainings pillars of the Temple of Apollo (ca. 540 B.C.), which was erected above the market place.

Korinth, etched by Eugène Edouard Adler-Mesnard for the portfolio *Ansichten aus Griechenland und Italien* (see no. 22), was one of the prints reproducing the fourteen frescoes from the Villa Klose.[1] Apparently Klose based one of the frescoes on this drawing.

1. *Ansichten aus Griechenland und Italien: Vierzehn Blatt: Gemalt von Wilhelm Klose: Radirt* [sic] *von E. Adler-Mesnard,* Vienna: P. Kaeser, pl. VIII.

Albert Lang

Karlsruhe 1847 — Munich 1933

Lang was born in Karlsruhe on November 15, 1847. At first he studied architecture in Karlsruhe (1864-68) and then continued his studies under Johann Heinrich Strack at the Bauakademie of Berlin (1868-69). After spending 1869-70 in Italy, he decided to take up painting and went to the Academy in Munich to study under Alexander Straehuber. He was a student at the Karlsruhe Academy in 1873. From 1874 to 1888 he lived in Florence, and from 1888 to 1897 in Frankfurt am Main. In 1897 he moved to Munich, where he died on December 1, 1933.

Lang is known primarily for his landscapes, portraits, and figure compositions. During his early years in Munich he was one of a group of artists including Charles Schuch, Theodor Alt, Wilhelm Trübner (no. 64), Ernst Sattler, and Rudolf Hirth du Frênes who gathered around the towering figure of Wilhelm Leibl. Throughout the first stage of his career which ends about 1875, Lang's works were strongly influenced by the painterly realism of Leibl. In 1874 he joined Hans Thoma (nos. 57-63) on the latter's first trip to Italy, accompanying him as far as Florence, where he remained until 1888. Here Lang met the painters Hans von Marées, Arnold Böcklin, and Karl von Pidoll, and the sculptor Adolf Hildebrand. The companionship he shared with these artists influenced both the style and the subject of his work. The monumentality of Marées' landscape and figure compositions led to a fundamental shift in Lang's attitude towards art. He turned away from his monochromatic, highly painterly technique of the early 1870's towards a linear conception visible in his later portraits, figure compositions and even his landscapes. This stylistic change also shows the influence of his friend Emil Lugo (nos. 27-28).

24. Rocky Pathway near Lerici with Group of Figures in the Background

[*Felsiger Weg bei Lerici mit Figurengruppe im Hintergrund*], 1874.
Pencil with highlights in white gouache (partially oxidized) on grayish blue paper, 29.2 x 43.4 cm.
Inscribed in pencil lower right: *Lerici 28 July 1874/Albert Lang* (*Albert Lang* apparently added at a later date with a different pencil).

Provenance: Acquired in 1936 from Ella Geissler-Thoma, Berlin; formerly part of the estate of Hans Thoma (Lugt S. 2395a). Inv. no. 1936-28.
Bibliography: Theilmann and Ammann, 1978, I, p. 354, no. 2222, illus. II, p. 164.

Even though this work was executed in Italy, it still maintains the tradition of the painters in the circle around Wilhelm Leibl. This picture shares the same subject matter and even the same details, especially on the left side, with a painting from the same period, *Landschaft bei Lerici (Landscape near Lerici),* which hangs in the Staatliche Kunsthalle Karlsruhe.[1] Another version differing only in the position of the figures was sold at auction by Dr. Helmut Tenner of Heidelberg.[2]

1. Staatliche Kunsthalle, Karlsruhe, inv. no. 2010; see Theilmann and Ammann, 1971, pp. 149-50, illus. p. 254.
2. Auction 55, Dr. Helmut Tenner, Heidelberg, April 23, 1966, no. 3878, illus. pl. XXIX.

Karl Lindemann-Frommel

Markirch 1819 — Rome 1891

The adoptive son and later the pupil of Carl Ludwig Frommel (nos. 12-13), Lindemann-Frommel was born in Markirch (Alsace) on August 19, 1819. After spending his early years in Karlsruhe, he went to Munich, where he studied under Carl Rottmann. He spent the years 1845-49 away from Germany, living in Paris and Rome. In 1856 he moved to Rome, living there till his death on May 16, 1891.

The landscape painter Karl Lindemann-Frommel, like Wilhelm Klose (nos. 22-23), is one of several artists who were strongly influenced by Carl Rottmann. His longing for the classical landscape of Italy was so deep that eventually he took up permanent residence in the South. The marvelous color contrasts in his numerous paintings of the area around Rome, La Spèzia, and Naples, as well as of the island of Capri, demonstrate his mastery of this type of subject although his oil compositions seem somewhat stylized and stage-managed. The freshness and immediacy of the Italian landscape is best captured in his meticulous drawings and watercolors (see no. 25). Those works, which were composed for the series *Vignetten aus Rom (Vignettes from Rome),* 1847 and *Skizzen aus Rom und Umgebung (Sketches from Rome and Its Vicinity),* 1855, combine the immediacy of his watercolors with the more deliberate sense of planning and composition typical of his oils, thus achieving, as Franz Kugler described it, "a most fortunate unity . . . and a most effective artistic impact."[1]

1. Franz Kugler in *Deutsches Kunstblatt* II (1851), p. 296.

25. View of Ariccia

[*Blick auf Ariccia*], 1845.
Pencil with highlights in white gouache on brownish paper, 17.6 x 23.2 cm.
Inscribed in pencil lower left center: *Ariccia, am 2 Aug 45.*

Provenance: Acquired in 1900 from the estate of Manfred Lindemann-Frommel, the artist's son. Inv. no. VIII 1870-2.
Exhibition: Badischer Kunstverein, Karlsruhe, 1900 (an exhibition of works from the artist's estate, without catalogue).
Bibliography: Theilmann and Ammann, 1978, I, p. 364, no. 2273, illus. II, p. 166.

The city of Ariccia lies between Lake Nemi and the Albanese Mountains. It was conquered by the Romans in 338 B.C. During the Middle Ages it became part of the holdings of the Savelli. Pope Alexander VII, a member of the Chigi family, acquired the city in 1661, and he commissioned Lorenzo Bernini in 1661 to build both the Palazzo Chigi and the church of S. Maria dell'Assunzione, which has a central domed structure with an attached portico. This drawing shows the apse of the church flanked by two towers.[1]

1. Max von Boehn, *Lorenzo Bernini: Seine Zeit, sein Leben, sein Werk,* Bielefeld and Leipzig, 1927, illus. no. 56.

26. View of Rome from Monte Mario

[*Blick vom Monte Mario auf Rom*], 1848.
Watercolor over pencil with touches of gum arabic on cream cardboard, 22.6 x 33.7 cm.
Signed in pen and brown ink lower left center: *Karl Lindemann-fromel;* inscribed lower right center: *Rom, 11 Mai 1848.*

Provenance: Part of the Grand Ducal private collection until 1855. Inv. no. VIII 1871.
Bibliography: Theilmann and Ammann, 1978, I, pp. 364-65, no. 2274, illus. II, p. 166.

This view is from Monte Mario, located northwest of Rome. Lindemann-Frommel used the same composition with only a few changes for a landscape in his portfolio *Lindemann-Frommels Skizzen aus Rom und der Umgebung: Aus Neu Rom, II. Theil (Lindemann-Frommel's Sketches of Rome and its Vicinity: From New Rome, part II).* The lithograph is entitled *Rom von Monte Mario aus (Rome as Seen from Monte Mario)* and is inscribed and dated: *Rom 1848.*[1] There is a related composition in the Staatliche Graphische Sammlung in Munich,[2] which is taken from a somewhat different point of view. In 1881 the artist used the same motif in his painting *Blick auf Rom von der Villa Mellini auf Monte Mario, bei Sonnenuntergang (Sunset: View of Rome from the Villa Mellini on Monte Mario).*[3]

1. *Kunstblatt,* No. 37 (1851), pp. 295-96.
2. Staatliche Graphische Sammlung, Munich, inv. no. 21846.
3. Boetticher, 1891-1901, I/2, p. 876, no. 22; see also *Jubiläums-Ausstellung der Königlichen Akademie der Künste,* Berlin, 1886, no. 692.

Emil Lugo

Stockach 1840 – Munich 1902

Lugo was born in Stockach on June 26, 1840. He received his first drawing instruction from Joseph Anton Geßler and Karl Rösch at the Gymnasium in Freiburg im Breisgau. In 1856 he began his studies under Johann Wilhelm Schirmer (nos. 37-43) at the Academy in Karlsruhe, where he remained until 1865. In the fall of 1869 he made a study trip to Dresden to visit Ludwig Richter and Julius Schnorr von Carolsfeld, and continued to Weimar to visit Friedrich Preller, Sr. Lugo spent the years 1871-74 in Italy. He moved from Karlsruhe to Munich in the late summer of 1888, dying there on June 4, 1902.

A contemporary critic called Lugo "the last romantic of our sober age."[1] He is one of the most significant and most individualistic of Baden's landscape artists of the latter half of the nineteenth century. Lugo pursued Schirmer's artistic ideals to their limits. He was totally opposed to the simple compositions of his Munich colleagues grouped around Eduard Schleich and Adolf Lier. He could not begin to understand their tendency to discount the content of a work in favor of its execution. "For me, nature is a festival, a holiday," he proclaimed, "and I want it to lift me up out of the drudgery of everyday life."[2] Lugo's numerous early oil studies and drawings from nature do not yet reflect his strong philosophical notions of the principles of composition (see no. 27). But by the 1860's, his work begins to reveal a rigor and dogmaticism which increasingly served to isolate him both artistically and socially (see no. 28).

The greatest influences on Lugo were the works of Schirmer and the poetical, classical landscapes of Claude Lorrain. He associated frequently with the aesthetic philosopher Konrad Fiedler, who acquainted him with the works of Hans von Marées and Arnold Böcklin – works which Lugo felt were essentially similar to his own. Lugo was the last significant representative of the school of heroic landscape painting in Germany.

1. *Kunstchronik,* N.F. XVI (1905), column 395.
2. Beringer, 1912, p. 85.

27. Landscape with Oak Tree under Stormy Sky

[*Landschaft mit Eiche unter gewittrigem Himmel*], [ca. 1856].
Watercolor over pencil, gouache, with highlights in white gouache on thin beige cardboard, 34.4 x 43.0 cm.
Signed in pen and ink lower left: *Emil Lugo.*

Provenance: Formerly part of the Grand Ducal private collection. Inv. no. P. K. 1675-3-140.
Bibliography: Beringer, 1912, p. 90; Beringer, 1925, p. 18, illus. p. 12; Schneider, 1935, p. 82, illus. pl. 46 b; Schneider, 1968, p. 110, illus. no. 106; Theilmann, 1971, p. 150, note 660, illus. no. 51; Theilmann and Ammann, 1978, I, p. 375, no. 2330, illus. II, p. 170.

This is sheet no. 140 of the "Heidelberger Friedrich – Luisen – Album," a gift of German artists on the occasion of the marriage of Grand Duke Friedrich I of Baden and Princess Luise of Prussia on September 20, 1856 (see nos. 7, 14, 16, 65-66).

This watercolor was probably executed immediately after Lugo entered the Karlsruhe Academy in 1856. It shows the outstanding talent of this young student and at the same time reveals the strong influence of Schirmer, his teacher. There are numerous works of Schirmer's which contain similar ancient, gnarled oaks stretching out their limbs to a storm-laden sky.

28. Italian Mountain Road with Peasants and Shepherds

[*Italienische Gebirgsstraße mit aufsteigenden Bauern und Hirten*], 1866.
Pencil on ivory paper, 39.4 x 58.5 cm.
Signed and dated in pencil lower left: *E. Lugo. 1866.*

Provenance: Acquired in 1908, gift of Mathilde Lugo, Freiburg im Breisgau, the artist's sister. Inv. no. VIII 1889-33.
Bibliography: Theilmann, 1971, p. 157 (entitled *Heroische Felsenlandschaft*), note 705; illus. no. 81; Theilmann and Ammann, p. 382, no. 2398, illus. II., p. 171.

The tiny parallel shading strokes executed with hard pencil are typical of Lugo's works around 1865-66. The scale of composition corresponds more to that of a painting than of a drawing, and it reflects Lugo's belief in a "magnificent nature" which he was determined to capture and portray in his art. Several aspects of the drawing show a familiarity with the works of Friedrich Preller, Sr.: the compositional scheme with a series of trees and rocky cliffs, an emphasis on the middle ground, and the narrow gap at the lower left with a view into the far distance. This work, probably drawn in Freiburg im Breisgau, is an imaginary landscape evocative of the Italian countryside, which Lugo did not visit until 1871. There is a closely related work dated the same year in the Augustinermuseum Freiburg im Breisgau.[1]

1. Augustinermuseum, Freiburg im Breisgau, inv. no. 12392; see Theilmann, 1971, illus. 82.

Friedrich Mosbrugger

Constance 1804 – St. Petersburg 1830

Mosbrugger was born in Constance on September 19, 1804. He was the brother of Josef Mosbrugger and the son of Wendelin Mosbrugger, who was apparently his first drawing and painting instructor. Friedrich studied at the Academy in Munich from 1822 to 1826, then was active in Karlsruhe between 1826 and 1827. He spent about two years in Italy, from late November 1827 until the summer of 1829, visiting Rome, Olevano, Civitella, Capri, Naples, and Venice. From January to August of 1830 he was again in Karlsruhe. He then undertook a journey to Russia, and was in St. Petersburg when he died on October 17, 1830.

Friedrich Mosbrugger was one of Baden's earliest painters of genre scenes. Even though his oeuvre was limited by his untimely death, the few examples which he produced show the great talent he had for capturing mood and personality, a talent which he developed through his study of seventeenth century Dutch painting. Mosbrugger also devoted himself to the execution of portraits in both oil and pencil which are characterized by a solid, realistic approach to their subjects. He regards his models with a cold, objective eye; there is no trace of romanticizing emotionalism in his images. During his stay in Italy (1827-29) Mosbrugger turned his hand to landscape composition, and a number of remarkable drawings survive from this period.

29. Leopold Mosbrugger in His Study

[*Leopold Mosbrugger in seiner Studierstube*], 1825.
Pencil on off-white paper, 20.8 x 25.7 cm.
Inscribed in pencil by another hand lower center: *Prfeßor der Mathematik Leopold Mosbrugger in Arau;* inscribed lower right: *Konst 1825.*

Provenance: Unknown; part of the museum's collection before 1885. Inv. no. VIII 2003-11.
Exhibition: Constance, 1969, no. 87.
Bibliography: Bringmann and Blanckenhagen, 1974, p. 95, no. F 18a; Theilmann and Ammann, 1978, I, p. 415, no. 2640, illus. II, p. 172.

Leopold Mosbrugger (1796-1864), Friedrich's step-brother,

> *studied mathematics in Heidelberg, Karlsruhe, and Freiburg, and finally secured a position as teacher at the Lyzeum in Constance. Joseph Mosbrugger gave a penetrating description of him in his memoirs: "He was completely uninterested in art. . . . Although he had a quick temper, he was really a good sort; and quite individualistic: even in his later years he was unable to adapt to the norms of society, perhaps because he did not want to."*[1]

The drawing is a preliminary study of a portrait painted in 1825 entitled *Leopold Mosbrugger in seiner Studierstube (Leopold Mosbrugger in His Study),* a work now in a private collection in Aarau.[2]

1. Bringmann and Blanckenhagen, 1974, p. 95.
2. Ibid., pp. 95-96 and following illus.

30. Self Portrait with Bandaged Cheeks

[*Selbstbildnis mit verbundenen Backen*], 1827.
Pencil on off-white paper (watermark: J WHATMAN / TURKEY MILL), 18.7 x 14.3 cm.

Signed and dated in pencil lower left: *FMoßbrugger 1827 (F* and *M* linked together).

Provenance: Acquired in 1950 from Gertrud Baumeister, Karlsruhe; formerly part of the estate of the architect Friedrich Eisenlohr. Inv. no. 1950-60.
Exhibition: Constance, 1969, no. 118.
Bibliography: Bringmann and Blanckenhagen, p. 95, illus. no. 44, cat. no. F 166; Theilmann and Ammann, 1978, I, pp. 417-18, no. 2667, illus. II, p. 400.

"Mosbrugger used this composition, without the tragic expression, for a self portrait which he executed later."[1] This *Selbstbildnis im Malerkittel* [*Self Portrait in an Artist's Frock*] was executed in 1829.[2]

1. Bringmann and Blanckenhagen, 1974, p. 95.
2. Ibid., cat. no. F 55, illus. no. 71.

31. Portrait of the Painter Joseph Unger

[*Brustbildnis des Malers Joseph Unger*], n.d.
Pencil on ivory paper, 22.1 x 14.3 cm.
Inscribed in pencil lower right: *Unger / aus / Würzburg / Maler.*

Provenance: Acquired in 1885 from Mr. Gagg, Constance; formerly part of the artist's estate. Inv. no. VIII 2003-12.
Bibliography: Bringmann and Blanckenhagen, 1974, p. 102, cat. no. F 462; Theilmann and Ammann, 1978, I, p. 418, no. 2670, illus. II, p. 171.

Unger was born in Würzburg on July 15, 1808, the son of a Saxon merchant named Heinrich Gottlob Unger and his wife Margarethe, neé Schmitt. In 1826 the family moved to Lohr am Main, but the following year Joseph was back in Würzburg, apparently serving as an apprentice to a painter. In 1838 he became a drawing instructor at the Royal Gewerbeschule, a school of applied arts. He received his painter's license from the city parliament on April 28, 1840, and on July first of the same year he married Auguste Josepha de Malampré. Unger died in Würzburg on April 26, 1841.

Wilhelm Riefstahl

Neustrelitz 1827 – Munich 1888

Riefstahl was born in Neustrelitz in the province of Mecklenburg on August 15, 1827. He began his studies at the Berlin Academy in 1843 under August Wilhelm Ferdinand Schirmer. He lived in Karlsruhe from 1868 to 1878. From 1870 till 1873 he was a professor at the Karlsruhe Academy; from 1875 until 1877 he served as its director. In 1878 he moved to Munich. His many journeys took him to the island of Rügen, to Mecklenburg and Westphalia, along the Rhine, to Switzerland, Tyrol (in the 1850's), and to Rome (1869-70, 1874-75, 1877). He died in Munich on October 11, 1888.

Riefstahl's reputation was established by his large alpine landscapes of Switzerland and Tyrol. His sense of the landscape was well complemented by his knowledge of the life and customs of the area. Writing shortly after the artist's death, H. E. von Berlepsch observed:

> *Riefstahl was one of those rare artists who did not merely make a number of studies so that later he could combine them in a large painting. He was more interested in solving a much larger problem, that of bringing both the space and the surroundings of his pictures into full harmony with the figures within it; in other words, he presented in a painting the totality of what he had experienced and perceived.*[1]

Before undertaking his first trip to the mountains in 1860, Riefstahl spent much of the late 1850's in Westphalia, where he executed from nature a number of landscape studies to be used for an extensive publication on the Westphalian countryside. The drawings of Corvey and Arnsberg were produced as part of this project.

1. H. E. von Berlepsch, "Wilhelm Riefstahl," *Zeitschrift für bildende Kunst,* N.F. I (1890), p. 185.

32. Corvey Abbey from the Southeast

[*Blick von Südosten auf die Abtei Corvey*], 1857.
Pencil and watercolor on beige paper, 21.6 x 29.4 cm.
Inscribed in pencil lower left: *Abtei Corvey. 31/8. 57.;* inscribed lower right center: *weiße Ränder auf den Schornsteinen* (white borders on the chimneys).

Provenance: Acquired from a private source in 1966; formerly part of the collection of a niece of the artist. Inv. no. 1966-2.
Bibliography: Jahrbuch IV (1967), p. 145; Theilmann and Ammann, 1978, I, p. 466, no. 3049, illus. II, p. 178.

This is the preliminary study for illustration 13 in *Bilder aus Westfalen(Scenes from Westphalia).*[1] The abbey of Corvey, located northeast of Höxter in Westphalia, was founded in 816. Construction of a Carolingian church was begun in 822; the nave, which served the Emperor as "his" church during his visits to the abbey, was added between 873 and 885. Only the nave has survived the destruction of the original structure in 1665. The monastery buildings adjoining the church to the north and south date from the seventeenth and eighteenth centuries.

1. Schücking, 1860, illus. pl. 13.

33. View of Arnsberg an der Ruhr

[*Blick vom Klosterberg am Eichholz auf Arnsberg an der Ruhr*], 1859.
Watercolor over pencil on beige paper, 21.6 x 29.3 cm.
Inscribed in pencil lower left: *Arnsberg 19/9. 59.*

Provenance: Acquired from a private source in 1966; formerly part of the collection of a niece of the artist. Inv.no. 1966-3.
Exhibition: Karlsruhe, 1978, p. 20.

Bibliography: Jahrbuch IV (1967), p. 145; Theilmann and Ammann, p. 466, no. 3050, illus. II, p. 178.

This is the preliminary study for plate 10 of *Bilder aus Westfalen (Scenes from Westphalia).*[1] The view is taken from a coffeehouse at the north edge of the Eichholz forest looking north toward the old city of Arnsberg with the Schloßberg and the Stadtkapelle St. Georg in the center. The bridge at the right side leads across the Ruhr.

1. Schücking, 1860, illus. pl. 10; see also W. O. Zerbin, ed., *Arnspergum,* Arnsberg, 1970, n.p.

Philipp Röth

Darmstadt 1841 – Munich 1921

Röth was born in Darmstadt on March 10, 1841. After receiving his first instruction in the studio of the Darmstadt artist August Lucas in 1855, he studied at the Karlsruhe Academy under Johann Wilhelm Schirmer (nos. 37-43) from 1859 to 1860. Here he became a close friend of Eugen Bracht (no. 2) and Hans Thoma (nos. 57-63). In 1861 he moved to Düsseldorf, where he stayed until moving permanently to Munich in 1871. He journeyed to Heidelberg (1858, 1859), the Black Forest (1860, 1861, 1862), Dresden and Paris (1867), and to Holland (1869) in addition to making numerous shorter trips throughout Bavaria. In 1903 he was given the honorary title of Professor. He died in Munich on May 29, 1921.

After moving to Munich, Röth was quickly accepted into the circle of prominent exponents of the *paysage intime,* the French style of intimate landscape. This circle included Otto Frölicher, Ludwig Willroider, and Otto Strützel. There are scores of drawings which testify to Röth's persistent efforts to intensify his contact with nature and to incorporate within his simple compositions a high degree of coloristic refinement. His masterfully composed and brilliantly executed works of the 1890's represent the high point of his career, and they place him within the ranks of the most accomplished landscape artists of the day.

During his studies in Karlsruhe, Röth made numerous sketches from nature. His talent for such works is evident in his tree studies. He preferred to use pencil to capture the effect of intertwined branches in the crowns of trees, but turned to brush and ink to reproduce the nuances and painterly charm of large groves of trees and clumps of bushes.

It did not take Röth long to free himself from the classical formulations of his instructor Schirmer. Even his earliest works (nos. 34-36) attest to his interest in the representation of the nature of his homeland. For him and for many of his contemporaries, the landscape of Italy, which had been considered the model of perfection for generations of landscape artists, became totally meaningless.

34. Heidelberg Castle from the South

[*Blick von Süden auf das Heidelberger Schloß*], 1859.
Pencil on ivory paper, 34.2 x 43.2 cm.
Inscribed in pencil lower right: *Heidelberg, 17. August 59.*

Provenance: Acquired in 1922 from Waldemar Bracht, Darmstadt; formerly part of the estate of the painter Eugen Bracht. Inv. no. VIII 1150-8.
Bibliography: Theilmann, 1971, p. 171, note 810, illus. no. 91 (incorrectly listed as a drawing by Eugen Bracht, corrected in appendix VI, p. 428); Schefold, 1971, II, no. 25260 (incorrectly listed as a drawing by Eugen Bracht); Theilmann and Ammann, 1978, I, p. 468, no. 3062, illus. II, p. 179.

The view is taken from the south towards the bell tower. During his August 1859 stay in Heidelberg, Röth worked together with his friend Eugen Bracht. He made a second, slightly different drawing of this scene which is in the Städelsches Kunstinstitut Frankfurt am Main.[1] Other drawings made during this stay are in the Kurpfälzisches Museum Heidelberg.[2]

1. Städelsches Kunstinstitut, Frankfurt am Main, inv. no. 15884.
2. Kurpfälzisches Museum, Heidelberg, inv. nos. Z 1365, Z 1367 A,[1] Z 1367 B[2], Z 1368, Z 1370.

35. Grove of Trees in Beiertheimer Allee, Karlsruhe

[*Große Baumgruppe in der Beiertheimer Allee in Karlsruhe*], 1860.
Pen and brush and ink over pencil with highlights in white gouache on grayish beige paper, 44.7 x 56.9 cm.
Inscribed in pen and ink lower right: *Ph. Röth. Carlsruhe Beyertheimer. Allee./Juni 1860.*

Provenance: Unknown. Inv. no. VIII 2231.
Bibliography: Theilmann, 1971, p. 191, note 959, illus. no. 149; Theilmann and Ammann, 1978, I, p. 469, no. 3066, illus. II, p. 180.

The Beiertheimer Allee, at that time outside the city proper, had groves of trees which were favorite sketching subjects for the Academy's students. The sense of volume in Röth's impressive drawing is enhanced by his effective use of contrasts between light and dark.

36. The Kaiserberg near Bernau

[*Am Kaiserberg bei Bernau*], 1860.
Brush and grayish blue wash over pencil on cream paper (watermark: NIDDA), 23.7 x 30.4 cm.
Inscribed in pencil lower right: *Kaiserberg, 30 August 60.*

Provenance: Unknown. Inv. no. VIII 2249.
Bibliography. Schefold, 1965, illus. p. 218, no. 166; Theilmann, 1971, p. 192, note 968, illus. no. 156; Schefold, 1971, II, nos. 21336 and 21342; Theilmann and Ammann, 1978, I, p. 469, no. 3068, illus. II, p. 180.

This drawing was composed during the summer holidays of 1860 when Röth and Eugen Bracht visited their friend Hans Thoma in his home town of Bernau.

The scale of gray tones suggests a transparent surface. The lively arrangement of the details emphasizes the naturalness of the scene. A second view of the Kaiserberg, closely related to this one and dated September of the same year, is in the Staatliche Kunsthalle Karlsruhe.[1]

1. Staatliche Kunsthalle, Karlsruhe, inv. no. VIII 2248; see Theilmann and Ammann, 1978, I, p. 469, no. 3069, illus. II, p. 180.

Johann Wilhelm Schirmer

Jülich 1807 – Karlsruhe 1863

Schirmer was born in Jülich, a small town to the west of Cologne, on September 5, 1807. After completing an apprenticeship as a bookbinder in 1824, he entered the Düsseldorf Academy in March of 1825, where he studied under Wilhelm von Schadow. At this time he met Carl Friedrich Lessing, whose landscapes exerted a strong influence on him. In the winter of 1827 Schirmer, Lessing, and a number of fellow students established a society of landscape composition in Düsseldorf. In 1829 Schadow asked Schirmer to take over responsibility for the Academy's newly established class in landscape painting. While at Düsseldorf, Schirmer traveled to the Eifel (1828, 1829), to Belgium (1830), the Black Forest and Switzerland (1835, 1837, 1853), and to Normandy (1836). In 1839 he was named a professor of landscape painting at the Düsseldorf Academy. He spent the years 1839 and 1840 in Italy and later undertook trips to Kassel and Schloß Elmarshausen (1849), Paris (1850), and southern France (1851). He served as director of the Karlsruhe Academy from 1854 until 1863. Schirmer died in Karlsruhe on September 11, 1863.

Schirmer was one of the most significant and one of the best known landscape artists in Germany during the first half of the nineteenth century. Strictly speaking, he is considered a member of the Düsseldorf school of painting, yet after his appointment as the director of the Karlsruhe Academy, which he organized along the patterns established in Düsseldorf, he became the most influential painter in Baden. His reputation as a pedagogue attracted many students. By all accounts, Schirmer is one of the most important representatives of the school of classic historical landscape painting inspired by the works of Claude Lorrain, Poussin, and the Dutch artists of the seventeenth century.

It was in Karlsruhe that Schirmer produced his large, complex cycles of Biblical landscapes, the best known of which is the group *Die Vier Tageszeiten mit Szenen aus dem Gleichnis vom Barmherzigen Samariter (The Four Times of Day with Scenes from the Parable of the Good Samaritan* – 1856-57), an effort which Schirmer himself described as his most significant accomplishment. Schirmer was deeply convinced of the validity of his approach to art, considering it to be of far greater worth than the more objective type of landscape art. The cycle of the Good Samaritan reveals his belief in an idealistic and imaginative art of ideas. The Biblical parable serves as an evocative, symbolic basis for the action portrayed; the cycle itself is organized around the various times of day. Schirmer follows the baroque tradition of placing figures in idealized landscapes which echo and comment upon the action. Although Schirmer executed numerous realistic sketches and drawings during all phases of his work on this cycle (no. 43), he felt that they had no lasting value – as far as he was concerned, they were simply small nature studies or travel notes.

37. View of the Mamelles from the Sabine Hills

[*Landschaft im Sabinergebirge mit Blick zu den Mamellen*], [1839].
Watercolor over pencil on roughed cream paper, 28.2 x 43.5 cm.
Verso inscribed in pencil by another hand: *Schirmer/Die Mamellen im Sabinergebirge.*

Provenance: Unknown. Inv. no. VIII 2362-2.
Bibliography: Zimmermann, 1919-20, p. 69, no. 204; Theilmann and Ammann, 1978, I, p. 499, no. 3269, illus. II, p. 76.

Schirmer probably composed this piece in Rome after nature studies which he had made during a trip in 1839 from September 28 to October 6, visiting Subiaco, the Mamelles, and the monasteries of St. Benedetto and Sta. Scholastica.[1] The background of this drawing showing the Mamelles is identical to that in the picture *Italienische Landschaft (Italian Landscape)* in the Stiftung Kunsthaus Heylshof Worms.[2]

1. Zimmermann, 1919-20, p. 30.
2. Stiftung Kunsthaus Heylshof, Worms, inv. no. 1961-2975.

38. Forest Landscape with View towards Olevano and Mons Artemisio

[*Waldlandschaft mit Blick auf Olevano und den Mons Artemisio*], [1839].

Watercolor over pencil on brown paper (watermark: M inside laurel branches), 43.3 x 54.2 cm.

Provenance: Acquired in 1921 by exchange. Inv. no. VIII 2359.
Exhibition: Karlsruhe, 1966, no. 71; Karlsruhe, 1978, p. 23.
Bibliography: Theilmann, 1971, p. 153, note 676, illus. no. 62; Theilmann and Ammann, 1978, I, pp. 499-500, no. 3273, illus. II, p. 77.

This large scale composition, whose style approaches that of an oil painting, is based on nature studies done around Rome in 1839.

39. The Grotto of Egeria

[*Die Grotte der Egeria*], [1840-41].
Black chalk, pen and brush and brown ink, watercolor on grayish blue paper (watermark: P. M FABRIANO 1833), 58.4 x 84.1 cm.

Inscribed in pencil lower right by another hand: *Z 3689;* verso inscribed by another hand: *J. W. Schirmer.*

Provenance: Unknown. Inv. no. VIII 2367.
Bibliography: Theilmann and Ammann, I, p. 501, no. 3282, illus. II, p. 77.

The grotto of Egeria lies south of Rome in the vicinity of the Via Appia; it is a nymphaeum sacred to the brook Almo, and was formerly clad in marble.

This drawing, composed between 1840 and 1841, is a preliminary study for the famous painting *Die Grotte der Egeria (The Grotto of Egeria),* dated 1841, now in the Museum der bildenden Künste, Leipzig.[1] Another version was exhibited in 1869 in the Kunsthandlung Sachse in Berlin.[2]

In the Germanisches Nationalmuseum Nürnberg there is a nature study dated 1840 which antedates this drawing and shows the background in a slightly different configuration.[3] Another version of this drawing which differs only in minor details is in the Staatliche Museen in Berlin.[4]

1. Museum der bildenden Künste, Leipzig, inv. no. 219; see Maria Buchsbaum, *Deutsche Malerei im 19. Jahrhundert: Realismus und Naturalismus,* Vienna and Munich, no. 41, illus. color.
2. Boetticher, 1891-1901, II/2, p. 567, no. 29.
3. Germanisches Nationalmuseum, Nürnberg, inv. no. Hz 5583; See *Anzeiger des Germanischen Nationalmuseums,* Nürnberg, 1966, pp. 203-4, illus. p. 202, no. 21.
4. Kupferstichkabinett und Sammlung der Zeichnungen, Staatliche Museen, Berlin, no. 8.

40. Sawmill on the Upper Rhine

[*Landschaft aus dem Hinterrheintal mit Sägemühle*], [1853-54].
Charcoal with highlights in white gouache and varnish on brown paper, 44.6 x 63.9 cm.
Signed in charcoal lower right: *J. WSchirmer.*

Provenance: Acquired in 1863 from Emilie Schirmer, Karlsruhe, the artist's widow; formerly part of the artist's estate. Inv. no. VIII 2364.
Bibliography: Zimmermann, 1919-20, p. 69, no. 206; Theilmann and Ammann, 1978, I, p. 505, no. 3321, illus. II, p. 78.

A preliminary nature study, probably made in 1853 during a trip through Switzerland en route to Chiavenna, is in the Städelsches Kunstinstitut, Frankfurt am Main.[1] This is probably a scene from the upper Rhine valley between Andeer and Splügen in Graubünden. The drawing exhibited here was completed ca. 1853-54 in Karlsruhe after Schirmer's return from the trip; it relies heavily on the sketch now located in Frankfurt am Main.

1. Städelsches Kunstinstitut, Frankfurt am Main, inv. no. 5399.

41. Landscape with the Good Samaritan

[*Landschaft mit dem barmherzigen Samariter*], [1853-55].
Charcoal and varnish on light beige paper, 41.7 x 55.2 cm.
Signed in charcoal lower right: *J. WSchirmer.*

Provenance: Unknown. Inv. no. VIII 2365.
Exhibition: Munich, 1929, no. 449 and supplement no. 526.
Bibliography: Zimmermann, 1919-20, pp. 43 and 69, no. 208; Theilmann and Ammann, 1978, I, p. 506, no. 3324, illus. II, p. 78.

Beginning in the 1850's, Schirmer devoted himself to Biblical subjects.[1] Schirmer borrowed the figures in this composition from Alfred Rethel's drawing of the same title,[2] even retaining the bent legs of the victim. The same figures are also found in a Schirmer painting currently in a private collection in Marburg; with only slight variations Schirmer again used them in a charcoal drawing owned by the city of Düren.[3] The greatest difference between the version in this exhibition and the later versions of the same theme lies in the extensive development of the landscape. Here Schirmer seems to focus his interest primarily on the landscape, reducing the Biblical story to mere figurative decoration. For a later example see a drawing in the Kunstmuseum, Düsseldorf.[4] A similar landscape without figures was once in the possession of Liesel Schirmer, Munich. The same composition, this time with the figures from *Überfall (The Assault on the Traveler,* see no. 42), is owned by the city of Jülich. An oil study made between 1853 and 1855 of a bare rocky landscape similar to that of this drawing is in the Hamburger Kunsthalle.[5]

1. Zimmermann, 1919-20, p. 43.
2. Städelsches Kunstinstitut, Frankfurt am Main, inv. no. 13047; see Heinrich Schmidt, *Alfred Rethel,* Neuß, 1959, illus. p. 130.
3. City of Düren, inv. no. 1948-274.
4. Kunstmuseum, Düsseldorf, inv. no. 51/17; see also *Abend (Evening)* from the cycle of the Good Samaritan in the Staatliche Kunsthalle, Karlsruhe, inv. no. 615; see Lauts and Zimmermann, 1971, illus. p. 367.
5. Hamburger Kunsthalle, Hamburg, inv. no. 1313; see Krafft and Schümann, 1969, illus. p. 302.

42. The Assault on the Traveler

[*Der Überfall auf den Wanderer*], [1855].
Fixed charcoal on brown paper, 55.0 x 74.3 cm.
Signed in charcoal lower right: *J. WSchirmer.*

Provenance: Acquired in 1863 from Emilie Schirmer, Karlsruhe, the artist's widow; formerly part of the artist's estate. Inv. no. VIII 2366.
Bibliography: Zimmermann, 1919-20, p. 69, no. 207 (incorrectly titled *Schäfer vom Blitz erschlagen);* Theilmann and Ammann, 1978, I, p. 506, no. 3325, illus. II, p. 79.

This is one of the scenes illustrating the parable of the Good Samaritan, a variation of the composition entitled *Mittag (Noon)* is in the Staatliche Kunsthalle Karlsruhe.[1] The same composition but with a different group of figures is also in the Staatliche Kunsthalle Karlsruhe.[2] The boulders in the center are reminiscent of those in the *Landschaft mit dem Barmherzigen Samariter (Landscape with the Good Samaritan)* in the Kunstmuseum Düsseldorf.[3] The city of Jülich owns an additional, slightly different version of the *Überfall.*

1. Staatliche Kunsthalle, Karlsruhe, inv. no. 614; see Lauts and Zimmermann, 1971, illus. p. 366.
2. Ibid., inv. no. 1411; see also illus. p. 368.
3. Kunstmuseum, Düsseldorf, inv. no. 51/17.

43. Section of the Upper Falls in Allerheiligen

[*Partie beim oberen Wasserfall in Allerheiligen*], 1857.
Black chalk with highlights in white gouache on brown paper, 56.5 x 41.9 cm.
Inscribed in pencil lower right (by another hand?): *J. 1/Baden/1857;* lower left by another hand: *5 fl;* verso in pen and dark brown ink by another hand: *Kunst Schul Inv. S. 3 N° 39;* to the right of this in pencil by another hand: *163/N° 26. Wasserfall bei Allerheiligen* (with the words crossed out).

Provenance: Extended loan from the Staatliche Akademie der bildenden Künste, Karlsruhe. Inv. no. Lg. 740 a.
Exhibition: Munich, 1929, no. 450.
Bibliography: Schefold, 1971, II, no. 20141; Theilmann and Ammann, 1978, I, p. 512, no. 3354, illus. II, p. 186.

Allerheiligen is situated in the Black Forest, northwest of Baiersbronn, between Ruhestein and Schliffkopf. This nature study was composed during one of Schirmer's trips to the Black Forest in 1857. It shows one of a group of five waterfalls which have a combined height of eighty-three meters.

Georg Philip Schmitt

Spesbach 1808 – Heidelberg 1873

Schmitt, the brother of Franz Schmitt and father of Guido Schmitt (no. 46) and Nathanael Schmitt, was born in Spesbach on October 28, 1808. He received his first instruction from Christian Xeller in Heidelberg. From 1825 to 1830 he studied at the Academy in Munich under Peter von Cornelius and Julius Schnorr von Carolsfeld. After completing his studies he moved to Heidelberg, where he lived until his death on January 19, 1873. During his lifetime he made numerous trips to Basel, Freiburg im Breisgau, Belgium, Luxembourg, France, and England.

Schmitt is one of the most significant members of the Heidelberg school of romantic painting, even if his name is not mentioned as often as the classical triad of Carl Philipp Fohr, Ernst Fries and Carl Rottmann. Although he was primarily a portraitist who also executed a number of still lifes, Schmitt's unusually restrained and highly objective landscape compositions represent a significant contribution to the realistic art of his era. He was also respected as a collector. Together with Charles de Graimberg, he was the founder of the Heidelberg Kunst- und Altertumssammlung, a collection which later became part of the Kurpfälzisches Museum.

44. Portrait of an Elderly Woman with Shawl

[*Brustbildnis einer älteren Frau mit Kopftuch*], 1829.
Brush, sepia and gray wash over pencil on light brown paper, 45.9 x 35.9 cm.
Signed and dated in pen and sepia lower right: *Ph: Schmitt. 1829.*

Provenance: Acquired in 1942, gift of the heirs of Nathanael Schmitt, the artist's son. Inv. no. 1942-20.
Exhibition: Städtische Sammlungen, Heidelberg, *Heidelberger Maler der Romantik*, 1919, no. 27; Kurpfälzisches Museum, Heidelberg, *Die Romantiker-Familie Schmitt*, 1923, no. 51.
Bibliography: Franzke, 1977, pp. 25 and 97, cat. no. Z 15, illus. p. 17; Theilmann and Ammann, 1978, I, p. 517, no. 3379, illus. II, p. 450.

This picture was created during Schmitt's studies in Munich. As Franzke states, the artist was primarily attempting to achieve "an objectification of material substances suggesting volume."[1] There are drawings which are stylistically related to this one: *Ältere Frau mit lang herabhängenden gewellten Haaren und Kopftuch (Elderly Woman with Long Hair and Shawl)* in the Kunstmuseum Düsseldorf,[2] and *Alte Frau mit Pelzbarett (Elderly Woman with Fur Beret)* in the Kurpfälzisches Museum Heidelberg.[3]

1. Franzke and Honold, 1977, p. 25.
2. Kunstmuseum, Düsseldorf, inv. no. 19-1099.
3. Kurpfälzisches Museum, Heidelberg, inv. no. Z 1517; see Franzke and Honold, illus. p. 25.

45. Courtyard of the Heidelberg Castle

[*Im Heidelberger Schloß*], [1838].
Watercolor over pencil with touches of gum arabic on thin beige cardboard, 29.7 x 23.2 cm.

Provenance: Acquired in 1920 from Guido Schmitt, Heidelberg, the artist's son, and Mrs. Nathanael Schmitt, the artist's daughter-in-law, Karlsruhe. Inv. no. VIII 2374-1.
Bibliography: Franzke and Honold, 1977, pp. 70 and 104, cat. no. Z 61; Theilmann and Ammann, 1978, I, p. 520, no. 3404, illus. II, p. 186.

This view, apparently composed in 1838 at the same time as the two watercolors *Das Elisabethentor des Heidelberger Schlosses (The Elizabeth Gateway of the Heidelberg Castle)* and *Der dicke Turm des Heidelberger Schlosses (The Wide Tower of the Heidelberg Castle),*[1] shows the badly ruined curved staircase on the east side of the library. Schmitt's direct, unpretentious style enhances the charm of this study. Wilhelm Trübner executed a similar composition dated 1873.[2]

1. Franzke and Honold, 1977, illus. p. 70.
2. Josef August Beringer, *Trübner: Des Meisters Gemälde,* Stuttgart and Berlin, 1917, illus. p. 37.

Guido Schmitt

Heidelberg 1834 – Miltenberg am Main 1922

Guido Schmitt was born in Heidelberg on February 23, 1834, the son of Georg Philipp Schmitt (nos. 44-45) and the brother of Nathanael Schmitt. He studied under his father and then was active as a portrait painter in London from 1859 to 1896, when he returned to live in

Heidelberg. Schmitt died in Miltenberg am Main on August 7, 1922.

Before Schmitt left for England in 1859, where he would embark upon a successful career as a portraitist, painting Queen Victoria, among others, his work was strongly influenced by his father. This influence is seen not only in his portraits of children, but also in the drawing exhibited here, which was executed during a visit to Heidelberg for the Christmas holidays in 1861, after Schmitt had taken up residence in London. The delicate and precise group portrait of his family with its cozy, idyllic setting shows the continued impact of his father on his work.

46. The Painter Georg Philipp Schmitt and His Family

[*Der Maler Georg Philipp Schmitt im Kreis seiner Familie*], 1861. Pencil on grayish ivory paper, 26.3 x 32.1 cm (window dimensions). Inscribed in pencil lower left: *Guido Schmitt, del./Heidelberg im Dezember 1861.*

Provenance: Acquired in 1942 from the heirs of Nathanael Schmitt, the artist's brother. Inv. no. 1942-53.
Bibliography: Theilmann and Ammann, 1978, I, p. 521, no. 3418, illus. II, p. 186.

The figures are: Guido's father, Georg Philipp Schmitt, at the easel; his mother, Eva Katharina Schmitt (1800-88) crocheting; at the extreme left her brother-in-law Ludwig Schmitt (1810-71), her husband's brother, who later became attorney general of the Palatinate in Zweibrücken; at the extreme right the youngest son, Nathanael, who later also became an artist (1847-1918); and in the background the daughters Amalie (1840-88), Josephine (1842-1911), Katharina (1838-1918), and Elise (1836-1918). In the middle of the wall is a preliminary sketch for Georg Philipp Schmitt's last but never completed oil painting entitled *Maria, Johannes und Magdalena trauernd auf Golgatha (The Virgin, St. John, and Mary Magdalene Mourning on Golgotha).* An oil study for his father's composition is in the Staatliche Kunsthalle Karlsruhe.[1]

1. Staatliche Kunsthalle, Karlsruhe, inv. no. 2097; see Lauts and Zimmermann, 1971, illus. p. 381.

Gustav Schönleber

Bietigheim 1851 – Karlsruhe 1917

Schönleber was born in Bietigheim in the kingdom of Württemberg on December 3, 1851. In 1866 he began a program of training as a machine builder, then entered the Polytechnikum in Stuttgart in 1869. From 1870 to 1873 he studied in Munich under Adolf Lier. Schönleber took up residence in Munich and made several study trips to Italy, reaching Riva, Verona, Venice, and Genoa. In 1880 he was appointed a professor of landscape painting in Karlsruhe. He took numerous trips to Holland (beginning in 1873), as well as to the North Sea and the Baltic (1875, 1876), to the Italian Riviera (1892-93), to Belgium and to France. He died in Karlsruhe on February 1, 1917.

According to Johann Wilhelm Schirmer (nos. 37-43), Schönleber was the most important landscape painting instructor at the Karlsruhe Academy. It was largely to his credit that the school achieved such a high reputation toward the end of the century. Among his best known students were Friedrich Kallmorgen, Gustav Kampmann, Paul von Ravenstein, Hans Richard von Volkmann, and Julius Bergmann. Schönleber's masterful achievements in capturing atmosphere and mood, and his success in communicating painterly impressions are accounted among the most significant achievements in German art of his day.

His teacher in Munich, Adolf Lier, introduced him to the fresh and unpretentious approach to landscape characteristic of the French painters of the Barbizon school. Schönleber adopted as his own credo Lier's proclamation that "the true poetry of landscape painting lies in the beauty of nature herself; it can not be conjured up by artificial means."[1] Schönleber sought out subjects for his compositions during his many travels to Italy and Holland, as well as in the area of his native Swabia. After the turn of the century, Schönleber's choice of subject matter and the execution of his works became somewhat routine, but his Dutch landscapes from the early 1880's show him in full possession of great and far-reaching creative powers.

1. Theodor Mennacher, *Adolf Lier und sein Werk*, Munich, 1928, p. 14.

47. Half-timbered House in Eßlingen on the Neckar ("am Kesselwasen")

[*Fachwerkhaus "am Kesselwasen" in Eßlingen am Neckar*], 1870. Watercolor over pencil on ivory cardboard, 26.1 x 16.2 cm. Inscribed in pencil lower left: *Eßlingen, Juli 70.*

Provenance: Acquired in 1942, gift of Mrs. M. von Clossmann, Freiburg im Breisgau, the artist's daughter. Inv. no. 1942-122.
Bibliography: Schefold, 1974, no. 1724 f; Theilmann and Ammann, 1978, I, p. 537, no. 3547, illus. II, p. 460.

Schönleber's parents moved to Eßlingen in 1869 after his father had sold the family's textile mill in Bietigheim. In his diary Schönleber reminisced about this time of his life:

> *In 1870 I assumed I was going to be a machine builder; there was nothing I liked more than weaving machinery—I had no plans at all to become a painter. But then because of the longer vacation which came about because of the war, I found I had a lot of time to spend in the old imperial city of Eßlingen, and I sat around with my sketchbook and drew ancient walls, moats, and buildings. . . .*[1]

This half-timbered house no longer exists. In 1872 Schönleber executed an oil painting of the same subject with only a few changes of detail which is now in the Staatsgalerie Stuttgart.[2]

1. *Die Rheinlande*, Heft 1 (1906), pp. 1-2.
2. Staatsgalerie, Stuttgart, inv. no. GVL 49.

48. Half-timbered House in Eßlingen on the Neckar ("am Kesselwasen")

[*Fachwerkhaus "am Kesselwasen"* in *Eßlingen am Neckar*], [1870]
Watercolor over pencil on ivory cardboard, 23.4 x 17.8 cm.
Signed in pencil lower left: *G. Schoenleber;* inscribed lower right: *Esslingen.*

Provenance: Acquired in 1942, gift of Mrs. M. von Clossmann, Freiburg im Breisgau, the artist's daughter. Inv. no. 1942-123.
Bibliography: Schefold, 1974, no. 1724 a; Theilmann and Ammann, 1978, I, p. 537, no. 3548, illus. II, p. 460.

The name "am Kesselwasen" (roughly equivalent to "Kettle Place") is first encountered in mercantile documents of 1594, presumably referring to the coppersmiths and coopers once prevalent in this part of town. This 1870 drawing belongs to a series of thirteen views of the city.

Adolf Schrödter

Schwedt an der Oder 1805 — Karlsruhe 1875

Schrödter was born in Schwedt an der Oder on June 28, 1805. His father was an engraver and Schrödter received his earliest training from him. In 1820 he began to study at the Berlin Academy under Ludwig Buchhorn, then in 1829 he began further studies under Wilhelm von Schadow at the Academy in Düsseldorf. He lived in Frankfurt am Main from 1848 to 1854, when he returned to Düsseldorf. In 1859 he was appointed a professor of ornamental arts at the Polytechnikum in Karlsruhe. He died in Karlsruhe on December 9, 1875.

His humorous interpretation of literary subjects (Shakespeare, Cervantes, Goethe, Uhland, Musäus, Münchhausen, Till Eulenspiegel) established Schrödter as the outstanding genre painter of the Düsseldorf artists. His contemporaries saw in his works the embodiment of Rhineland wit and lightheartedness. His many series of works, such as his varied and popular *Triumph des Königs Wein (Triumph of King Wine)* and above all his extensive output of prints reveal his inexhaustible reservoir of decorative motifs. During his later years he was known fondly and respectfully as "König der Arabeske" (Lord of the Arabesques) for his skill in producing gracefully profuse intertwining branch ornaments dotted with figures.[1] He also created several portraits which show him to be a sensitive observer capable of capturing the finest nuances of character of those persons whom he knew well. These intimate portraits of his family and friends, however, remained hidden from the public, who knew Schrödter's work only through his comic drawings.

1. Wolfgang Müller von Königswinter, *Düsseldorfer Künstler aus den letzten fünfundzwanzig Jahren,* Leipzig, 1854, p. 210.

49. Portrait of Luise Heuser, the Artist's Mother-in-Law

[*Bildnis Luise Heuser, die Schwiegermutter des Künstlers*], 1840.
Pencil, with border in pen and red ink on ivory paper (watermark: [fragment]HATMAN), 17.3 x 13.8 cm.
Inscribed in pencil lower right: *18 [corkscrew] 40/Ddorff;* below that (by Alwine Schrödter, the artist's wife): *Louise Heuser/meine Mutter.*

Provenance: Acquired in 1959, gift of I. and M. Schroedter, Karlsruhe, the artist's granddaughters. Inv. no. 1959-6.
Bibliography: Oberbergische Volkszeitung, No. 47 (25 February 1977), illus.; Theilmann and Ammann, 1978, I, p. 553, no. 3655, illus. II, p. 192; Wittichen, [1980], illus. p. 32, no. 12.

Luise Heuser, née Jügel, had two daughters: Alwine, who was married to Schrödter, drew still lifes; the other daughter was married to the painter Carl Friedrich Lessing. Born in Remagen on April 24, 1776, Luise was married to Daniel Heuser (no. 50). She died in Gummersbach on December 31, 1841. Her brother was Carl Jügel, a prominent book dealer in Frankfurt am Main.

50. Portrait of Heinrich Theodor Daniel Heuser, the Artist's Father-in-Law

[*Bildnis Heinrich Theodor Daniel Heuser, der Schwiegervater des Künstlers*], n.d.
Pencil and light gray wash on ivory paper, 17.3 x 13.7 cm.
Inscribed in pencil lower right (by Alwine Schrödter, the artist's wife): *Daniel Heuser/Senior.*

Provenance: Acquired in 1959, gift of I. and M. Schroedter, Karlsruhe, the artist's granddaughters. Inv. no. 1959-5.
Bibliography: Oberbergische Volkszeitung, No. 47 (25 February 1977), illus.; Theilmann and Ammann, 1978, I, p. 553, no. 3656, illus. II, p. 192; Wittichen, [1980], illus. p. 32, no. 13.

Heinrich Theodor Daniel Heuser, born in Gummersbach on April 16, 1767, married Luise Jügel on August 21, 1804. He was a partner in the prominent firm of Johann Peter Heuser Söhne in Gummersbach. Heuser died in 1848.

51. Couple in Costume: "Lady Kiss" and "The Junker"

[*Kostumiertes Paar "(Dame Kuß" und der "Junker")*], 1850.
Watercolor over pencil on light beige paper, 27.0 x 25.4 cm.
Inscribed in yellow wash left margin and in pencil right margin: *18 [corkscrew] 50.*

Provenance: Acquired from Auction 24, Galerie Gerda Bassenge, Berlin, 1974, no. 1016, illus. p. 167; formerly part of the collection of Dr. Heinrich Stinnes, Cologne (Lugt S. 1376a); Auction 87, Karl und Faber, Munich, 1963, no. 936; Auction 97, Karl und Faber, Munich, 1965, no. 943. Inv. no. 1974-25.
Bibliography: Jahrbuch, XII (1975), p. 295; Theilmann and Ammann, 1978, I, pp. 554-55, no. 3664, illus. II, p. 193.

This is a study of a detail for the ninth painting of the cycle *Triumph des Königs Wein (Triumph of King Wine)* in the Staatliche Kunsthalle

Karlsruhe.[1] The following text accompanies the painting:

und der glänzende, schwänzende junker komt dan: genuß;
er führet geziret das fräulein heran: dame kuß;
nach schleichet ein schlimer und grimer kumpan: der schluß;
daß genuß u. der kuß den schluß ach zum genossen doch
haben muß!
(The gleaming and beaming young esquire arriveth: Sir Bliss;
To escort his consort the lady he striveth: Dame Kiss;
But after comes faster a vicious, malicious dark knave: Finis;
Should Sir Bliss and Dame Kiss be parted by Finis then much
is amiss!)

There are three other studies now in a private collection which show slight differences in their clothing and posture. There is a watercolor dating from 1850 entitled *Maskiertes Paar (Masked Couple)* which belongs with this group of drawings, which was also formerly part of the collection of Dr. Heinrich Stinnes, Cologne.[2] This was a theme to which Schrödter devoted himself intensely during the time he spent in Frankfurt am Main from 1850 to 1852.[3]

1. Staatliche Kunsthalle, Karlsruhe, inv. no. 1409/8; see Lauts and Zimmermann, 1971, illus. p. 405.
2. Auction 9, Galerie Wolfgang Ketterer, Munich, 1973, no. 2200.
3. Boetticher, 1891-1901, II/2, p. 660, paintings nos. 54 and 59, watercolors and drawings nos. 5, 6, 10, and 11.

Ernst Schweinfurth

Karlsruhe 1818 – Rome 1877

Schweinfurth was born in Karlsruhe on March 2, 1818. Beginning in 1832 he studied steel engraving in Karlsruhe under Carl Ludwig Frommel (nos. 12-13), and continued his studies in the early 1840's at the Academy in Munich. After 1845 he settled in Baden-Baden. In 1852 he undertook a study tour to Dalmatia; in autumn of the same year he moved to Rome. From there he made several trips back to Baden and to Munich. In 1876 he journeyed to Estonia, to the Scandanavian countries, and to St. Petersburg. He died in Rome on October 24, 1877.

Schweinfurth was well-known for his views of Baden's towns and castles, some of which were published as steel engravings in *Das malerische und romantische Baden (Painterly and Romantic Baden).*[1] His decision to live in Italy was of great importance for the development of his art. In Rome he served repeatedly as president of the German artists' association. He made numerous landscape and figure studies of the area of the Campagna, Frascati, Tivoli, Genzano, Nemi, Bagnaia, Ronciglione, Rome, Florence, and Ariccia. From this extensive inventory of subjects he later executed his oils. Schweinfurth's primary success lies in his ability to combine narrative genre scenes of Italian peasant life with evocative landscapes.

1. J. Bader, *Das malerische und romantische Baden*, II, 1844-45; see Theilmann and Ammann, 1978, I, pp. 566-71, nos. 3773-3805, illus. II, pp. 470-73.

52. Forest Landscape in Italy

[*Waldige Landschaft in Italien*], [1860's].
Pencil with highlights in white gouache on beige paper, 42.6 x 60.5 cm.
Inscribed in pencil lower right by another hand: *Schweinfurt.*

Provenance: Acquired in 1878 from Mr. Schweinfurth, Karlsruhe, milliner to the court; formerly part of the artist's estate. Inv. no. VIII 2416-20.
Bibliography: Theilmann and Ammann, 1978, I, p. 573, no. 3827, illus. II, p. 195.

53. Pine Grove in the Roman Campagna

[*Pinienhain in der römischen Campagna*], [1860's].
Watercolor over pencil on cream paper (watermark: [fragment] L KENT), 24.2 x 42.5 cm.

Provenance: Acquired in 1878 from Mr. Schweinfurth, Karlsruhe, milliner to the court; formerly part of the artist's estate. Inv. no. VIII 2416-23.
Bibliography: Theilmann and Ammann, 1978, I, p. 573, no. 3828, illus. II, p. 195.

Schweinfurth's nature studies are quite painterly. They are normally drawn on toned paper with highlights in white gouache. Part of their charm derives from a careful and contrasting use of parallel shading strokes and clear outlines, which gives a strong sense of depth and volume. This sense of space and proportion is also found in the watercolors he completed in Italy, with their vivid contrast between light and shadow. It is in these watercolors that Schweinfurth shows himself to be a representative of the classical ideal of landscape painting.

Moritz von Schwind

Vienna 1804 – Niederpöcking 1871

Schwind was born on January 21, 1804, in Vienna. After studying at the University in Vienna, he decided to become an artist and entered the Vienna Academy in 1821 where he remained until 1823, studying under Ludwig Schnorr von Carolsfeld and Peter Krafft. For the most part, however, he developed his art independently. From 1828 to 1840 he lived in Munich, studying under Peter von Cornelius. In 1832 he executed frescoes for the palace in Munich and for Schloß Hohenschwangau. His stay in Munich was interrupted by an extended trip to Italy in 1835. In 1840 he moved to Karlsruhe, and in 1844 to Frankfurt am Main; he was appointed a professor of the Academy in Munich in 1847. Schwind owes his reputation to the extensive, complex cycles of frescoes he executed in late romantic style. In 1832-34, he decorated the palace in Munich with a series of scenes illustrating Ludwig Tieck's *Phantasus.* In 1854-55, he painted seven scenes illustrating the history of Thuringia for the castle

Wartburg near Eisenach. Finally, in 1866-67, he prepared for the Vienna Opera a series of scenes from *The Magic Flute* and works of other composers. Schwind died in Niederpöcking on Lake Starnberg on February 8, 1871.

Schwind's activity in Karlsruhe was limited to the period between 1840 and 1844.[1] In 1841 and 1842 he executed the designs for the Upper House of the former Ständehaus, or parliament building. The frescoes depicted eight virtues, six political caricatures, and a portrait of Grand Duke Leopold surrounded by allegorical figures; all of these frescoes have since been destroyed. During the same time he carried out the decorations for the main entrance hall of the Gemäldegalerie, now the Staatliche Kunsthalle Karlsruhe, designed by Heinrich Hübsch (no. 17). Apparently on the basis of a recommendation from Julius Schnorr von Carolsfeld, Hübsch had worked out an agreement with Schwind on March 19, 1838, while work on the structure was still in progress, agreeing on the subject matter of the decorations. The major composition was to be *Die Einweihung des Freiburger Münsters durch Herzog Konrad von Zähringen (Count Konrad von Zähringen Dedicating the Cathedral of Freiburg),* an allegory which, according to Schwind, was to show "Architecture being safeguarded by both the Church and the State." On December 10, 1842, Schwind signed another contract for two side frescoes and lunettes, representing Sculpture and Painting (see no. 55). In addition Schwind designed the *Philostratische Gemälde* (based on works by Goethe) for the first floor of the building as well as several scenes from Roman mythology and allegorical representations of various cities. These works were then carried out by his students.[2]

At one time Schwind had referred to Karlsruhe as "the most exciting city in the world,"[3] but he left the city with great bitterness towards it. There had been numerous differences of opinion between him and the Duchy's architectural authorities. Finally his designs for the Trinkhalle at Baden-Baden were rejected because his fees were too high. Around Easter of 1844 he moved to Frankfurt am Main, from where he let it be known that matters were "much different than in Karlsruhe, where I was fed up with everything."[4]

1. Beringer, 1915, pp. 137-200.
2. Theilmann and Ammann, 1978, I, pp. 589-600, nos. 3899-3944, illus. II, pp. 478-81.
3. Moritz von Schwind letter, December 17, 1841 in Otto Stoessl, ed., *Moritz von Schwind: Briefe*, Leipzig, n.d., p. 137.
4. Ibid., May 3, 1844, p. 174, note 2.

54. Allegory of Mathematics

[*Allegorie der Mathematik*], [1840].
Watercolor over pencil on ivory paper (watermark: D & C BLAUW), 25.7 x 45.7 cm.
Inscribed in pencil lower right: *Freund Becker zum Andenken/Schwind.*

Provenance: Acquired from Auction 13, Arno Winterberg, Heidelberg, 1976, no. 1074, illus. p. 232. Inv. no. 1976-61.
Bibliography: Theilmann and Ammann, 1978, I, p. 581, no. 3868, illus. II, p. 196.

This is a sketch for the left lunette over the major fresco illustrating the dedication of the cathedral in Freiburg im Breisgau. The three lunettes in the entrance hall of the Staatliche Kunsthalle Karlsruhe were executed between late September and mid-December of 1840.[1]

In a letter to the art historian Ernst Förster postmarked November 23, 1844, Schwind described this picture:

> *Mathematics: the designs for the building* [*i.e., floorplan and cross-section of the main wing of the current Kunsthalle, designed and built by Heinrich Hübsch*] *in one hand, a compass in the other hand. A boy filling a lamp with oil* [*symbol of intelligence*]. *On a board* [*at the boy's right hand*] *the chain which Hübsch designed to calculate the degree of arch.*[2]

This description of the fresco was made after Schwind had left Karlsruhe, and it corresponds precisely to the watercolor in this exhibition. But in the actual fresco the figure of Mathematics is holding in one hand an open book with geometric figures and in the other a compass with which she is measuring a plan lying on the floor, eliminating the references and homage to Hübsch. There is a preliminary sketch for this watercolor, which has other symbols and a slightly different composition, in the Staatliche Kunsthalle Karlsruhe.[3]

Schwind's friend "Becker," to whom the drawing is dedicated, has not been identified with certainty. Perhaps this is one of Schwind's associates during the time he was in Frankfurt am Main, e.g., Christian Becker (1809-85), a historical painter, or Jakob Becker (1810-72), a genre and landscape painter.

1. Weigmann, 1906, illus. p. 210; see also Beringer, 1915, pp. 144, note 1, 149-50.
2. Otto Weigmann, "Brief Moritz von Schwind an Ernst Förster," *Die Rheinlande*, 16, Heft 6 (1916), p. 8.
3. Staatliche Kunsthalle, Karlsruhe, inv. no. 1964-13; see Theilmann and Ammann, 1978, I, p. 581, no. 3867, illus. II, p. 475.

55. The Art of Painting: Hans Baldung Grien Executing a Portrait of Christoph, Margrave of Baden

[*Die Malerei: Hans Baldung Grien porträtiert Markgraf Christoph von Baden*], [1842-43].
Pen and dark brown ink and watercolor over pencil on light gray paper, 19.9 x 21.6 cm (border 16.7 x 18.5 cm).

Provenance: Acquired from Auction 92, Karl und Faber, Munich 1964, no. 907, from the collection of Dr. von Ravenstein, Frankfurt am Main, the artist's grandson; formerly part of the artist's estate. Inv. no. 1964-14.
Bibliography: Beringer, 1915, p. 154; *Jahrbuch* II (1965), p. 287; Bernhard, II, illus. p. 1785; Theilmann and Ammann, 1978, I, p. 583, no. 3879, illus. II, p. 196.

This is a design for the cartoon of the fresco to the right of the central fresco in the main entrance hall of the Karlsruhe museum. The cartoon was executed between late December 1842 and early February 1843, and the fresco itself was completed in November 1843.[1]

Hübsch and Schwind came to an agreement on December 10, 1842, concerning the subject matter of the two side frescoes: "The surfaces over the doorways on both sides of the main picture are to be decorated; the one side is to represent Hans Baldung Grien making a portrait of Count Berthold the Rich. . . ."[2]

The fresco corresponds fairly well with this preliminary study, executed in late 1841 or in early 1842. But in place of Count Berthold, Schwind substituted Margrave Christoph. In the watercolor exhibited here the features of the Margrave are not those of the portrait executed by Baldung in 1515.[3] In the fresco, however, the features portrayed by the renaissance artist are unmistakable.

1. Weigmann, 1906, illus. p. 207.
2. Beringer, 1915, p. 152, note 1.
3. Christian A. zu Salm and Gisela Goldberg, *Alte Pinakothek München:* II, *Altdeutsche Malerei,* Munich, 1963, illus. p. 262.

56. Hübsch, Schwind, and Lotsch Presenting the Plans for the Kunsthalle

[*Hübsch, Schwind und Lotsch überreichen die Pläne für den Bau der Kunsthalle*], [ca. 1842].
Pen and dark brown ink over pencil on light beige paper, 28.0 x 21.2 cm.
Inscribed in pen and dark brown ink between pencil lines lower center margin (by another hand?): *empfehlen Euer Excellenz hoher Protection diese wenigen Pläne.;* in pencil by another hand below the first inscription: *Baurath Hübsch, Schwindt/Bei der Erbauung der Carlsruher Academie/in der Mitte Schwindt, 1839.;* lower right by another hand: *v. Schwindt.*

Provenance: Acquired in 1941 from Wolf Freiherr von Blittersdorff, Munich; formerly part of the album of Maximiliane Freifrau von Blittersdorff, Karlsruhe, wife of the Baden Secretary of State, Friedrich Karl Landolin Freiherr von Blittersdorff. Inv. no. 1950-1.
Bibliography: Beringer, 1915, p. 187, illus. no. 3 following p. 200; Schneider, 1968, p. 58, illus. 47; Theilmann and Ammann, 1978, I, p. 586, no. 3887, illus. II, p. 197.

This caricature represents the persons involved in the construction and decoration of the Karlsruhe Academy (Großherzogliche Kunsthalle). The architect Heinrich Hübsch with long coat, a self portrait of Schwind with palette, and the sculptor Christian Lotsch with hammer and trowel present a pile of plans and documents for approval. The building was designed by Hübsch and was constructed between 1837 and 1846. Lotsch (1790-1873) executed the idealized portrait busts of Raphael and Dürer for the main entrance hall, while Schwind was responsible for the frescoes.

Hans Thoma

Bernau 1839 – Karlsruhe 1924

Thoma was born on October 2, 1839, in Bernau in the Black Forest. After serving several short apprenticeships in art-related trades – under a lithographer and a housepainter in Basel, and even one under a clockface painter in Furtwangen – he went to the Karlsruhe Academy where he studied under Ludwig Des Coudres and Johann Wilhelm Schirmer from 1859 to 1866. In 1867 he moved to the Academy in Düsseldorf, where he became close friends with Otto Scholderer, the painter. In 1868 Scholderer took him to Paris, where Thoma was greatly impressed by the works of Gustave Courbet. After his return from Paris he lived in Karlsruhe. From 1870 to 1873 he was in Munich, where he associated himself with a group of artists that had formed around Victor Müller. He then lived for a short time in Frankfurt am Main. In 1874 he took his first trip to Italy. In 1875 he moved back to Munich, then in 1877 he settled in Frankfurt am Main, where he remained for several years. He did not return to Italy until the 1880's, when he visited Adolf von Hildebrand in Florence in 1887 and began his long friendship with the art historian Henry Thode in 1889. In 1895 he traveled to Venice. In 1899 he was appointed director of the Gemäldegalerie and was simultaneously named a professor of the Karlsruhe Academy. In 1904 he made his first trip to Switzerland. In 1905 he spent some time at Lake Garda near Verona and visited Switzerland for a second time. On October 2, 1909, the Thoma-Museum in Karlsruhe was formally dedicated. Thoma stepped down from his position as director of the museum in May of 1919. He died in Karlsruhe on November 7, 1924.

Thoma was the most significant student of Johann Wilhelm Schirmer (nos. 37-43) at the Karlsruhe Academy. In the 1860's and 1870's Thoma was one of several German artists who rebelled against the restrictive academic notions of art. Like those artists around Wilhelm Leibl, Thoma advocated the principles of realism found in the work of Gustave Courbet.

> *To do this, however, you have to free yourself completely from everything that has been taught you. You have to achieve an intimacy with nature, and you have to have a clear idea about the essence of painting and even of its methods as well. That is what today's realism needs; it is democratic and for that reason will have the entire narrow-minded world against it, especially Germany.*[1]

Two aspects of this realistic art created a great deal of unease among a public which had been trained to perceive and think in traditional categories: the portrayal of relatively banal subjects which derived from the artist's personal life, rather than heroic idealizations, and the realist's choice of more natural coloration. Thoma saw himself being forced to play the role of a revolutionary against his will. Thoma's style of painting, which attempted to reproduce the reality of its subject matter, combined with the mundane nature of his subjects, outraged many gallery visitors. It took years for his pictures to gain any kind of recognition. Well into the 1870's, the jurors of exhibitions regularly rejected his submissions. Thoma finally received acclaim from the general public when he started to retreat from his position of strict realism and began to give expression to his poetic fantasy. But as the allegorical and religious compositions of his later life increased in narrative content, they decreased in artistic quality.

In the early 1890's Thoma began to occupy himself with printmaking, which served to make his work even more widely known, and by the end of his career Thoma was inundated with honors and awards. Throughout his life he maintained a deep affection for his native landscape and continually referred to it as the true source of all his art. He continued to celebrate its beauties in his paintings, his drawings, and his prints.

Thoma drew constantly. He thought of his drawings both as preliminary studies for oil paintings and as independent artistic works. In the 1860's, precise and detailed pencil portraits or nature studies dominate his output. Later he tended to use pastels or the more painterly media of brush and ink or watercolor. Despite the brilliance of Thoma's draftsmanship, his drawings avoid falling into mere virtuosity for its own sake. Thoma perceived nature as God's creation, and this perception is evident in his works, which seek to convey to their viewers a sense of awe and humility.

1. Hans Thoma letter to Eugen Bracht, January 2, 1868, in Beringer, 1929, p. 81.

57. Portrait of the Painter Gustav Osterroht

[*Bildnis des Malers Gustav Osterroht*], [1863-64].
Black chalk with touches of red chalk, brush and ink, and pencil on cream paper, 25.3 x 21.9 cm (border 23.6 x 20.4 cm).
Signed in pencil lower right: *HTh* (letters linked together).

Provenance: Acquired in 1909, gift of the artist to the Hans Thoma-Museum, Karlsruhe. Inv. no. VIII 2964.
Exhibition: Karlsruhe, 1930, no. 50; Karlsruhe, 1939, no. 38; Karlsruhe, 1966, no. 95, illus. no. 21; Karlsruhe, 1978, p. 28; Reutlingen, 1978, p. 88, no. 10.
Bibliography: Koelitz, 1915, Thoma-Museum no. 36; Koelitz, 1920, Thoma-Museum no. 36; Fischel, 1929, p. 157, no. K 32; Schneider, 1932, p. 13, pl. 14 (dated in the 1860's); Martin, 1946, pl. 6 (dated ca. 1870); Ammann, 1967, no. 35, illus. no. 20; Theilmann, 1971, note 1129; Theilmann, 1973, note 141; Wilhelm Brauer, "Gustav Osterroht 1836-1874: Ein unbekannter Landschaftsmaler aus der Kaschubei," *Unser Danzig: Mitteilungsblatt des Bundes der Danziger* 28, No. 15 (1976), p. 6, illus. p. 7; Wilhelm Brauer, "Gustav Osterroht (1856-1874): Ein unbekannter Landschaftsmaler aus der Kaschubei," in Wilhelm Brauer, ed., *Der Kreis Karthaus: Ein westpreußisches Heimatbuch,* Lübeck, 1978, p. 312, illus. p. 311; Theilmann and Ammann, 1978, I, p. 631, no. 4098, illus. II, p. 205.

Gustav Osterroht was born on September 10, 1836, in Stendsitz near Danzig. He studied in Karlsruhe under Johann Wilhelm Schirmer from 1857 to 1864, where he remained after his artistic training was completed. After many trips to Tyrol, the Baltic, the Black Forest, and to the Bavarian Alps, he died in Karlsruhe on November 2, 1874.

Thoma and Osterroht became close friends at the Karlsruhe Academy.[1] Apparently this portrait was executed in the winter of 1863-64, "during a time of intense cooperation."[2] Edith Ammann suggests that the picture was made shortly before Thoma's departure for Munich in the spring of 1870.[3]

Thoma's close friend Eugen Bracht (no. 2) described Osterroht as a "fanatic smoker."[4] Thoma attests to Osterroht's passion for tobacco by portraying him with a cigar.

There is another portrait of Osterroht from this same time which is also in the Staatliche Kunsthalle Karlsruhe.[5]

1. See Hans Thoma's letters to his sister Agathe from the years 1863 to 1869 in Beringer, 1929, pp. 38, 39, 42, 43, 45, 66 and 92.
2. Theilmann, 1971, note 1129.
3. Theilmann and Ammann, 1978, I, p. 631, no. 4098.
4. Theilmann, 1973, p. 68.
5. Staatliche Kunsthalle, Karlsruhe, inv. no. VIII 2926; see Theilmann and Ammann, 1978, I, p. 631, no. 4097, illus. II, p. 490.

58. Willow by a Brook

[*Weide am Bach*], 1866.
Pencil with highlights in white gouache on brownish paper, 49.3 x 25.3 cm. (The upper right corner has been restored and the drawing has been continued onto it, possibly by another hand.)
Inscribed in pencil lower right (thereby darkening the original but faded date): *Bernau/9.* VIII. *66.;* under this an oval red stamp with diagonal grid and the letters: *H Th.*

Provenance: Acquired in 1909, gift of the artist to the Hans Thoma-Museum, Karlsruhe. Inv. no. VIII 2953.
Exhibition: Basel, 1924, no. 191; Kunsthaus, Zurich, *Hans Thoma: Ausstellung von Gemälden, Zeichnungen und graphischen Arbeiten 1855-1920,* 1924, no. 139; Bern, 1924, no. 204; Karlsruhe, 1930, no. 21; Karlsruhe, 1939, no. 17; Busch-Reisinger Museum, Harvard University, Cambridge, Mass., *German Master Drawings of the 19th Century,* no. 90, illus.; Museum Boymans-van Beuningen Rotterdam, *Duitse tekeningen uit de 19e eeuw,* 1973, no. 78; Karlsruhe, 1978, p. 28; Reutlingen, 1978, p. 87, no. 5, illus.
Bibliography: Koelitz, 1915, Thoma-Museum, no. 29 (entitled *Baumstudie);* Koelitz, 1920, Thoma-Museum, no. 29; Willy F. Storck, *Zeichnungen von Hans Thoma,* Dresden, 1921, p. 12, illus. pl. 23; Fischel, 1929, p. 157, no. K 21 (entitled *Weidenstudie);* Martin, 1946, illus. pl. 3; Ammann, 1967, no. 29, illus. no. 17; Theilmann and Ammann, 1978, I, p. 630, no. 4092, illus. II, p. 93.

Thoma used this study for a painting dated 1870 entitled *Der Kahn (The Boat).* This painting is in a private collection in Mannheim.[1]

1. Thode, 1901, p. 32.

59. Study of Foliage against Rocks

[*Stauden vor Felsen*], 1870.
Pen and brush and ink on brownish paper, 42.4 x 30.3 cm (window dimensions).

Inscribed in pen and ink lower right: *St. Bl. 11 9/70.*

Provenance: Unknown. Inv. no. VIII 2641.
Exhibition: Kunsthalle, Basel, *Hans Thoma,* 1924, no. 209; Kunsthalle, Bern, 1924, no. 223; Karlsruhe, 1930, no. 33 (entitled *Äste mit Blättern).*
Bibliography: Ammann, no. 41 and jacket illus.; Theilmann and Ammann, 1978, I, p. 632, no. 4105, illus. II, p. 206.

This work is typical of those which Thoma executed in the 1870's; the soft, painterly effect of wash brings out a broad scale of values for the fundamental gray.

60. Portrait of the Artist's Mother

[*Bildnis der Mutter nach links*], 1878.
Black chalk with highlights in white gouache on brownish paper, 35.0 x 26.8 cm.
Signed in pencil lower right: *Hans Thoma.;* dated above this in black chalk: *2 Mai 78.*

Provenance: Acquired in 1909, gift of the artist to the Hans Thoma-Museum, Karlsruhe. Inv. no. VIII 2965.
Exhibition: Karlsruhe, 1930, no. 99.
Bibliography: Koelitz, 1915, Thoma-Museum, no. 38 (?); Koelitz, 1920, Thoma-Museum, no. 38 (?); Fischel, 1929, p. 158, no. K 33; Schneider, 1932, p. 26, pl. 37; Ammann, 1967, no. 55; Theilmann and Ammann, 1978, I, p. 634, no. 4118, illus. II, p. 491.

Rosa Thoma was born in Bernau-Oberlehen on February 24, 1804, the daughter of Josef Maier, a clockmaker. She married Franz Josef Thoma, who worked as a wood carver, sign painter and a miller. Her husband died on July 31, 1855. Rosa lived in relative poverty with her three children: Hilarius, who died at the age of twenty-two, Johannes (Hans), and Agathe. In a letter dated March 1, 1897, Thoma wrote to Countess Erdödy concerning his mother: "She had a powerful imagination, and I feel that my strength as an artist is based on her lively gift of fantasy."[1] After her son's marriage to Cella Berteneder (see no. 63) and his taking up residence in Frankfurt am Main in the autumn of 1877, she and her daughter Agathe, who remained unmarried, both moved there. Rosa Thoma lived there until she was well into her nineties; she died on February 23, 1897. Thoma portrayed his mother in numerous oils, drawings, and prints.[2]

1. Joseph August Beringer, ed., *Hans Thoma: Briefe an Frauen,* Stuttgart, 1936, p. 106.
2. See for example Thode, 1909, illus. pp. X, XII, XX, 5, 12, 56, 182, 241; see also Beringer, 1916, nos. 11 and 52. Additional portraits are in the Staatliche Kunsthalle Karlsruhe (inv. nos. VIII 2928, VIII 2949, VIII 2954, VIII 3044, VIII 3037; see Theilmann and Ammann, 1978, I, p. 625, no. 4065; p. 627, no. 4075; p. 629, no. 4089; pp. 633-34, no. 4113; p. 640, no. 4153; the illus. in II, pp. 488, 204, 490, and 493).

61. Portrait of a Neapolitan Girl

[*Bildnis einer jungen Neapolitanerin*], 1880.
Brush and ink over black chalk, watercolor and gouache with highlights in white gouache on gray paper, 40.3 x 29.7 cm.
Signed in pen and ink lower right: *Hans Thoma;* inscribed below this in black chalk: *Neapel 3. April 1880.*

Provenance: Acquired in 1951, gift of the Landesverein Badische Heimat on the occasion of the reopening of the Staatliche Kunsthalle Karlsruhe after World War II; formerly part of a private collection in Munich; formerly in the possession of the art dealer W. Bernt, in Munich. Inv. no. 1951-46.
Bibliography: Kurt Martin, "Zur Wiedereröffnung der Staatlichen Kunsthalle Karlsruhe," *Badische Heimat* 31, Heft 2 (1951), p. 88, illus. p. 89; Ammann, 1967, no. 68; Theilmann and Ammann, 1978, I, p. 637, no. 4131, illus. II, p. 208.

This is a preliminary study for a painting executed in 1882 and entitled *Italienerin (Italian Woman).*[1]

1. Thode, 1909, illus. p. 206.

62. Olive Trees near Tivoli

[*Ölbäume bei Tivoli*], 1880.
Black and blue chalk, watercolor with highlights in white gouache, squared with pencil on gray paper, 34.5 x 52.3 cm (window dimensions).
Inscribed in black chalk lower right: *Tivoli 1 Mai 80.*

Provenance: Acquired in 1909, gift of the artist to the Hans Thoma-Museum, Karlsruhe. Inv. no. VIII 2972.
Exhibition: Karlsruhe, 1930, no. 129 (entitled *Blick von Tivoli auf die Campagna);* Karlsruhe, 1939, no. 67; Staatliche Kunsthalle, Karlsruhe, *Hans Thoma: Gedächtnisausstellung zum 50. Todestag,* 1974, no. 39; Reutlingen, 1978, p. 89, no. 20.
Bibliography: Vorlagen für das Landschaftszeichnen an den Oberklassen der badischen Mittelschulen, Karlsruhe, Heft 1 (1898), pl. 5; Koelitz, 1915, Thoma-Museum no. 16; Koelitz, 1920, Thoma-Museum no. 16; Fischel, 1929, p. 158, no. K 40 (entitled *Landschaft bei Tivoli);* Ammann, 1967, no. 71, illus. no. 38; Uta Laxner-Gerlach, *Von der Heydt-Museum Wuppertal: Katalog der Gemälde des 19. Jahrhunderts,* Wuppertal, 1974, p. 236; Theilmann and Ammann, 1978, I, p. 637, no. 4134, illus. II, p. 208.

Thoma returned to this nature study several times for oil paintings executed in later years: *Unter Ölbäumen bei Tivoli (Under Olive Trees near Tivoli),* painted in 1880;[1] *Olivenbäume bei Tivoli (Olive Trees near Tivoli),* painted in 1890;[2] *Abend unter Ölbäumen bei Tivoli (Evening under Olive Trees near Tivoli),* painted in 1891.[3] Thoma also used the left group of trees but in a different orientation for his picture *Ölbäume bei Tivoli (Olive Trees near Tivoli),* painted in 1882.[4]

1. Thode, 1909, illus. p. 153.
2. Von der Heydt-Museum, Wuppertal, inv. no. 29; see Thode, illus. p. 321.
3. Thode, illus. p. 340.
4. Ibid., illus. p. 189.

63. Portrait of Cella Thoma

[*Bildnis Cella Thoma*], [ca. 1880].
Red and black chalk with highlights in white gouache on cream paper, 30.1 x 25.0 cm.
Signed in pencil lower right: *Hans Thoma.*

Provenance: Acquired in 1909, gift of the artist to the Hans Thoma-Museum, Karlsruhe. Inv. no. VIII 3035.
Exhibition: Karlsruhe, 1930, no. 166, illus. title page; Karlsruhe, 1939, no. 82; Reutlingen, 1978, p. 89, no. 21.
Bibliography: Koelitz, 1915, Thoma-Museum no. 37; Koelitz, 1920, Thoma-Museum no. 37; Fischel, 1929, p. 159, no. K 47; Kurt Martin, *Hans Thoma: Bildnisse der Familie,* Kunstbrief Nr. 17, Berlin, [ca. 1943], illus. no. 10; Ammann, 1967, no. 76, illus. no. 41; Theilmann and Ammann, 1978, I, p. 638, no. 4139, illus. II, p. 205.

Cella Thoma, née Berteneder, came from a peasant family. She was born in Landshut am Lech on April 14, 1858. At the age of eighteen she became Thoma's student, and developed into a talented flower painter.[1] She and Thoma were married in Säckingen on June 18, 1877. In the fall of the same year the couple settled in Frankfurt am Main where they shared a house with Thoma's mother (see. no. 60) and his sister Agathe, freeing Cella to continue her painting. She died while on a visit to Constance on November 23, 1901. Thoma portrayed his wife in numerous paintings, drawings, and prints.[2]

Arthur von Schneider, in the catalogue for the 1930 Karlsruhe exhibition, dates this drawing in the early 1880's.[3]

1. Lauts and Zimmermann, 1971, illus. p. 440; see also Hans-Joachim Ziemke, *Kataloge der Gemälde im Städelschen Kunstinstitut Frankfurt am Main: I, Die Gemälde des 19. Jahrhunderts,* Frankfurt am Main, 1972, illus. no. 197.
2. Thode, 1909, illus. pp. XXVIII, 86, 96, 98, 112, 174, 205, 264, 310, 350, 435; see also Beringer, 1916, nos. 27 and 119. The Staatliche Kunsthalle Karlsruhe has additional drawings portraying Cella Thoma, inv. nos. VIII 2647, VIII 2648, VIII 3032, 1950-19; see Theilmann and Ammann, 1978, I, p. 635, no. 4123; p. 636, no. 4126, p. 639, no. 4146, p. 642, no. 4166; the illustrations are found in II, pp. 490, 491, 209.
3. Karlsruhe, 1930, no. 166.

Wilhelm Trübner

Heidelberg 1851 – Karlsruhe 1917

Trübner was born in Heidelberg on February 3, 1851. After attending a goldsmith school in Hanau, he became acquainted with Anselm Feuerbach, who urged him to pursue a career as an artist. From 1867 to 1868 he studied at the Karlsruhe Academy under Karl Friedrich Schick and Hans Frederik Gude. In the following year, he moved to the Munich Academy and studied under Alexander Wagner, and in 1870 under Hans Canon (nos. 3-4) in Stuttgart. During this time he visited art galleries throughout Germany. In 1870 he returned to Munich and for the next two years he studied under Wilhelm Diez. While in Munich he associated with several members of the circle around Wilhelm Leibl. After his student years, he undertook several trips, visiting Italy (1872), Heidelberg (1872, 1873), Holland and Belgium (1874), the island of Rügen and the Chiemsee (1874). He lived in Munich from 1875 to 1895, but continued his travels, which included stays in Paris (1879, 1889) and London (1884-85), at Lake Constance (1894), and the Black Forest (1895). From 1896 to 1897 he taught at the Städelsches Kunstinstitut in Frankfurt am Main. In 1897 he opened a private art academy in Frankfurt am Main and the next year received the title of Royal Prussian Professor. He was married in 1900 to Alice Auerbach, one of his students. In 1902 he was one of the founding members of the "Frankfurt-Cronberger-Künstlerbund." He was appointed a professor at the Karlsruhe Academy in 1903. Twice he served as director of the Academy, in 1904-05 and in 1910-11. The first retrospective exhibition of his works was held in the Karlsruhe Kunstverein on the occasion of his sixtieth birthday in 1911. Trübner died in Karlsruhe on December 21, 1917.

Critics of Trübner's works tended to split into two groups: one was unreservedly enthusiastic while the other remained somewhat cool and distant, especially when dealing with Trübner's later works, which are indeed rather problematic.[1] Many writers considered Trübner, who matured within the group of artists around Leibl and whose radical devaluation of the content of pictorial art derived from theoretical views expressed within the Leibl circle, as the earliest representative of impressionism in Germany. As such, his pioneering work could hardly be underestimated, although Trübner himself did not accept this judgment of his work. Nevertheless, in a significant group of essays collectively published under the title *Personalien und Prinzipien (Personalities and Principles),*[2] he formulated his own understanding of art, in which he steadfastly proclaimed his support for *l'art pour l'art,* which he called the "pure artistic spirit."

> *The artistic value of a work of art depends solely on its method of execution. . . . The pure artistic spirit is contained within and is inseparable from the artistic capabilities of the artist, i.e., the art with which he portrays his subject matter.*[3]

Thoroughly convinced of his own significance as an artist, Trübner tried to insure that his reputation would not fade after his death. Writing shortly after Trübner's death, Julius Elias noted that Trübner "was very concerned about being treated in art history texts the way he wanted to be."[4] But as a draftsman Trübner was not able to get the kind of reputation he received as a painter. Since his drawings were not intended for the general public, art critics took little notice of them. Finally, however, Julius Elias worked with the artist to publish some of his important drawings and thus allowed a larger circle of interested persons to become acquainted with Trübner's graphic work.[5] In this publication Elias wrote:

> *The artist does not attempt to create master drawings, i.e., drawings which are works of art in and of themselves. He sees himself as standing in the tradition of Caravaggio and Vermeer, above all in a group with Courbet, Leibl, and Uhde. Indeed, the latter group produced very few master drawings, for they were all painters in the true sense of the word. Trübner's studies and*

sketches are "working drawings," just like those of Leibl; they accompany the painted works of his early career, arising as they did as notes for ideas or as inspirations for the composition of paintings on which he was working.[6]

1. Rohrandt, 1972, I, pp. 43-65.
2. Trübner, 1918.
3. Rohrandt, I, pp. 51, 53.
4. Julius Elias in *Die Neue Rundschau*, 19, I (1918), p. 275.
5. Julius Elias, *Wilhelm Trübner: Handzeichnungen*, Berlin, 1921.
6. Rohrandt, I, p. 207.

64. Seated Portrait of the Young Cavalryman Keller

[*Bildnis des Dragoner-Einjährigen Keller, in Halbfigur sitzend nach rechts gewendet*], [1874-75].
Charcoal on ivory paper, 31.4 x 24.0 cm.
Signed in pencil lower left: *W. Trübner* (*W* and *T* linked together.)

Provenance: Acquired in 1938 from Mrs. Jörg Trübner, the artist's daughter-in-law; formerly part of the artist's estate.
Inv. no. 1938-150.
Exhibition: Wilhelm Trübner-Ausstellung, Karlsruhe, 1911, nos. 3-6 (listed as drawings without further descriptions); Badische Kunsthalle, Karlsruhe, *Ausstellung von Werken aus Karlsruher Privatbesitz*, 1922, no. 284 (with incorrect signature); Karlsruhe, 1966, no. 98; Karlsruhe, 1978, p. 28.
Bibliography: Fischel, 1929, p. 160, no. K 57; Rohrandt, 1972, II, cat. no. Z 130; Theilmann and Ammann, 1978, I, p. 646, no. 4180, illus. II, p. 211.

This drawing was made during the year (1874-75) that Trübner served in the Third Baden Cavalry Regiment in Karlsruhe. It is a typical example of Trübner's work between 1872 and 1876, a time which Trübner himself characterized as his "early period." Typical for his style are the broad parallel charcoal strokes as well as the soft, almost painterly transitions which he achieved by modeling with a stump. Trübner also portrayed Keller standing in three different postures.[1]

1. Graphische Abteilung, Museen der Stadt, Nürnberg, inv. no. 1425; see also Auction 68, F.A.C. Prestel, Frankfurt am Main (auction of graphic works from the estate of Wilhelm Trübner), 1918, no. 131, illus. no. 22.

Theodor Verhas

Schwetzingen 1811 – Heidelberg 1872

Verhas was born in Schwetzingen on August 31, 1811. He studied in Karlsruhe under Ernst Fries until the latter's death in 1833. Verhas then moved to the Academy in Munich. He took up residence in Heidelberg in 1856. His extensive travels took him through the Palatinate, to Switzerland and Bavaria, and apparently also to France, Holland, England, and Scotland. He died in Heidelberg on November 1, 1872.

Verhas was strongly influenced by J. M. W. Turner's fantastic visions of light. Turner had painted landscapes of Heidelberg and the Neckar valley during the 1840's, and Verhas' delight in romantic light effects can be traced to Turner's works. His watercolors from the middle of the century reveal a style marked by precision and sensitivity; they normally have one dominant color, which is masterfully varied into a series of modulated tones. Verhas' landscapes are nearly always topographically accurate reproductions of actual scenes, but his virtuoso command of light effects gives his works a sense of fairy tale enchantment.

65. Heidelberg Castle from the Southwest

[*Blick auf das Heidelberger Schloß von Südwesten*], 1856.
Watercolor, pen and gray and dark brown ink over pencil on ivory cardboard, 24.4 x 33.2 cm.
Signed and dated in dark brown wash lower right: *TVerhas del. 1856* (*T* and *V* in monogram).

Provenance: Formerly part of the Grand Ducal private collection.
Inv. no. VIII 2773.
Bibliography: Schefold, 1971, II, no. 25871; Theilmann and Ammann, 1978, I, p. 654, no. 4230, illus. II, p. 213.

This is sheet no. 36 of the "Heidelberger Friedrich – Luisen – Album" of 1856 (see nos. 7, 14, 16, 27, 66). Responding to the invitation to participate in the album, Verhas wrote Ludwig Kachel in a letter dated January 7, 1856:

> *As far as a choice for the subject matter is concerned, the one that appeals most to me is the view from the Molkenkur; and should it not yet have been assigned elsewhere, I respectfully request that my selection thereof be approved.*[1]

In a letter written that April, Verhas reported with pleasure that he had been granted

> *some leeway . . . with respect to the composition of the "Molkenkur-view" which I promised to do for the Heidelberg album. This news is all the more pleasing, since I have come to realize that some changes are absolutely necessary before I can create an even half-way pleasing landscape, even though the view with regard to architectural detail is a complex and an interesting one. If the gentlemen of the committee had insisted on a completely accurate view, I would not have withdrawn from the project entirely; I simply said to Mr. Meder the last time he was in Munich that I would have to be excused from such a project because I simply didn't have the material necessary for it. I would have had to make a new study after nature, and given the circumstances that was simply impossible. . . . I have started the drawing, keeping it within the required format, and I hope to be able to send it to you quite soon.*[2]

The picture was finished three months later. On July 2, 1856, Verhas sent the picture with the following note:

I have the honor of sending to Your Eminence the enclosed drawing for the Heidelberg album (View of the Castle from the Molkenkur), and would have preferred to send it somewhat earlier, but circumstances in my family prevented my completing it. I have set my honorarium at 88 guilders; I hope that my efforts may receive your approval.[3]

The work shows the view from the Molkenkur towards the castle and to the Heiligenberg on the opposite bank of the Neckar. There is another version of this scene, also dated 1856, which agrees in practically every detail with this one.[4] A few years earlier Verhas had drawn the castle from the same vantage point for a work in the "König – Ludwig – Album."[5]

1. Theodor Verhas letter to Ludwig Kachel, January 7, 1856, in the Badisches Generallandesarchiv, Karlsruhe (hereafter BGK), Abt. 69, N 9, no. 19.
2. Verhas to Kachel, April 1856, in BGK, Abt. 69, N 9, no. 19.
3. Verhas to Kachel, July 2, 1856, in BGK, Abt. 69, N 9, no. 19.
4. Kurpfälzisches Museum, Heidelberg, inv. no. Z 1609.
5. Staatliche Graphische Sammlung, Munich, "König – Ludwig – Album," pl. no. 237; see also Adolf von Oechelhäuser, *Die Kunstdenkmäler des Amtsbezirks Heidelberg*, Tübingen, 1913, p. 369, fig. 250.

66. Heidelberg Castle from the Northeast by Full Moon

[*Blick von Nordosten auf das Heidelberger Schloß bei Vollmond*], [ca. 1856].
Watercolor over pencil with highlights in white gouache and touches of gum arabic on beige paper, 24.4 x 34.2 cm.
Signed in pen and ink lower left: *TVerhas. del.* (*T* and *V* in monogram).

Provenance: Formerly part of the Grand Ducal private collection. Inv. no. VIII 2774.
Bibliography: Schefold, 1971, II, no. 25057; Theilmann and Ammann, 1978, I, pp. 654-55, no. 4231, illus. II, p. 213.

This is sheet no. 37 of the "Heidelberger Friedrich – Luisen – Album" of 1856 (see nos. 7, 14, 16, 27, 65), although it was not originally intended as part of the album. The Heidelberg art dealer L. Meder decided to contribute the drawing to the album and wrote to Ludwig Kachel on September 17, 1856:

. . . I am quite pleased to be able to send you today Verhas' drawing of Heidelberg, which I would like to donate to the Heidelberg Album. I am sure you will be pleased with it, since Verhas considers it to be a companion-piece to his drawing from the Molkenkur. He has spent a good deal of time on it and even thinks it to be the better of the two works. I have had a frame made for this second drawing so that if I can get it mounted in the next few days it will be possible to put it in the exhibition as an addendum to the other picture, and Prof. Haeußer has included it in his catalogue.[1]

On December 22 Meder wrote again to Kachel:

Since the large moonlight drawing of Verhas was so well received and since this work is now part of my personal collection and is presently exhibited in the royal gallery at the castle, I commissioned the artist to produce another version of it so that I might contribute it to the album. In this way my drawing would be remembered but would not necessarily call attention to itself, a situation which I would by all means wish to avoid, since my main purpose of having made a worthy contribution to the album has been accomplished.[2]

This view is from the river bank at Neuenheim, showing from left to right the castle, the Heiliggeistkirche, the old bridge and to the rear the tower of the Providenzkirche. Under the north façade of the castle stands the former palace of the Prince of Sachsen-Weimar, now the home of the Portland-Stiftung. See also these views taken from the same standpoint: *Blick auf Heidelberg vom Neuenheimer Ufer (View of Heidelberg from the River at Neuenheim,* 1835), and *Heidelberg, Schloß und Stadt von Nordosten (Heidelberg: Castle and City Seen from the Northeast),* both in the Kurpfälzisches Museum Heidelberg.[3] There is another view from the same angle but taken at closer location in the Staatliche Kunsthalle Karlsruhe.[4]

1. L. Meder letter to Ludwig Kachel, September 17, 1856, in the Badisches Generallandesarchiv, Karlsruhe (hereafter BGK), Abt. 69, N 9, no. 19.
2. Meder to Kachel, December 22, 1856, in BGK, Abt. 69, N 9, no. 19.
3. Kurpfälzisches Museum, Heidelberg, inv. nos. Z 4393 and Z 2893.
4. Staatliche Kunsthalle, Karlsruhe, inv. no. VIII 2755; see Theilmann and Ammann, 1978, I, p. 655, no. 4232, illus. II, p. 213.

Karl Weysser

Karlsruhe-Durlach 1833 – Heidelberg 1904

Weysser was born in Karlsruhe-Durlach on September 7, 1833. He enrolled in the Polytechnikum in Karlsruhe in 1848, where he took classes in mathematics and technical subjects. He continued his scientific studies at the University in Berlin from 1853 to 1855, but then entered the Academy at Karlsruhe as a student of Johann Wilhelm Schirmer (nos. 37-43). Throughout his life, Weysser frequently moved between Karlsruhe and other cities. He lived in Munich during 1860-61, and then returned to the Karlsruhe Academy. He went back to Munich in 1863-64, and returned again to Karlsruhe, where he completed his studies under Hans Frederik Gude in 1865. He lived in Karlsruhe (until 1872), in Düsseldorf (1873-75) in Karlsruhe again (1875-80), in Heidelberg (1880-84), in Baden-Baden (1885-90), once again in Karlsruhe (1890-95), and finally in Heidelberg (1895-1904). He traveled extensively, visiting the valley of the Lahn (between 1857 and 1859), Württemberg (1862, 1866), Lake Constance (1862, 1867), the upper Rhine (1863), the Black Forest and southern Tyrol (1869), as well as Alsace (1872). He also traveled extensively throughout Baden. Weysser died in Heidelberg on March 28, 1904.

Weysser is best known for his architectural painting. He made countless drawings and paintings of scenes throughout large areas of south Germany. In particular he focused on charming street scenes, romantic alleyways, and striking rows of houses, as well as on the more significant architectural structures of villages and towns. Weysser's warm coloring, which he combined with his secure sense of draftsmanship, shows the influence of the Munich school. He avoided fussy details, yet was so precise in reproducing the elements of a scene or of a building that his drawings have been taken as the basis for a wide range of restoration projects, giving his pictures value as historical documents as well as works of art. Some of his drawings have been used as illustrations for volumes cataloguing the architectural treasures of Baden.[1] Weysser painted his oils in his studio, basing them on the drawings he had made of the scenes which interested him. These drawings reveal Weysser's sensitivity toward the beauty of intimate scenes and picturesque details, beauties which the less sensitive observer might fail to notice.

1. Theilmann and Ammann, 1978, I, p. 685, no. 4428, illus. II, p. 509.

67. Section of the Ottheinrich Wing of Heidelberg Castle

[*Partie am Ottheinrichsbau des Heidelberger Schlosses*], 1863.
Pencil, pen and brush and gray ink, wash on ivory paper (watermark: [lilies] / C & I HONIG), 44.8 x 33.6 cm.
Signed and dated in pen and ink lower right: *K. Weysser/1863*.

Provenance: Acquired in 1936 from the firm of Karl Groos, Heidelberg; formerly part of the artist's estate. Inv. no. 1936-3.
Exhibition: Kurpfälzisches Museum, Heidelberg, *Werke von Karl Weysser,* 1935, no. 3.
Bibliography: Schefold, 1971, II, no. 25982; Theilmann and Ammann, 1978, I, p. 685, no. 4427, illus. II, p. 219.

This drawing shows the two right windows of the outside section of the main floor. In the niche between them is a sculpture of David with the head of Goliath, carved by the Dutch sculptor Alexander Colin ca. 1558.[1]

This drawing was made during one of Weysser's visits to Heidelberg, just before his second trip to Munich. See also the following work drawn during the same visit: *Efeustock am Ludwigsbau des Heidelberger Schlosses (Ivy on the Ludwig Wing of the Heidelberg Castle).*[2]

1. Helga Dressler, *Alexander Colin,* Karlsruhe, 1973, illus. nos. 4 and 9.
2. Staatliche Kunsthalle, Karlsruhe, inv. no. 1936-2; see Theilmann and Ammann, 1978, I, p. 685, no. 4426, illus. II, p. 508.

Franz Xaver Winterhalter

Menzenschwand 1805 – Frankfurt am Main 1873

Winterhalter was born in Menzenschwand in the Black Forest on April 20, 1805. In 1818 he entered the Herdersches Kunstinstitut in Freiburg im Breisgau, where he was trained as a lithographer. He went to the Academy in Munich in 1824 and studied under Peter von Langer. In 1828 he moved to Karlsruhe, where he enjoyed some success as a portraitist. He lived in Rome in 1833-34. He returned to Karlsruhe for a short time during which he was named a court painter. He then moved to Paris, where he continued to live for the next thirty-odd years. King Louis Philippe advanced his career considerably, and in 1841 Queen Victoria invited him to come to London. Finally he returned again to Karlsruhe in 1871. Winterhalter died in Frankfurt am Main on July 8, 1873.

An article in the *Kunstblatt* of 1845 described Winterhalter as "having completely overshadowed everyone else. . . . You can call him the portraitist of princes just as easily as the prince of portraitists. . . ."[1] This extravagant praise reflects fairly accurately the esteem in which Winterhalter was held. Despite sharp criticism leveled against his work, he was the most sought after and the best known portraitist of his era. Although he executed a number of Italian genre scenes in the manner of Léopold Roberts,[2] his numerous portraits of upper European nobility carried his fame far and wide. He painted all the important members of the ruling families of England, Belgium, Prussia, Russia, and France. He was enormously effective in flattering his clients and in satisfying their vanities. There is little psychological depth in his works, doubtless because he did not attempt to achieve anything of the sort.

Winterhalter painted with dexterity and bravura. He had no desire to examine critically the superficial appearance of his clients, let alone seriously question it. As a result, he was often criticized for failing to penetrate beyond mere surface decoration. In his obituary, Max Schasler wrote that it was a shame that Winterhalter had adopted

> *a perfumed aristocratic bearing . . . which made him the pet painter of princes and especially of princesses. He strove to grasp and reproduce not pure, unadulterated nature, but rather elegance; not the fundamental truths of human life, regardless of its social class, but rather the refined charm of the ladies of "the court."*[3]

The collapse of the Second Empire in France and of the social class which supported it sealed the fate of Winterhalter's art. Too closely associated with the ideals and the values of its influential patrons, Winterhalter's work became meaningless for the new generation of realists and impressionists. Winterhalter's name was soon forgotten, but the kind of reputation he had enjoyed during his lifetime can be gauged by the value of the estate he left, which was placed at two million German marks.

In contrast with the pompous and artificial portraits commissioned during his later years, Winterhalter's early brush and ink or watercolor portraits reveal a simple, bourgeois charm. They show a love of detail and are marked by a delicate and refined sense of color. His careful distribution of light and shadow emphasizes the sense of volume in his figures and brings them forward from the bright background.

1. *Kunstblatt,* No. 64 (1845), p. 265.
2. Lauts and Zimmermann, 1971, illus. p. 515.
3. Max Schasler in *Dioskuren* XVIII (1873), p. 286.

68. Portrait of Dr. Johann Albert Wich

[*Brustbildnis Dr. Johann Albert Wich*], [1831].
Brush and ink over pencil on cream cardboard (watermark: J WHATMAN/1831), 36.4 x 29.2 cm.
Signed in pencil to the right under the image: *Winterhalter;* inscribed lower center by another hand: *Geh. Hofrat Dr Johann Nepomuck Wiech-.*

Provenance: Acquired in 1942 from Gräfin von Lamberg Ortenegg, Freiburg im Breisgau; formerly part of a private collection in Freiburg im Breisgau. Inv. no. 1942-9.
Exhibition: Freiburg, 1909, no. 191.
Bibliography: Sutter, 1909, p. 82, note 83; Theilmann and Ammann, 1978, I, p. 688, no. 4449, illus. II, p. 218.

Dr. Johann Albert Wich was born in Frauenalb. He began the practice of medicine in Bretten in 1809 and moved to Baden-Baden in 1826. In 1830 he settled in Karlsruhe, where he served as a private physician and held the title of Privy Medical Counselor. He died in Gaggenau on July 11, 1839. Winterhalter lived in the Wich's house from 1831 to 1833. This drawing was published as a lithograph by Kauffmann.

69. Portrait of Pauline Freifrau Seutter von Löfzen, née Wich

[*Halbfigurenbildnis Pauline Freifrau Seutter von Löfzen, geborene Wich*], [1833].
Brush and ink and watercolor over pencil on light beige cardboard (watermark: J WHATMAN/TURKEY MILL/1833; blind stamp: EXTRA LONDON BOARD), 36.8 x 31.0 cm.
Inscribed in pencil lower right by another hand: *2/87 a;* inscribed verso in indelible pencil by another hand: *Pauline von Seutter geb. Wich;* below this in pencil by another hand: *Tochter des Geh. Hofrats Dr Joh. Nep. Wich.*

Provenance: Acquired in 1942 from Gräfin von Lamberg Ortenegg, Freiburg im Breisgau; formerly part of a private collection in Freiburg im Breisgau. Inv. no. 1942-8.
Exhibition: Freiburg, 1909, no. 193; Karlsruhe, 1966, no. 105; Karlsruhe, 1978, p. 31.
Bibliography: Sutter, 1909, p. 82, with note and illus. p. 92; Theilmann and Ammann, 1978, I, p. 688, no. 4450, illus. II, p. 218.

Pauline Freifrau Seutter von Löfzen was the daughter of Dr. Johann Albert Wich (no. 68) and the sister of Karl Wich (no. 70).

70. Portrait of Karl Wich

[*Halbfigurenbildnis Karl Wich*], [1833].
Brush and ink over pencil on ivory cardboard (watermark: J WHATMAN/TURKEY MILL/1833; blind stamp: SUPERFINE LONDON BOARD), 37.1 x 30.6 cm.
Signed in pencil to the right under the image: *Winterhalter;* inscribed lower center by another hand: *Souvenir;* inscribed verso in indelible pencil by another hand: *Karl Wich.*

Provenance: Acquired in 1942 from Gräfin von Lamberg Ortenegg, Freiburg im Breisgau; formerly part of a private collection in Freiburg im Breisgau. Inv. no. 1942-10.
Exhibition: Freiburg, 1909, no. 195; Karlsruhe, 1966, no. 106.
Bibliography: Sutter, 1909, p. 82, note 83; Theilmann and Ammann, 1978, I, p. 688-89, no. 4451, illus. II, p. 218.

Karl Wich was the son of Dr. Albert Wich (no. 68) and the brother of Pauline Freifrau von Seutter (no. 69). There is another drawing which shows Karl Wich together with his sister Frida and a dog.[1]

1. Sutter, 1909, illus. p. 92.

Max Wolf

Gissigheim 1824 – Heidelberg 1901

Wolf was born in Gissigheim near Tauberbischofsheim on March 4, 1824. A pupil of Bernhard Fries, he taught classical languages and, sporadically, drawing and gymnastics, working occasionally at the Gymnasium in Bruchsal until 1868 and in Heidelberg between 1868 and 1890. From 1878 to 1893 he was the president of the Heidelberg artists' association. Wolf died in Heidelberg on December 25, 1901.

Wolf was primarily a language teacher, but his artistic talent drew him to painting. After his retirement in 1890 he was finally able to devote himself exclusively to art. Together with Bernhard Fries, the brother of the artist Ernst Fries, he painted scenes of Heidelberg and its surroundings. Wolf left a number of landscapes executed in the tradition of the Heidelberg romantics, and also a group of intimate oil sketches portraying forest scenes. These landscapes are fresh and direct, and they surprise the viewer with their unconventional realism. To this group of scenes belong his Heidelberg drawings. Wolf succeeds in capturing the picturesque qualities of the town with his quick, objective lines.

71. View of Heidelberg

[*Ansicht von Heidelberg*], n.d.
Pencil on beige paper, 24.9 x 33.4 cm.

Provenance: Acquired from Auction 94, Dr. Helmut Tenner, Heidelberg, 1973, no. 687, illus. Inv. no. 1973-3.
Bibliography: Jahrbuch XI (1974), p. 170; Theilmann and Ammann, 1978, I, pp. 690-91, no. 4465, illus. II, p. 219.

The view is taken from the northeast across the Neckar and toward the old section of town. To the left is the tower of the Jesuitenkirche, in the center the Heiliggeistkirche. At the extreme right is the gateway to the old bridge across the Neckar.

Selected Exhibitions and Bibliography

Exhibitions

Basel, 1924 — Basel, Kunsthalle, *Hans Thoma,* 1924.

Bern, 1924 — Bern, Kunsthalle, *Hans Thoma: Ausstellung von Gemälden, Zeichnungen und graphischen Arbeiten,* 1924.

Constance, 1963 — Constance, Wessenberghaus, *Gedächtnisausstellung Marie Ellenrieder,* 1963.

Constance, 1969 — Constance, Wessenberghaus, *Die Konstanzer Maler Wendelin, Friedrich, Joseph Mosbrugger,* 1969.

Freiburg, 1909 — Freiburg, Kunstverein, *Jahrhundert Ausstellung 1780-1880,* 1909, organized by the Freiburg Women's Club.

Furtwagen, 1967 — Furtwagen, *Johann Baptist Kirner,* 1967.

Karlsruhe, 1930 — Karlsruhe, Badische Kunsthalle, *Hans Thoma: Ausstellung von Aquarellen und Handzeichnungen,* 1930.

Karlsruhe, 1939 — Karlsruhe, Staatliche Kunsthalle, *Hans Thoma 1839-1924, Gedächtnisausstellung zum 100. Geburtstag,* 1939.

Karlsruhe, 1966 — Karlsruhe, Staatliche Kunsthalle, *Deutsche Zeichnungen des 19. Jahrhunderts aus der Staatlichen Kunsthalle Karlsruhe,* 1966.

Karlsruhe, 1978 — Karlsruhe, Staatliche Kunsthalle, *Deutsche Zeichnungen des 19. Jahrhunderts,* 1978.

Munich, 1929 — Munich, Neue Pinakothek, *Feuerbach-Ausstellung zur Feier des 100. Geburtstages des Meisters: Verbunden mit einer Ausstellung von Zeichnungen geistesverwandter Künstler des 19. Jahrhunderts,* 1929.

Reutlingen, 1978 — Reutlingen, Studio-Galerie, *Hans Thoma: Handzeichnungen-Graphik,* 1978.

Bibliography

Ammann, 1967 — Ammann, Edith, *Hans Thoma: Handzeichnungen aus der Staatlichen Kunsthalle Karlsruhe,* Karlsruhe, 1967.

Beringer, 1912 — Beringer, Josef August, *Emil Lugo,* Mannheim, 1912.

Beringer, 1915 — Beringer, Josef August, "Moritz von Schwinds Karlsruher Zeit," *Zeitschrift für die Geschichte des Oberrheins,* N.F. 30, (1915).

Beringer, 1916 — Beringer, Josef August, *Hans Thoma: Griffelkunst,* Frankfurt am Main, 1916.

Beringer, 1925 — Beringer, Josef August, *Emil Lugo,* 2nd ed. Karlsruhe, 1925.

Beringer, 1929 — Beringer, Josef August, *Hans Thoma: Aus achtzig Lebensjahren: Ein Lebensbild aus Briefen und Tagebüchern,* Leipzig, 1929.

Bernhard, 1973 — Bernhard, Marianne, ed., *Deutsche Romantik: Handzeichnungen,* 2 vols. Munich, 1973.

Boetticher, 1891-1901 — Boetticher, Friedrich von, *Malerwerke des neunzehnten Jahrhunderts,* 2 vols. Dresden, 1891-1901.

Bringmann and Blanckenhagen, 1974 — Bringmann, Michael and Blanckenhagen, Sigrid von, *Die Mosbrugger: Die Konstanzer Maler Wendelin, Friedrich und Joseph Mosbrugger,* Weißenhorn, 1974.

Fischel, 1929 — Fischel, Lilli, *Badische Kunsthalle Karlsruhe: Verzeichnis der Gemälde,* Berlin, 1929.

Fischer and Blanckenhagen, 1963 — Fischer, Friedhelm Wilhelm, *Marie Ellenrieder: Leben und Werk der Konstanzer Malerin:* with a work catalogue by Sigrid von Blanckenhagen, Constance, 1963.

Franzke and Honold, 1977 — Andreas Franzke, *Georg Philipp Schmitt (1808-1873): Ein Heidelberger Maler des 19. Jahrhunderts:* with a biographical study by Guido Florentin Honold, Karlsruhe, 1977.

Jahrbuch — *Jahrbuch der Staatlichen Kunstsammlungen in Baden-Württemberg* II-XII (1965-75).

Koelitz, 1915 — Koelitz, Karl, *Grossh. Kunsthalle zu Karlsruhe: Katalog der Gemälde-Galerie,* 7th ed. Karlsruhe, 1915.

Koelitz, 1920 — Koelitz, Karl, *Grossh. Kunsthalle zu Karlsruhe: Katalog der Gemälde-Galerie,* 8th ed. Karlsruhe, 1920.

Krafft and Schümann, 1969 — Krafft, Eva Maria and Schümann, Carl-Wolfgang, *Katalog der Meister des 19. Jahrhunderts in der Hamburger Kunsthalle,* Hamburg, 1969.

Lauts and Zimmermann, 1971 — Lauts, Jan and Zimmermann, Werner, *Staatlche Kunsthalle Karlsruhe, Katalog neuere Meister 19. und 20. Jahrhundert,* Karlsruhe, 1971.

Lugt — Lugt, Frits, *Les Marques de collections de dessins et d'estampes,* Amsterdam, 1921.

Lugt S. — Lugt, Frits, *Les Marques de collections de dessins et d'estampes . . . Supplément,* The Hague, 1956.

Martin, 1946 — Martin, Kurt, *Hans Thoma: 10 Zeichnungen,* Dietmannsried and Heidelberg, 1946.

Rohrandt, 1972 — Rohrandt, Klaus, "Wilhelm Trübner (1851-1917): Kritischer und beschreibender Katalog sämtlicher Gemälde, Zeichnungen und Druckgraphik: Biographie und Studien zum Werk," diss. Kiel, 1972, 2 vols.

Schefold, 1965 — Schefold, Max, ed., *Der Schwarzwald in alten Ansichten und Schilderungen,* Constance, 1965.

Schefold, 1971 — Schefold, Max, *Alte Ansichten aus Baden,* 2 vols. Weißenhorn, 1971.

Schefold, 1974 — Schefold, Max, *Alte Ansichten aus Württemberg: Nachtragsband zum Katalog,* Stuttgart, 1974.

Schneider, 1932 — Schneider, Arthur von, *Hans Thoma: Zeichnungen,* Freiburg im Breisgau, 1932.

Schneider, 1935 — Schneider, Arthur von, *Badische Malerei des 19. Jahrhunderts,* Berlin, 1935.

Schneider, 1968 — Schneider, Arthur von, *Badische Malerei des 19. Jahrhunderts,* 2nd ed. Karlsruhe, 1968.

Schücking, 1860 — Schücking, Levin, ed., *Bilder aus Westfalen,* Elberfeld, 1860.

Siebert, 1915 — Siebert, Klara, *Marie Ellenrieder,* Freiburg im Breisgau, 1915.

Sutter, 1909 — Sutter, Carl, "Die Freiburger Ausstellungen von 1908-1909," *Schau-ins-Land,* 36, (1909).

Theilmann, 1971 — Theilmann, Rudolf, "Johann Wilhelm Schirmers Karlsruher Schule," diss. Heidelberg, 1971.

Theilmann, 1973 — Theilmann, Rudolf, ed., *Die Lebenserinnerungen von Eugen Bracht,* Karlsruhe, 1973.

Theilmann and Ammann, 1978 — Theilmann, Rudolf and Ammann, Edith, *Staatliche Kunsthalle Karlsruhe, Kupferstichkabinett: Die deutschen Zeichnungen des 19. Jahrhunderts,* 2 vols. Karlsruhe, 1978.

Thode, 1909 — Thode, Henry, *Thoma: Des Meisters Gemälde,* Stuttgart and Leipzig, 1909.

Trübner, 1918 — Trübner, Wilhelm, *Personalien und Prinzipien,* 2nd and 3rd eds. Berlin, [1918].

Weigmann, 1906 — Weigmann, Otto, *Schwind: Des Meisters Werk,* Stuttgart and Leipzig, 1906.

Wittichen, 1980 — Wittichen, Ingeborg, *Oberbergische Malerinnen des 19. Jahrhunderts aus der Familie Jügel/Heuser,* Celle, [1980].

Zimmermann, 1919-20 — Zimmermann, Kurt, "Johann Wilhelm Schirmer," diss. Kiel, 1919, Saalfeld, 1920.

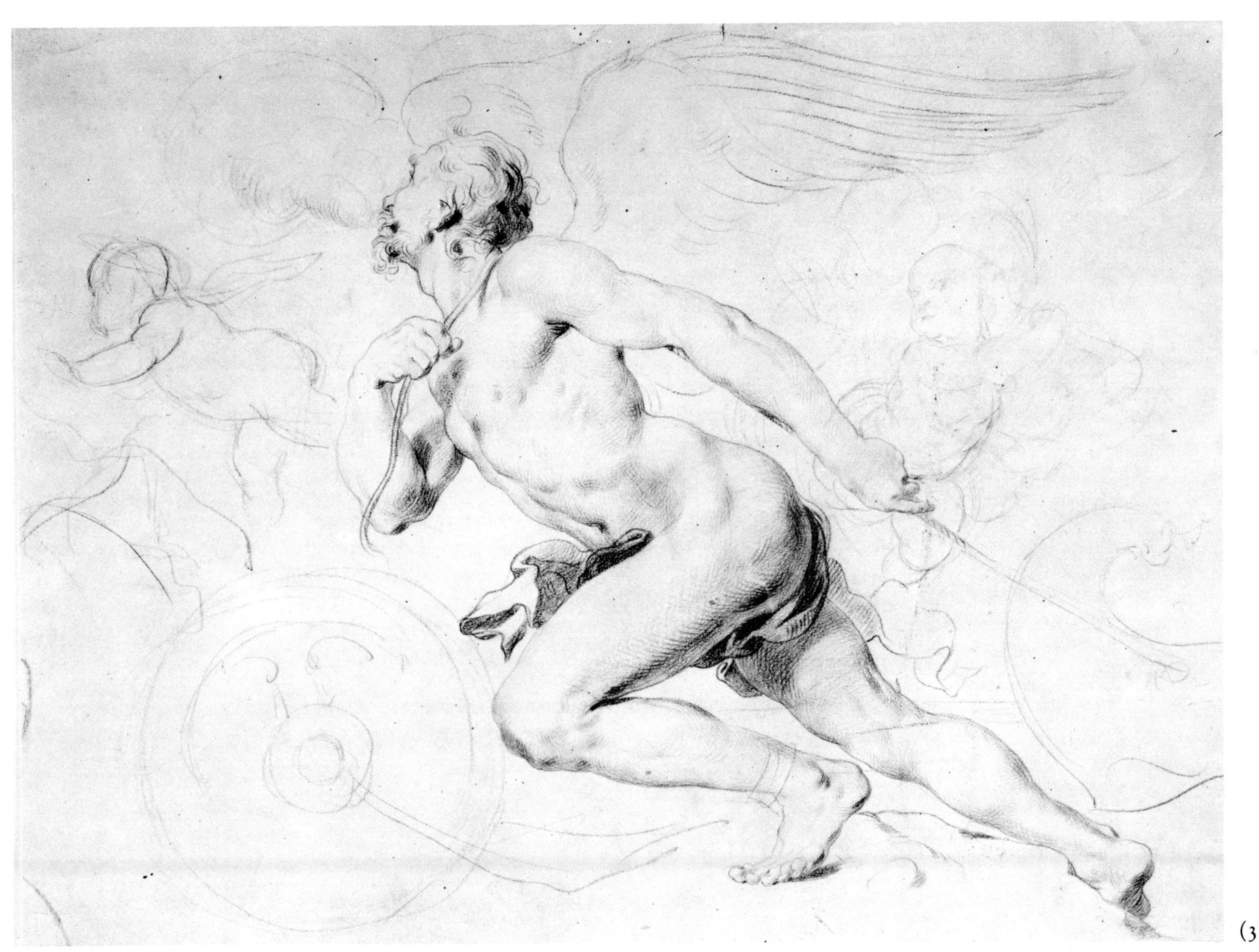

(3)

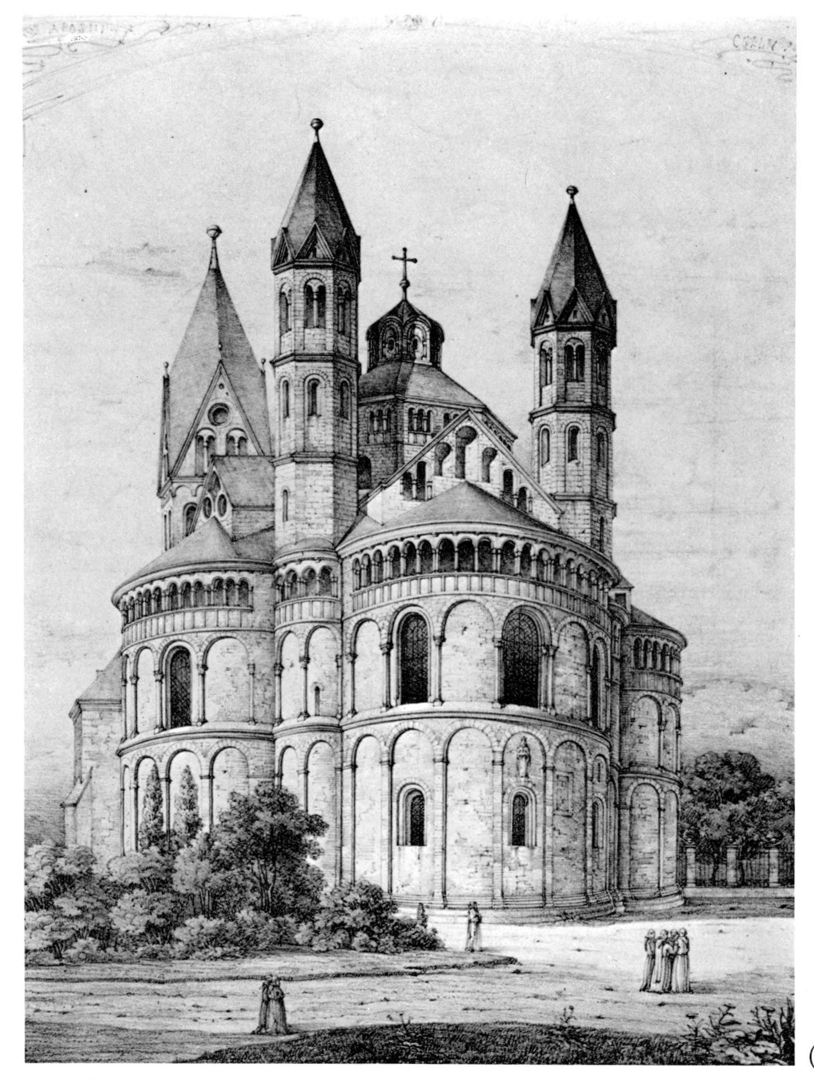

(5)

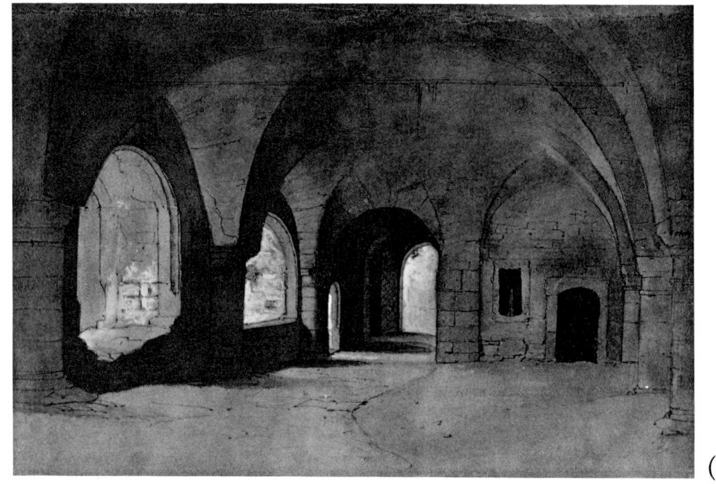

(2)

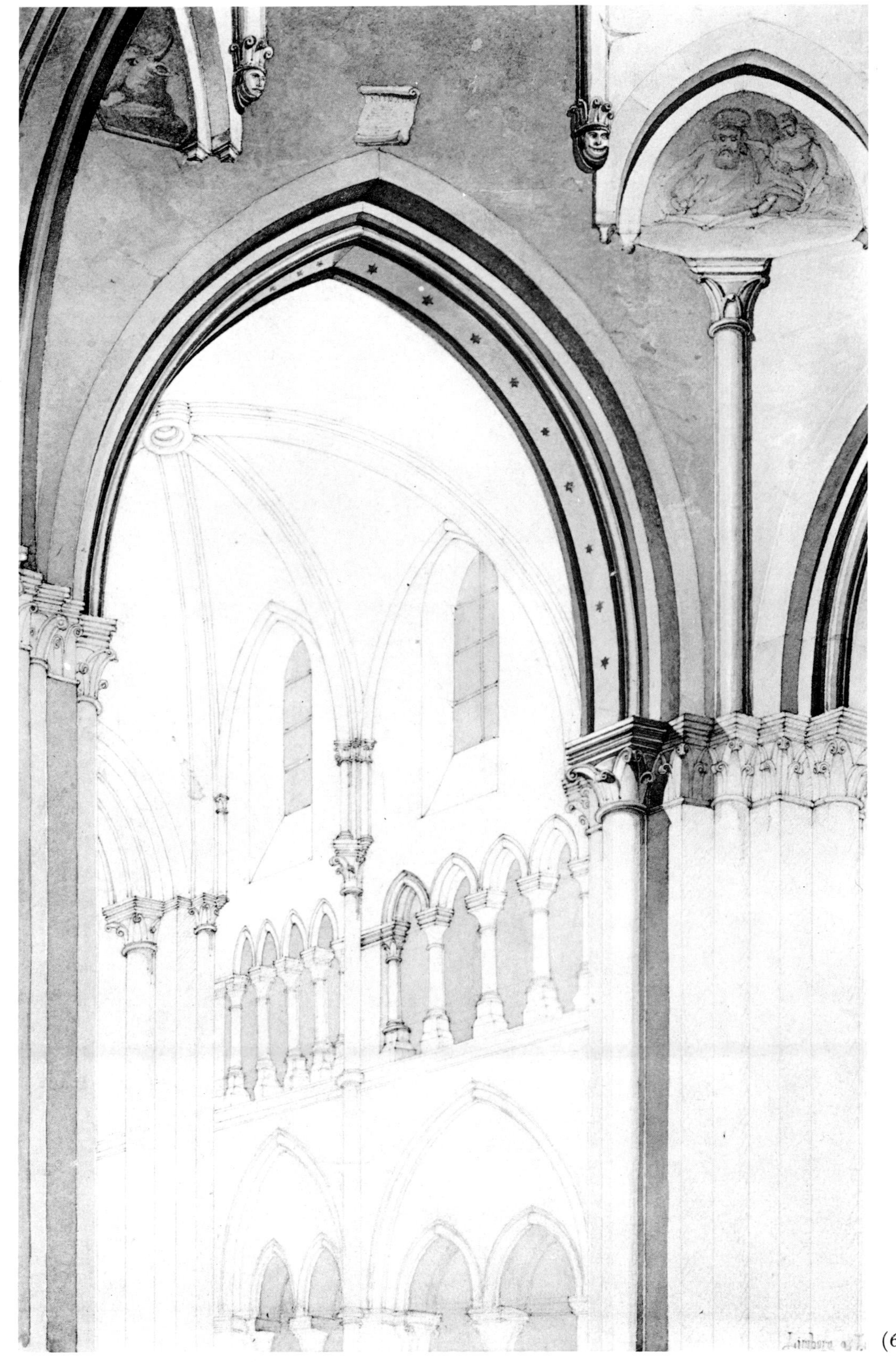
(6)

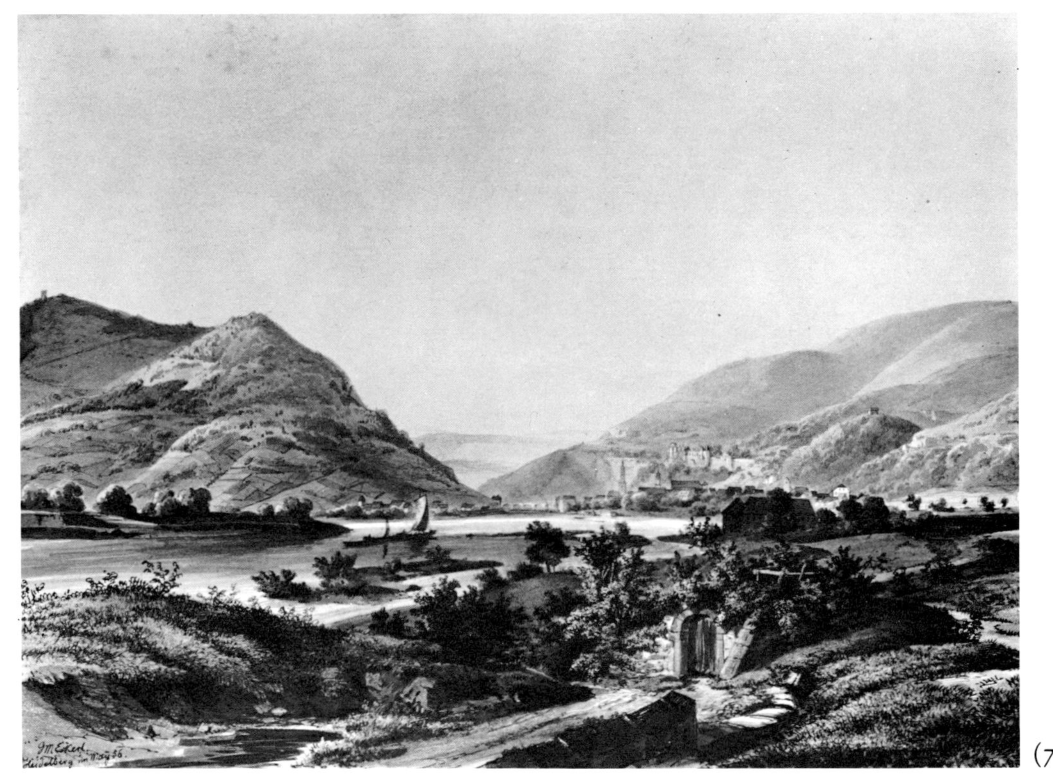

(7)

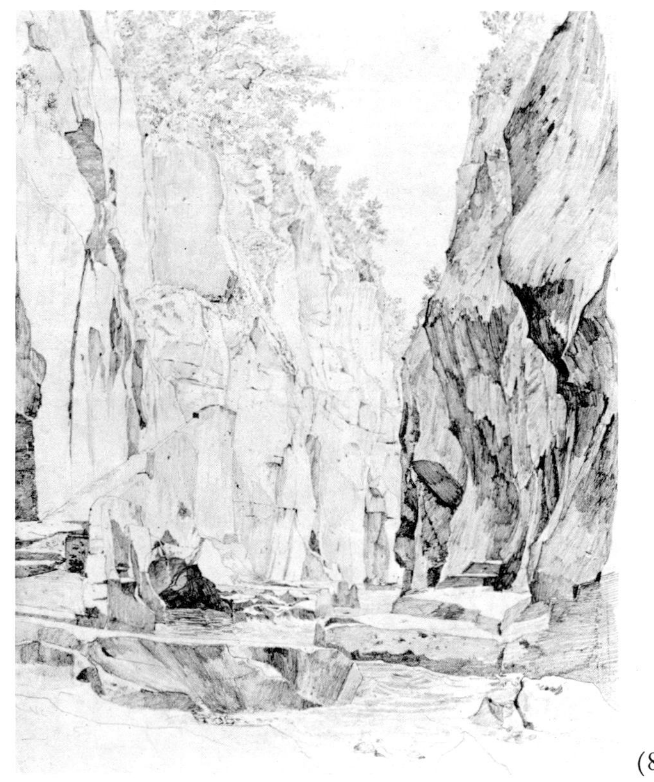
(8)

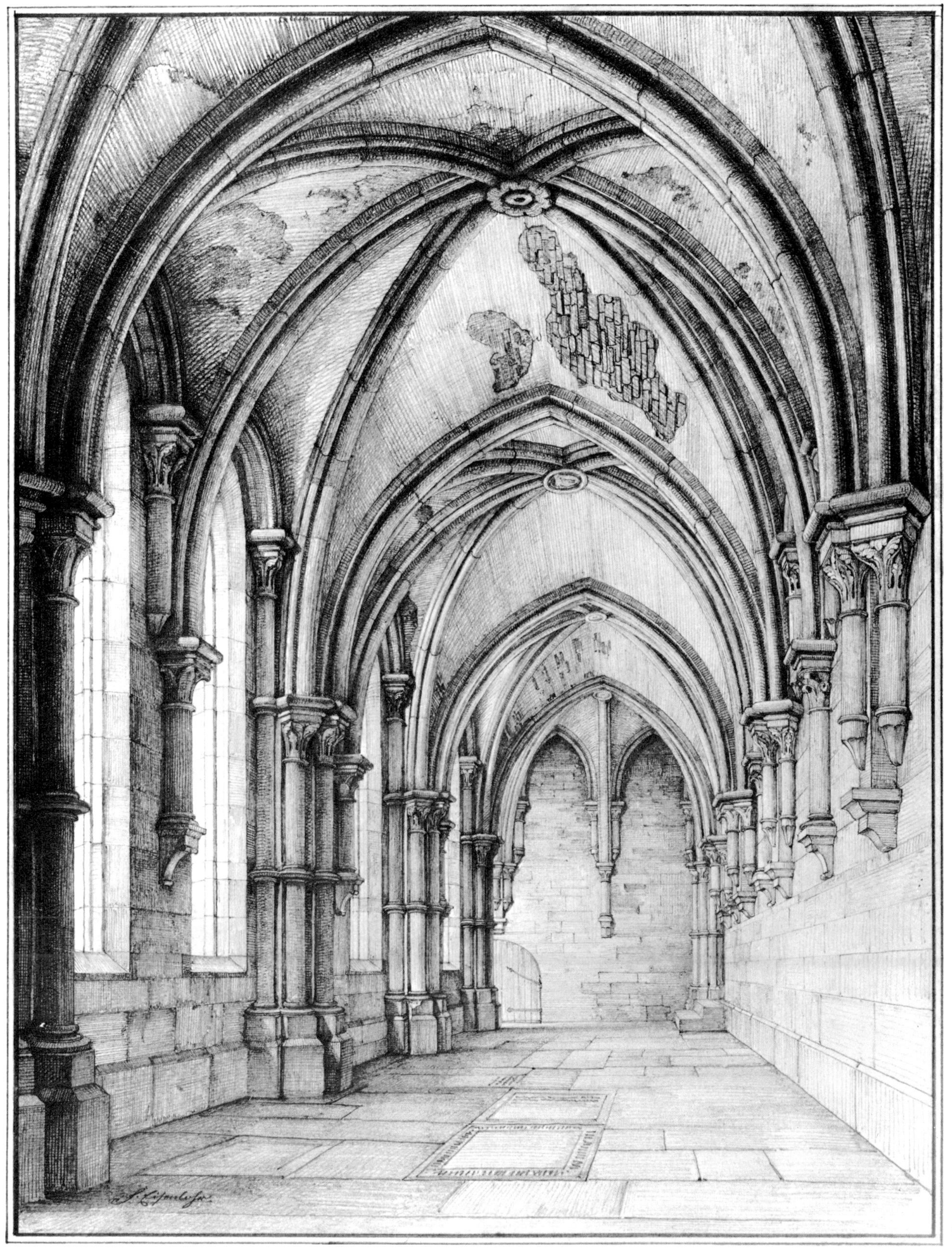

(9)

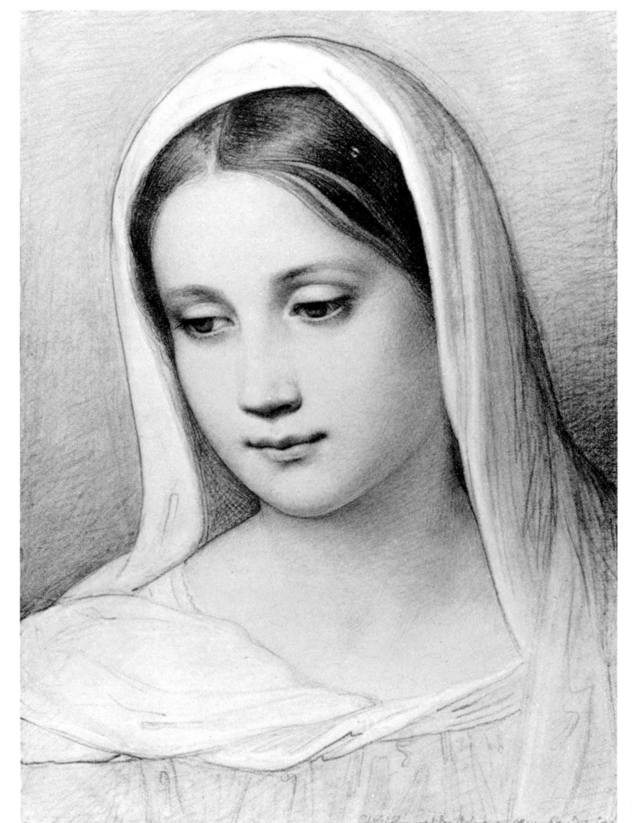

(10)

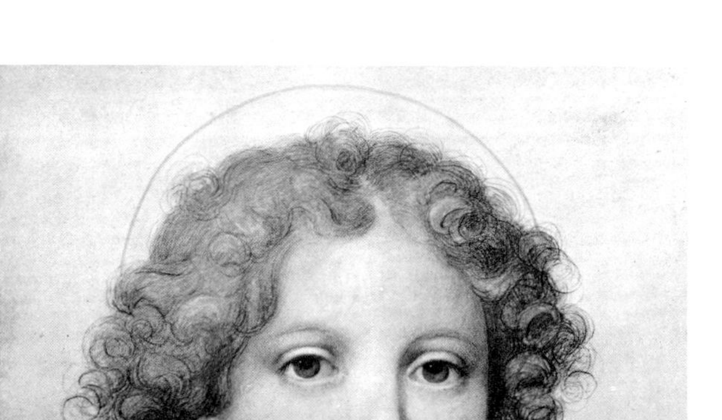

(11)

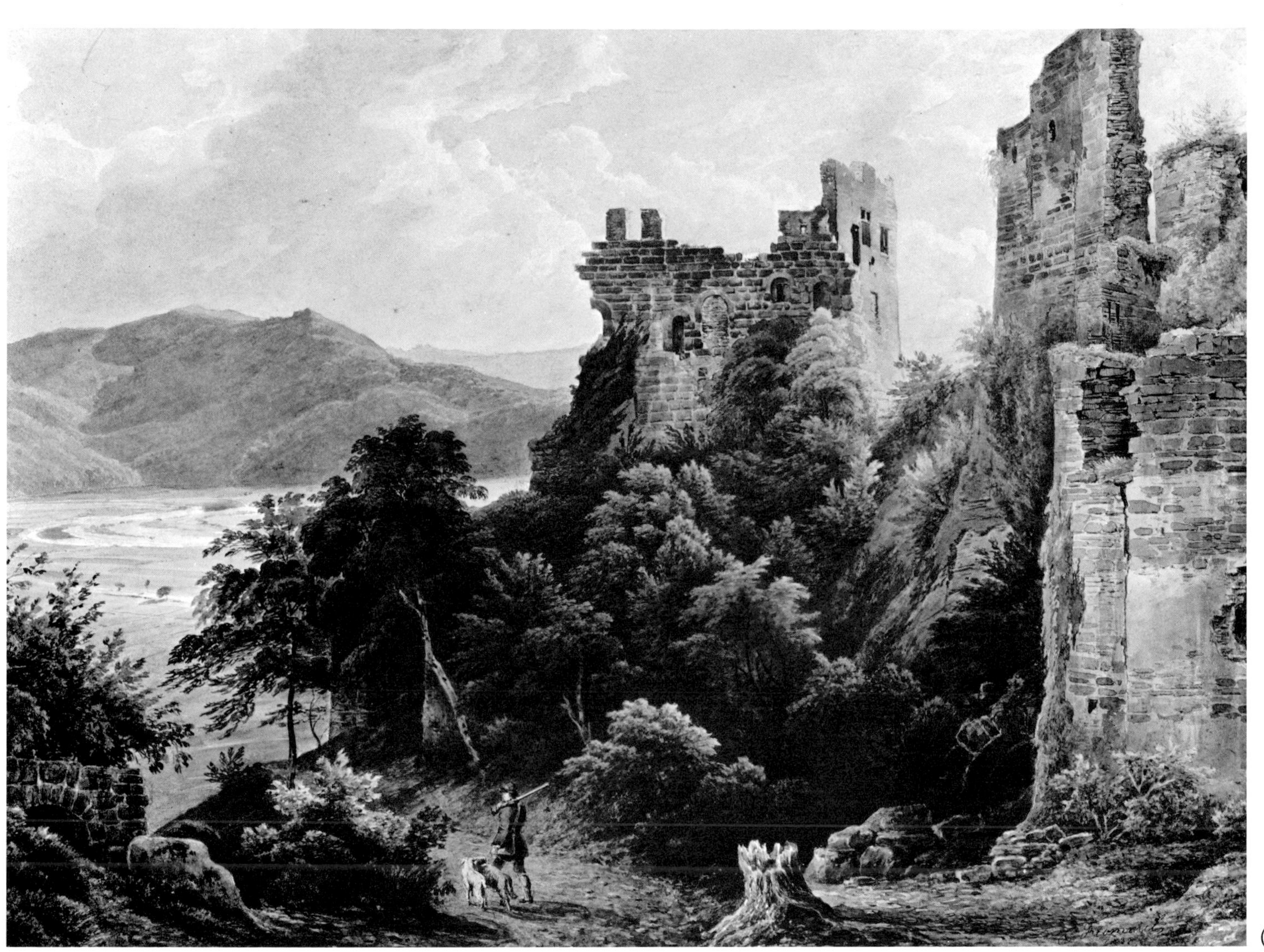

(12)

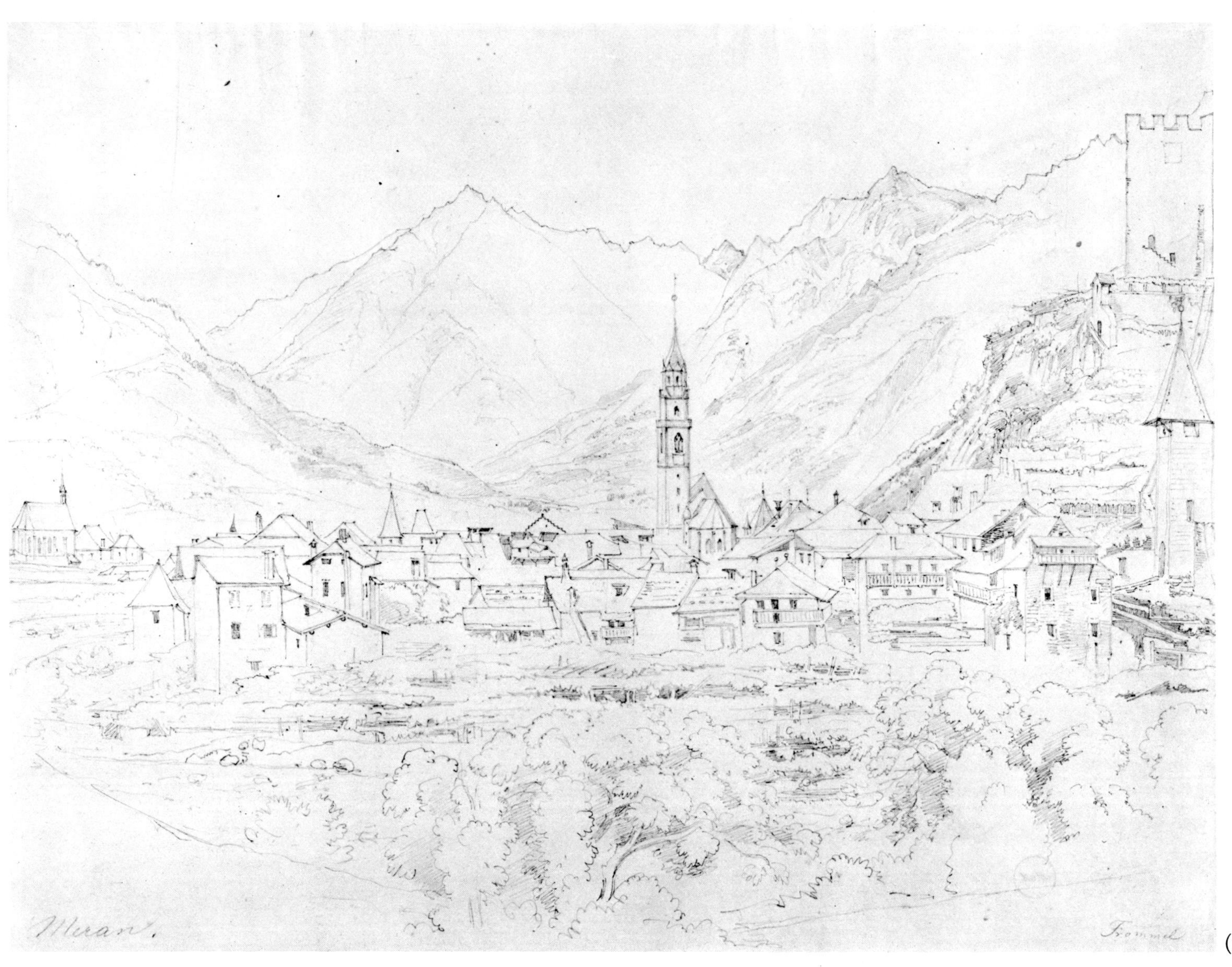

(13)

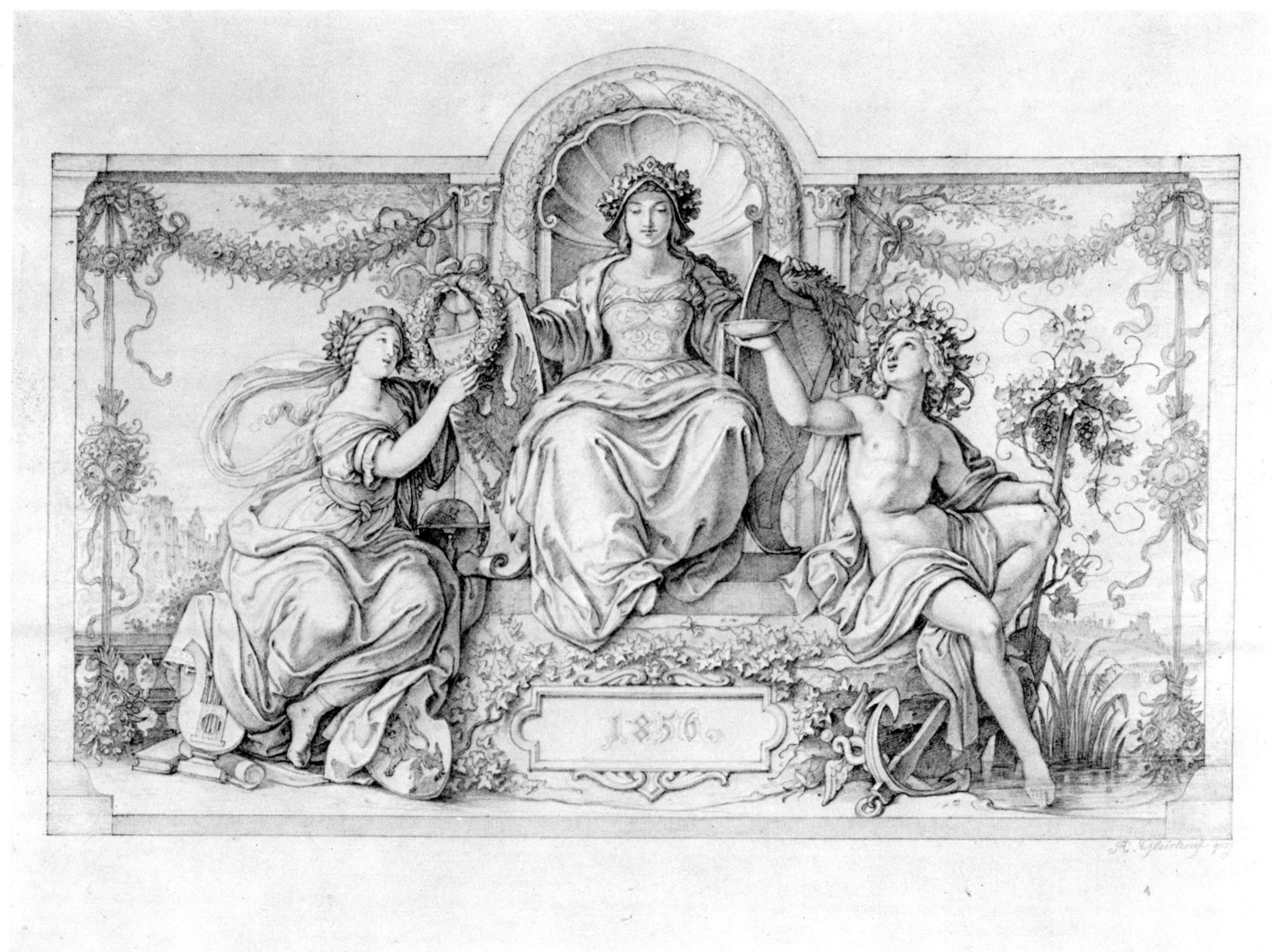

(14)

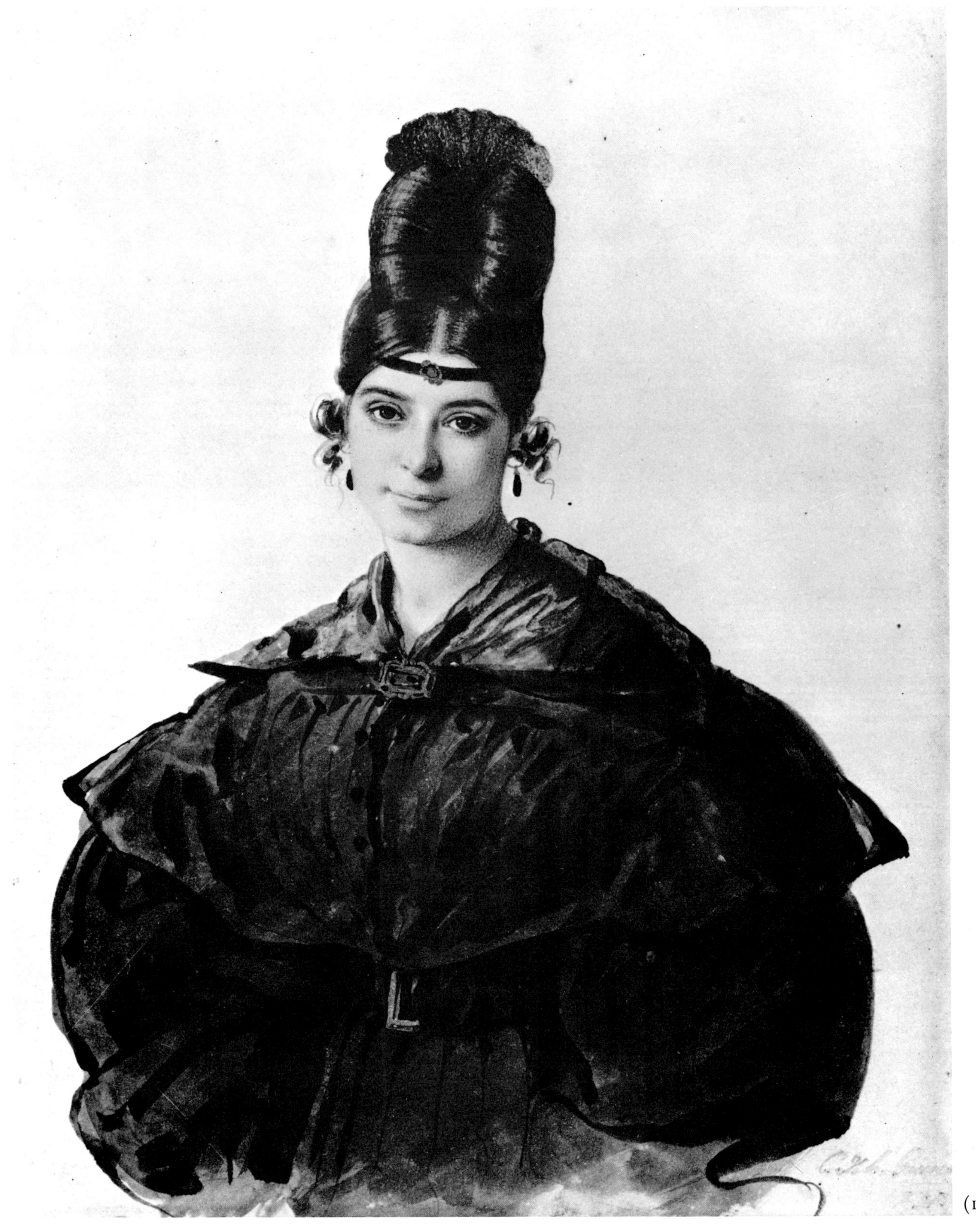

(15)

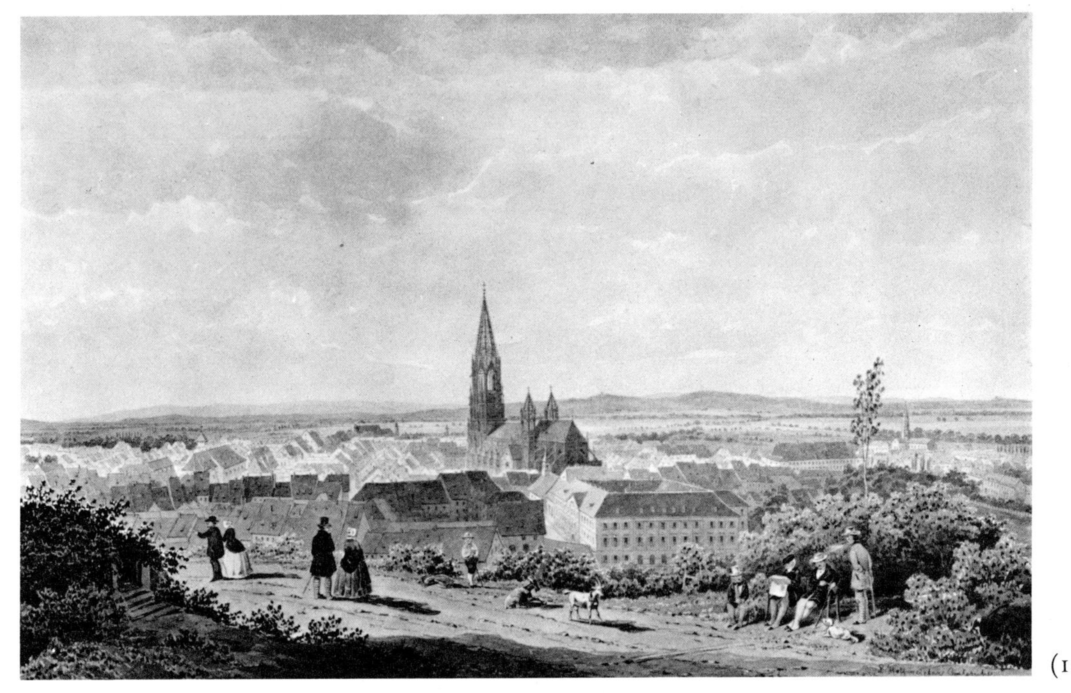

(16)

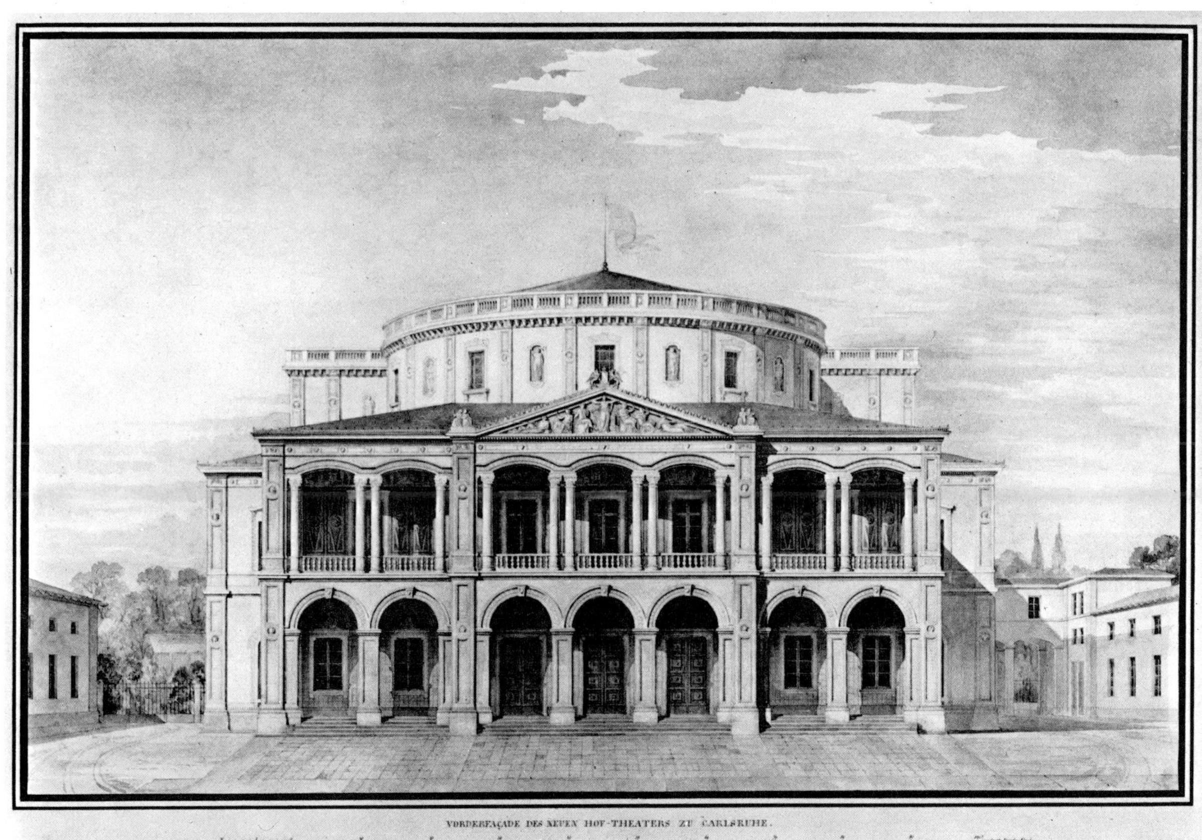

(17)

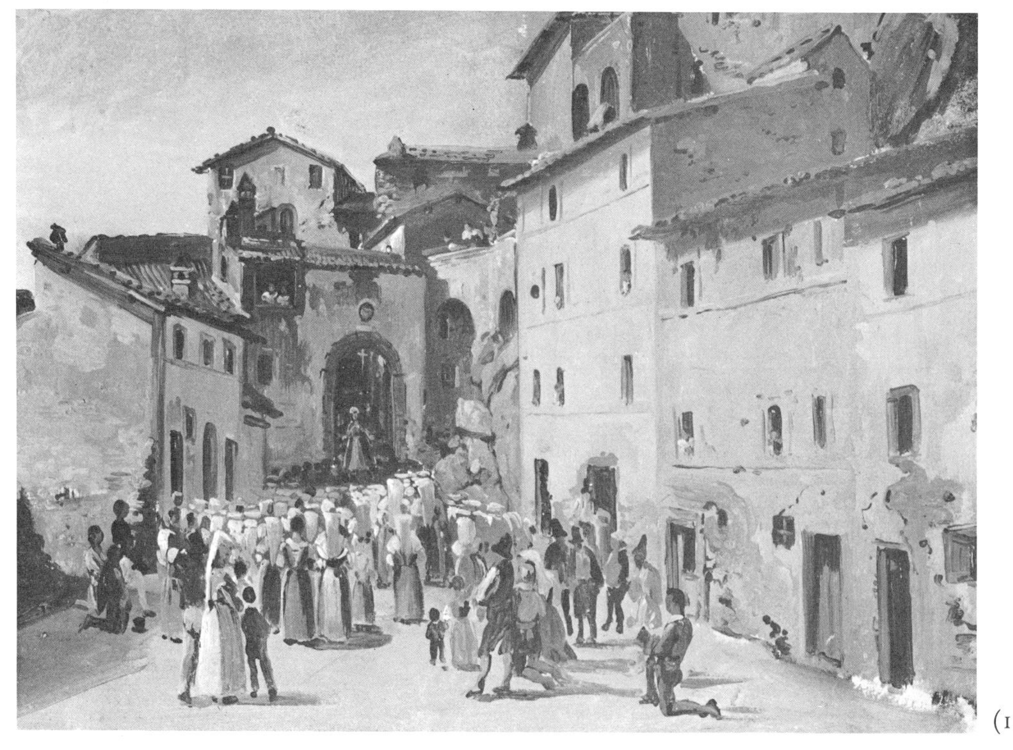
(18)

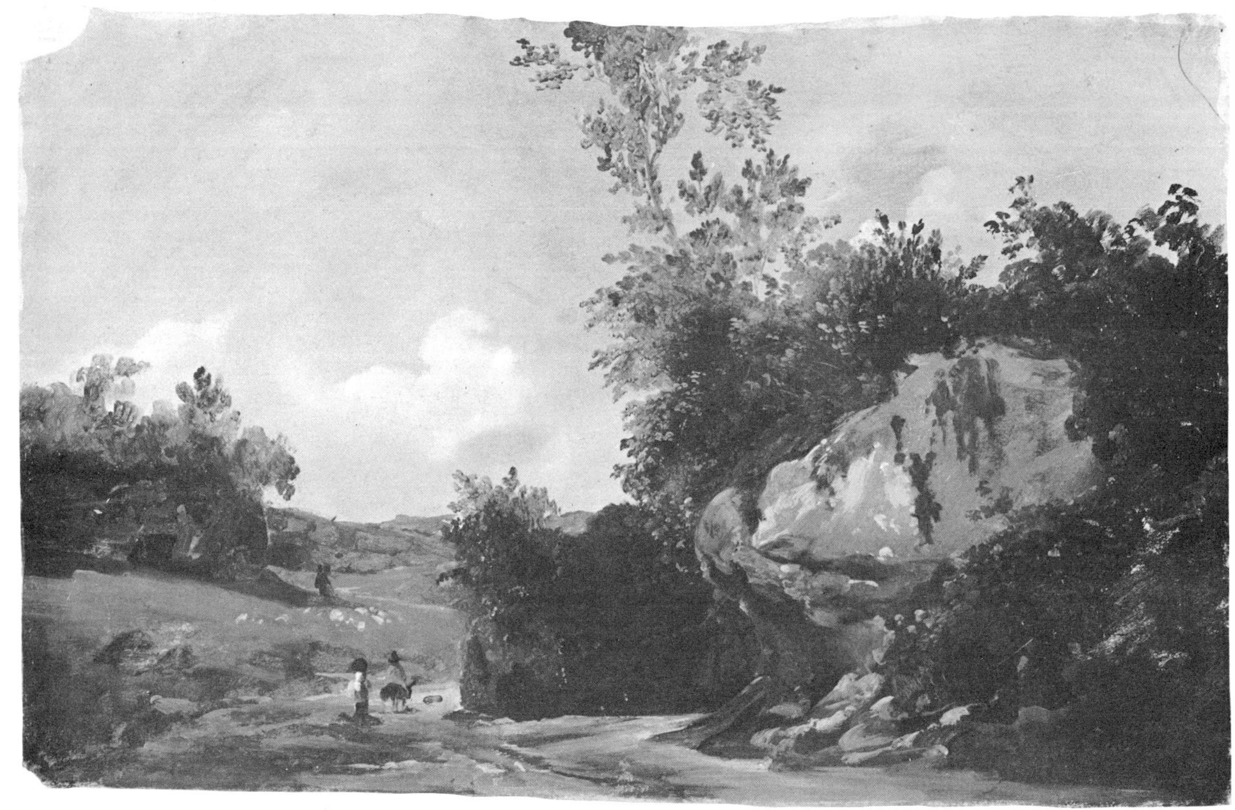
(19)

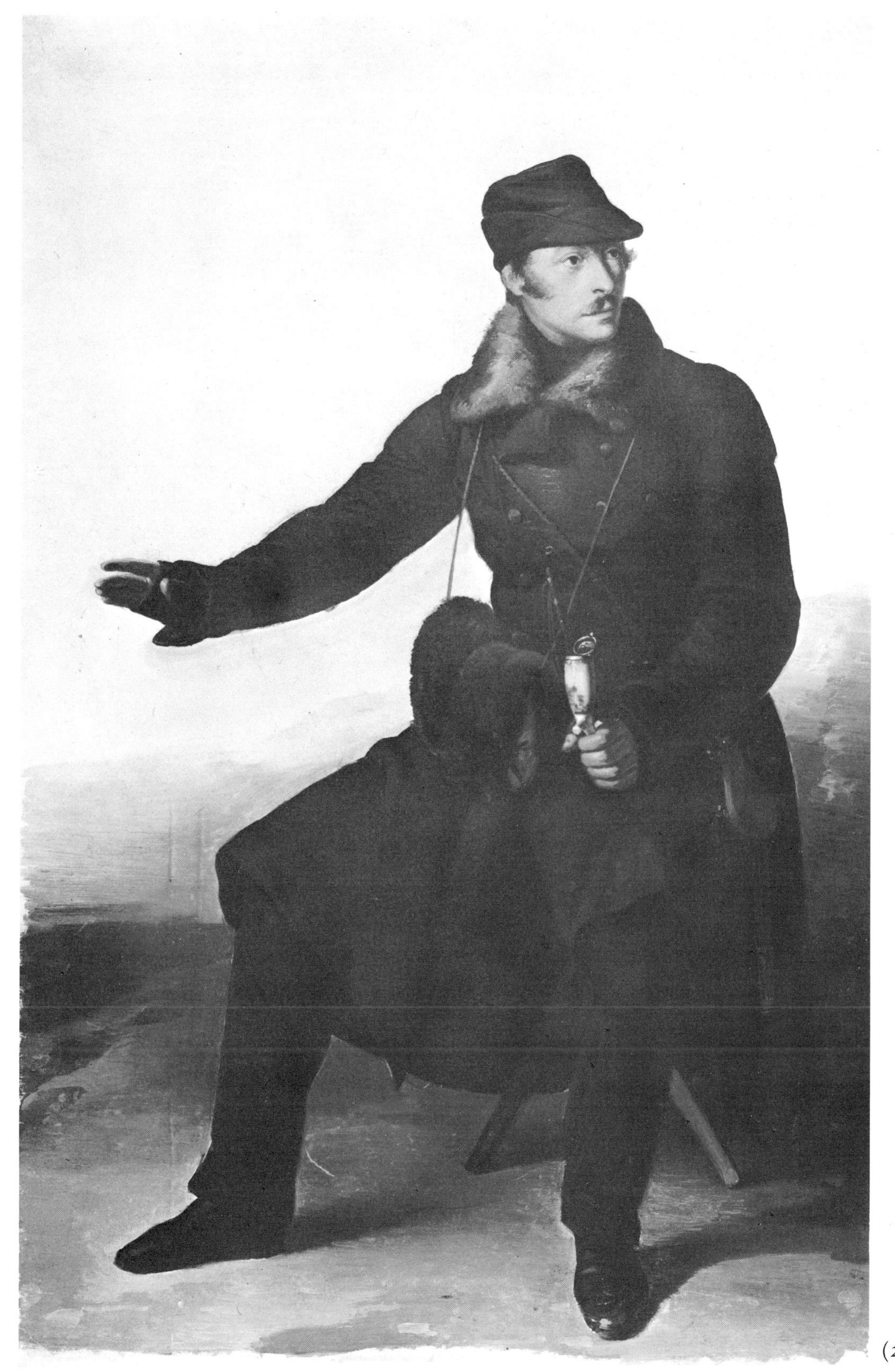

(20)

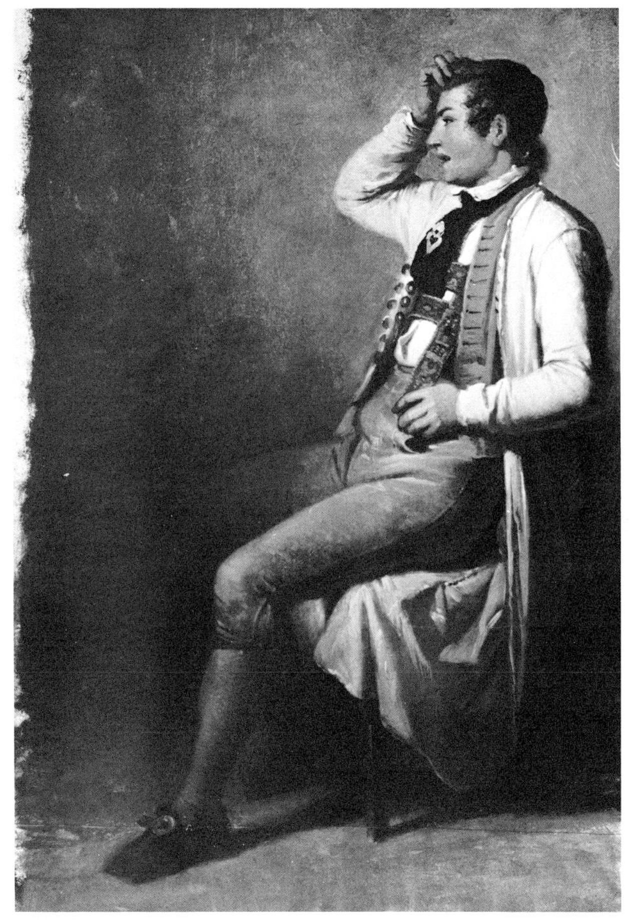

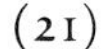

(21)

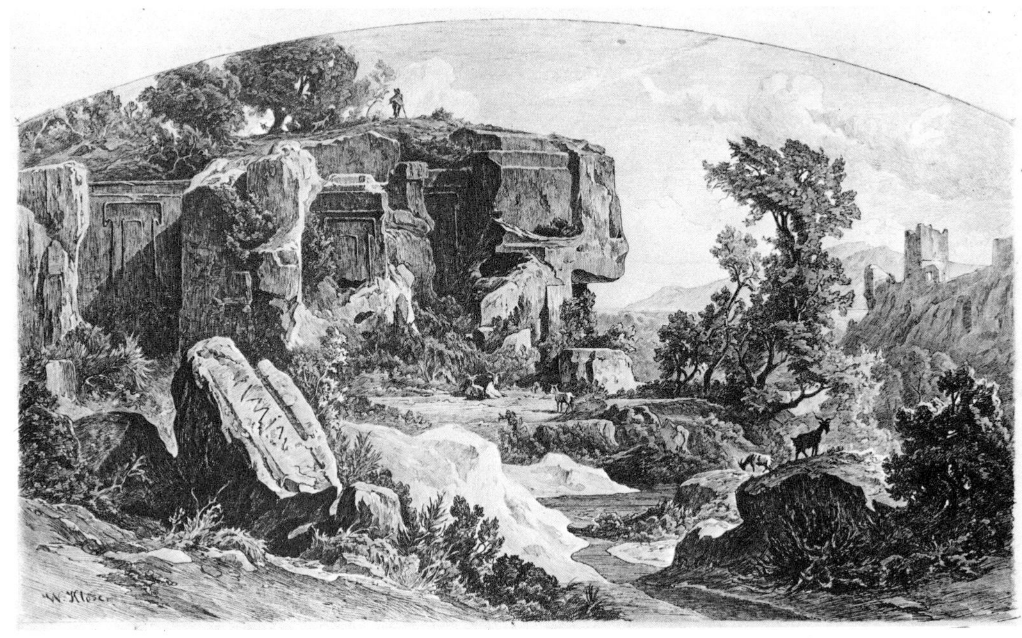

(22)

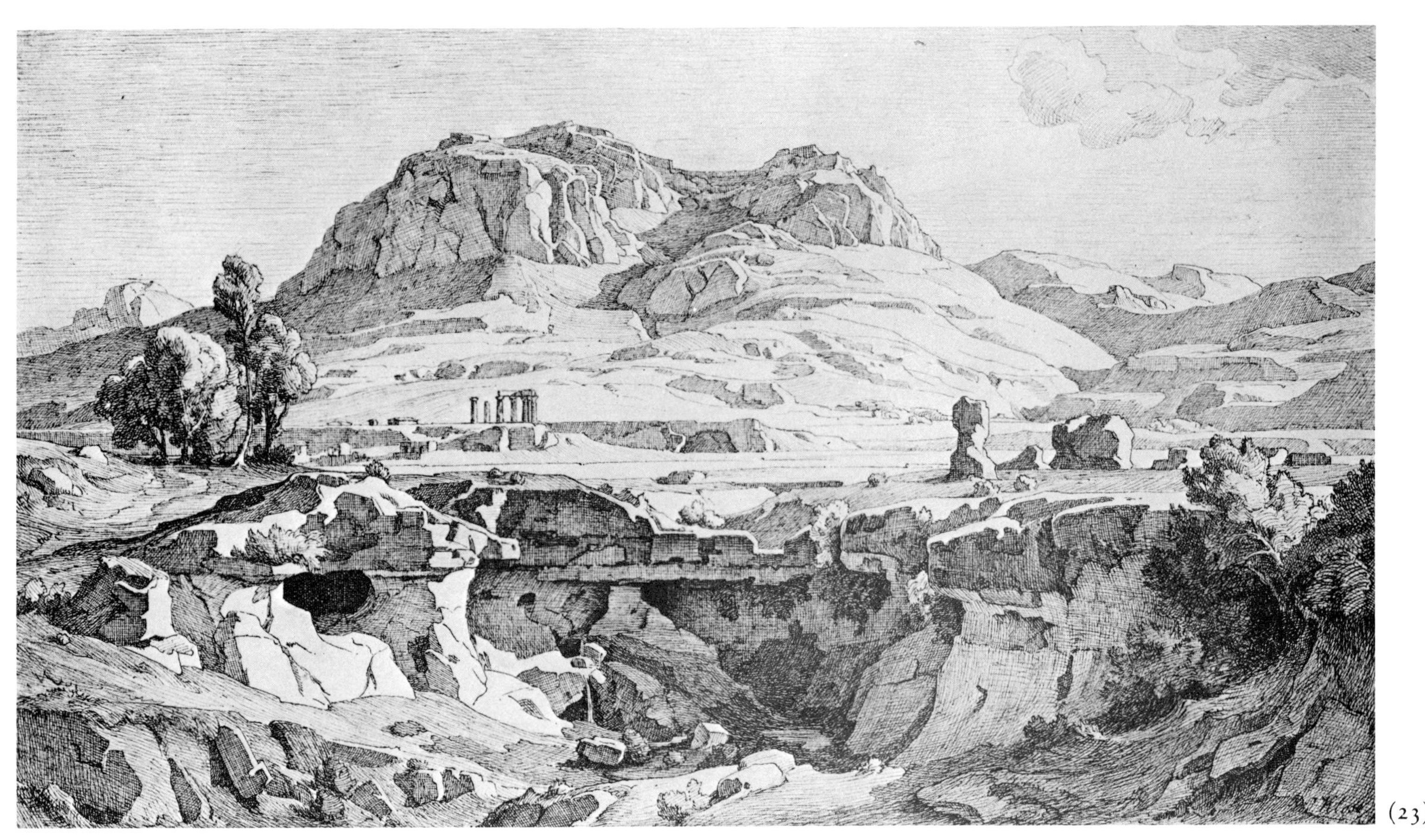

(23)

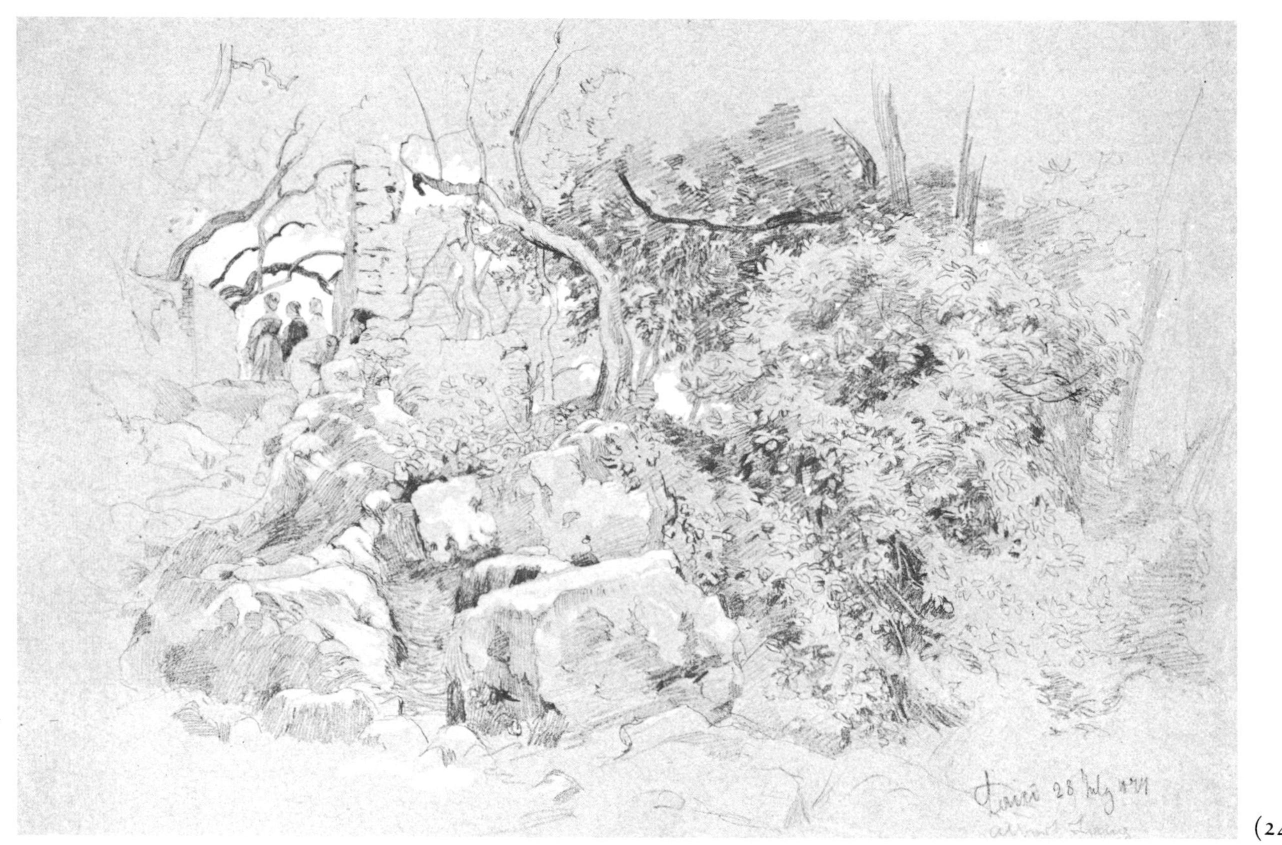
(24)

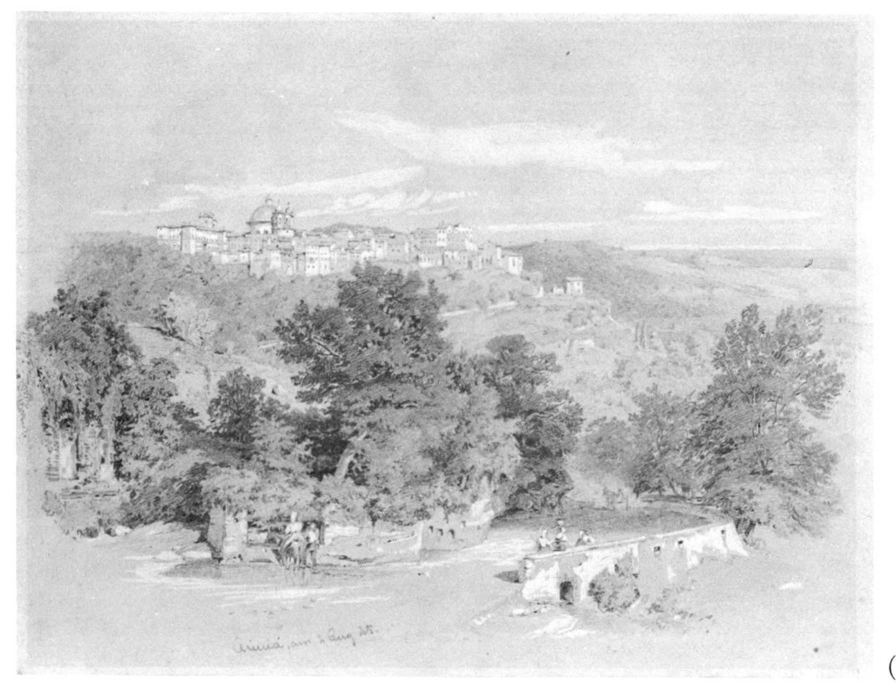
(25)

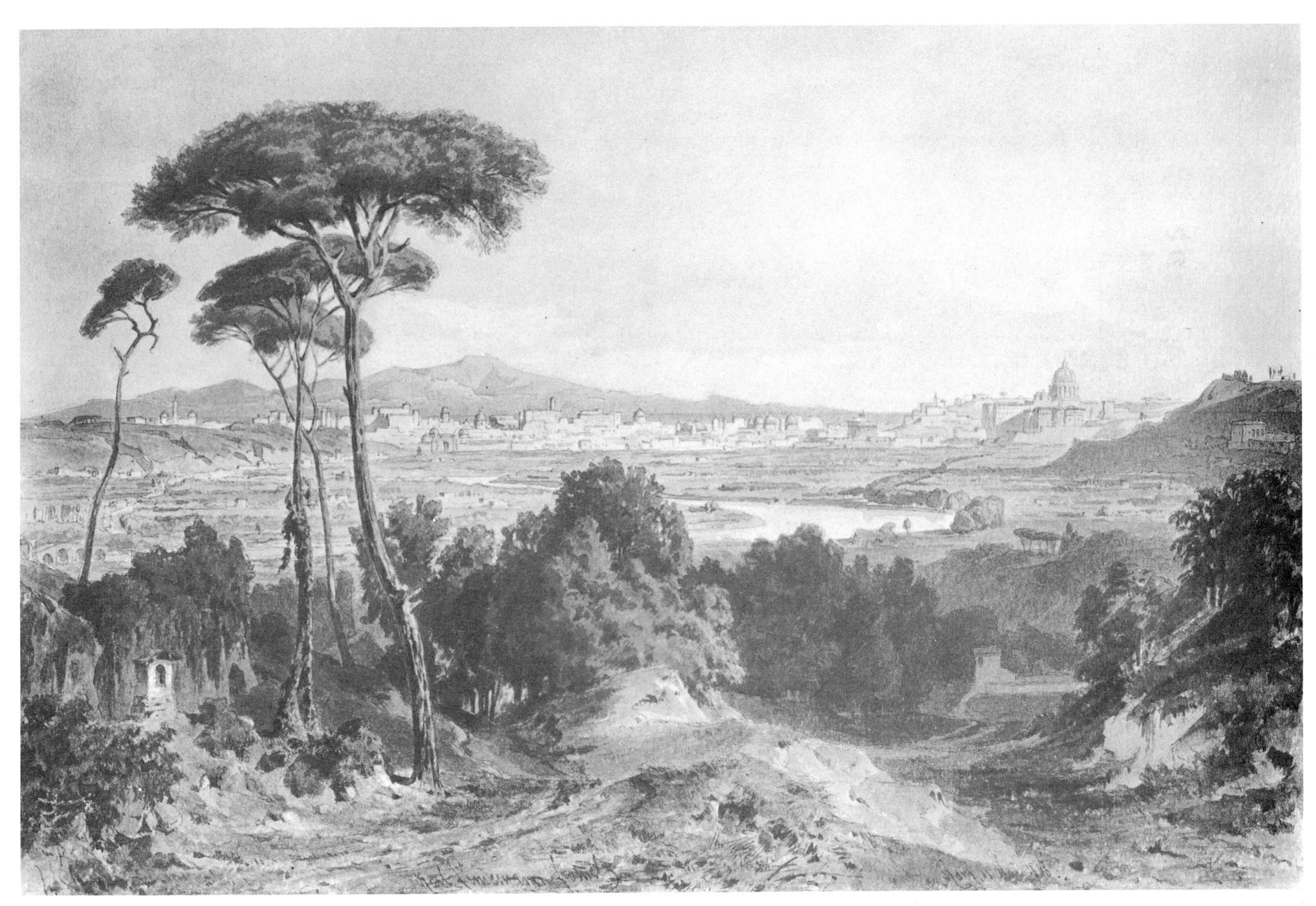

(26)

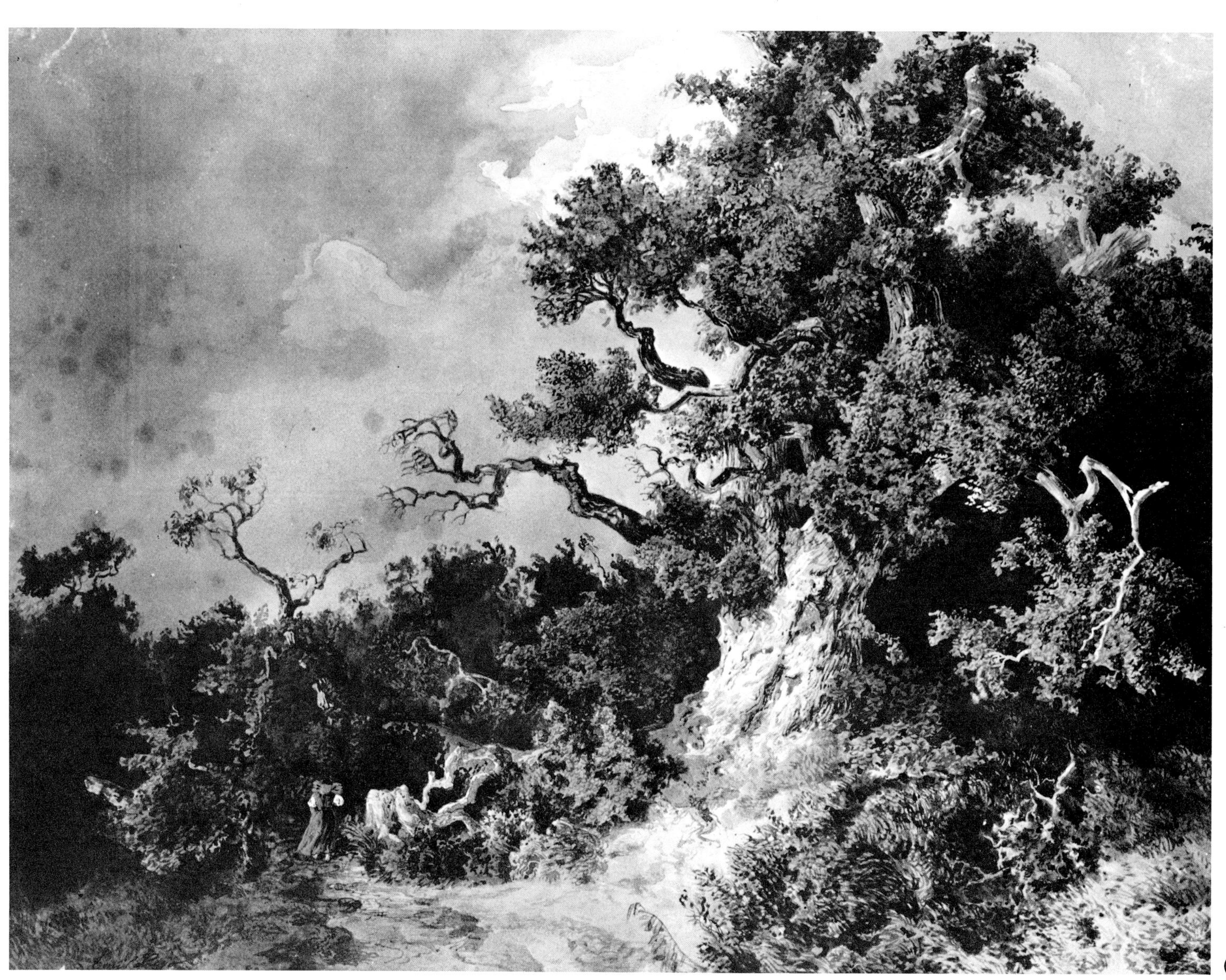

(27)

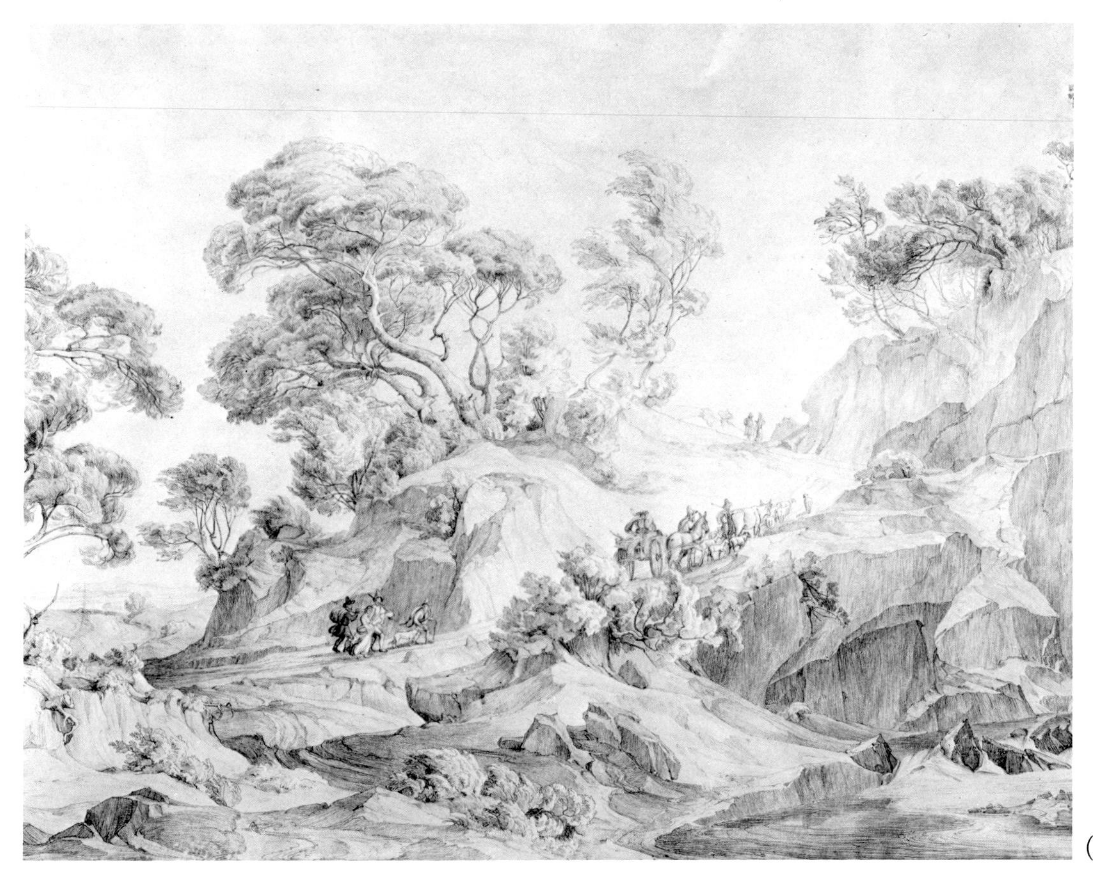

(28)

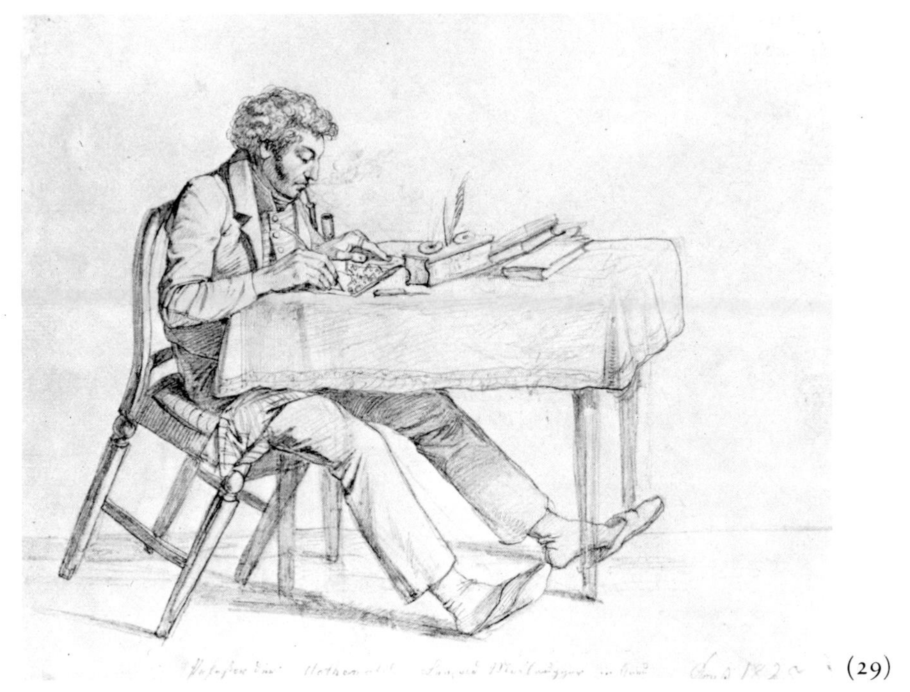

(29)

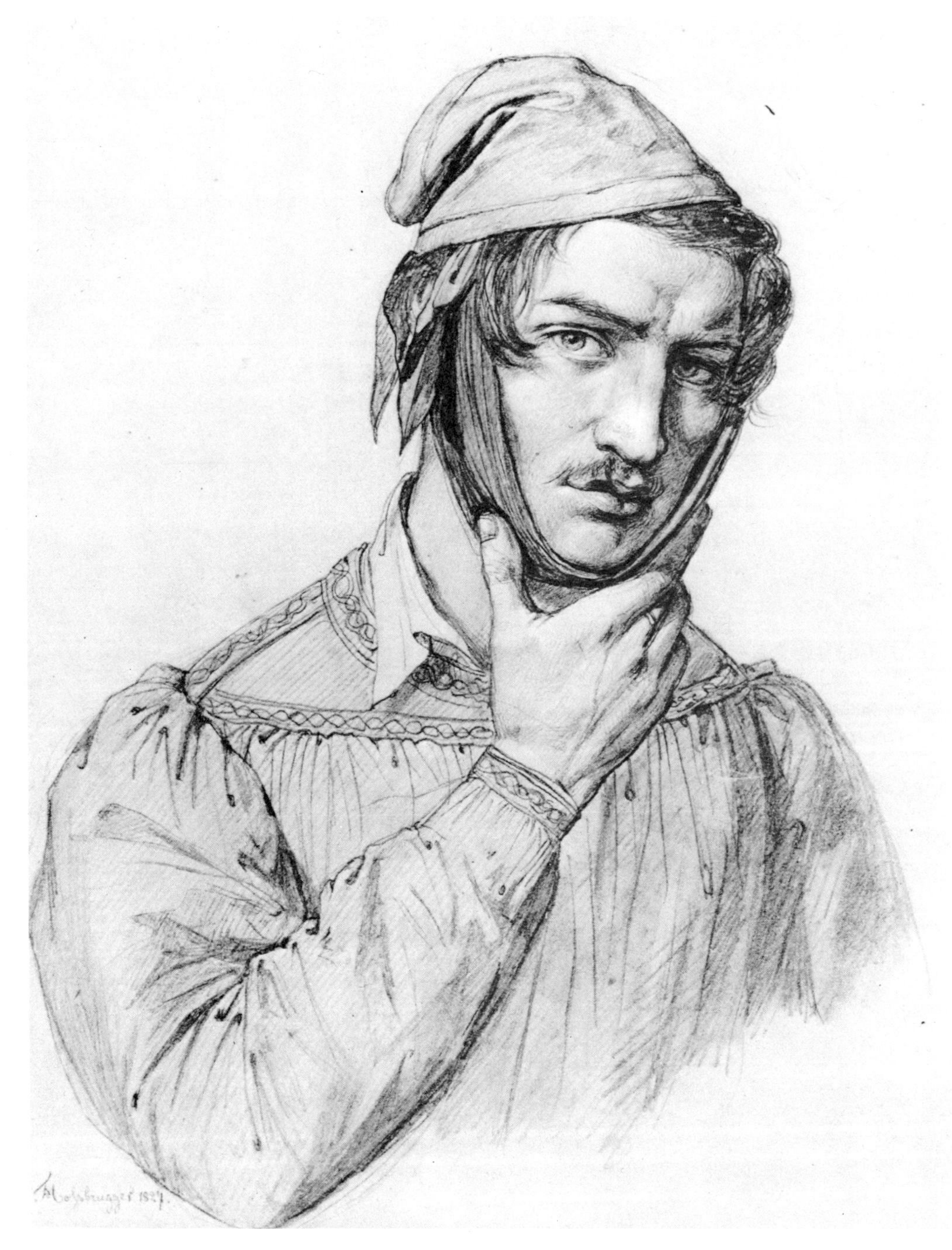

(30)

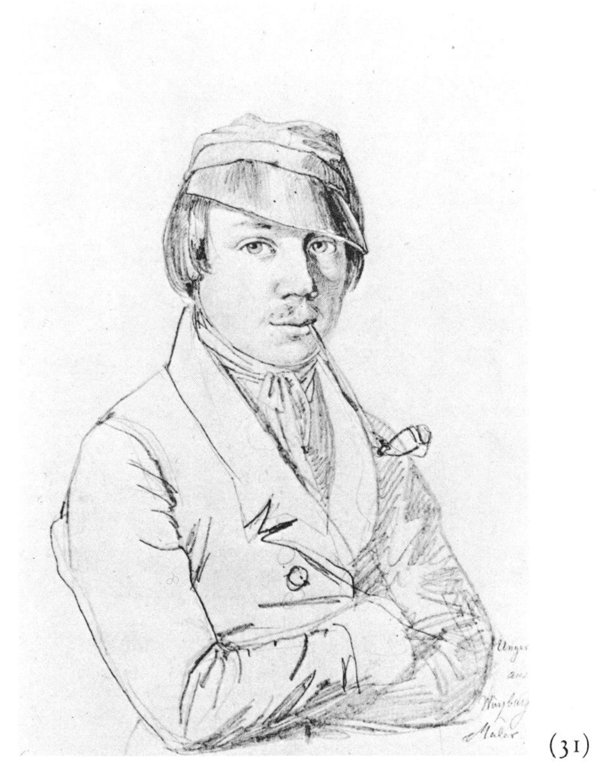

(31)

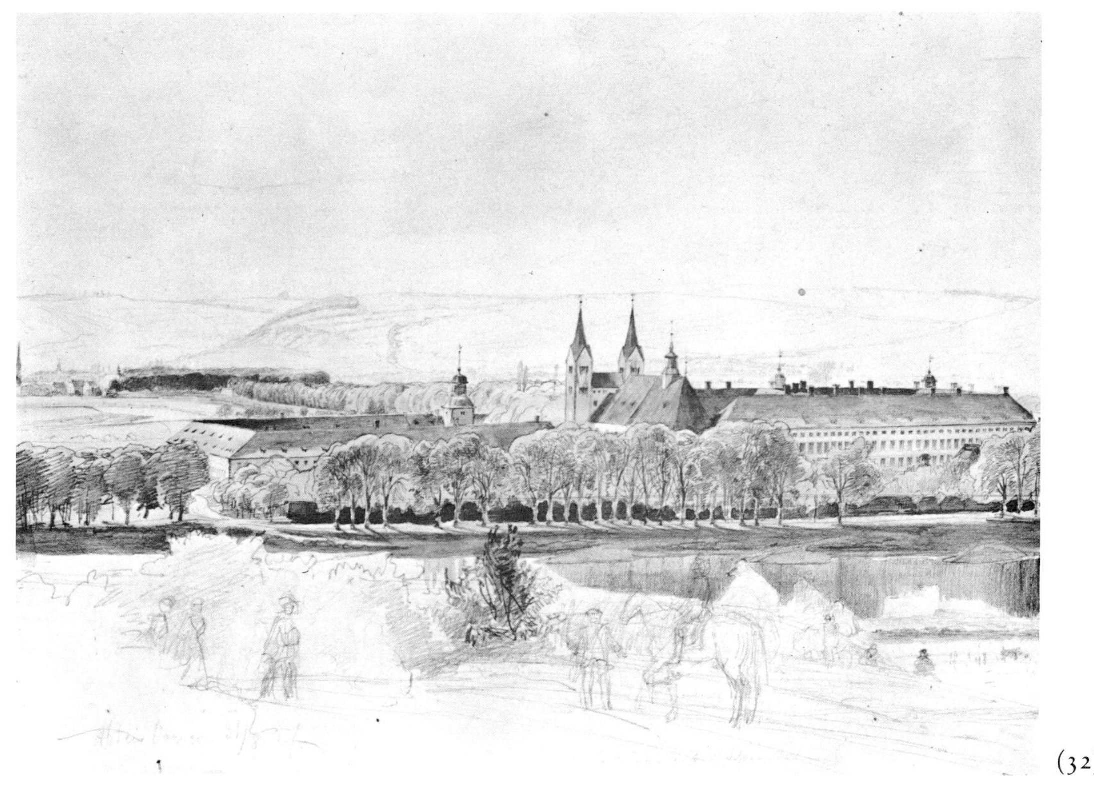

(32)

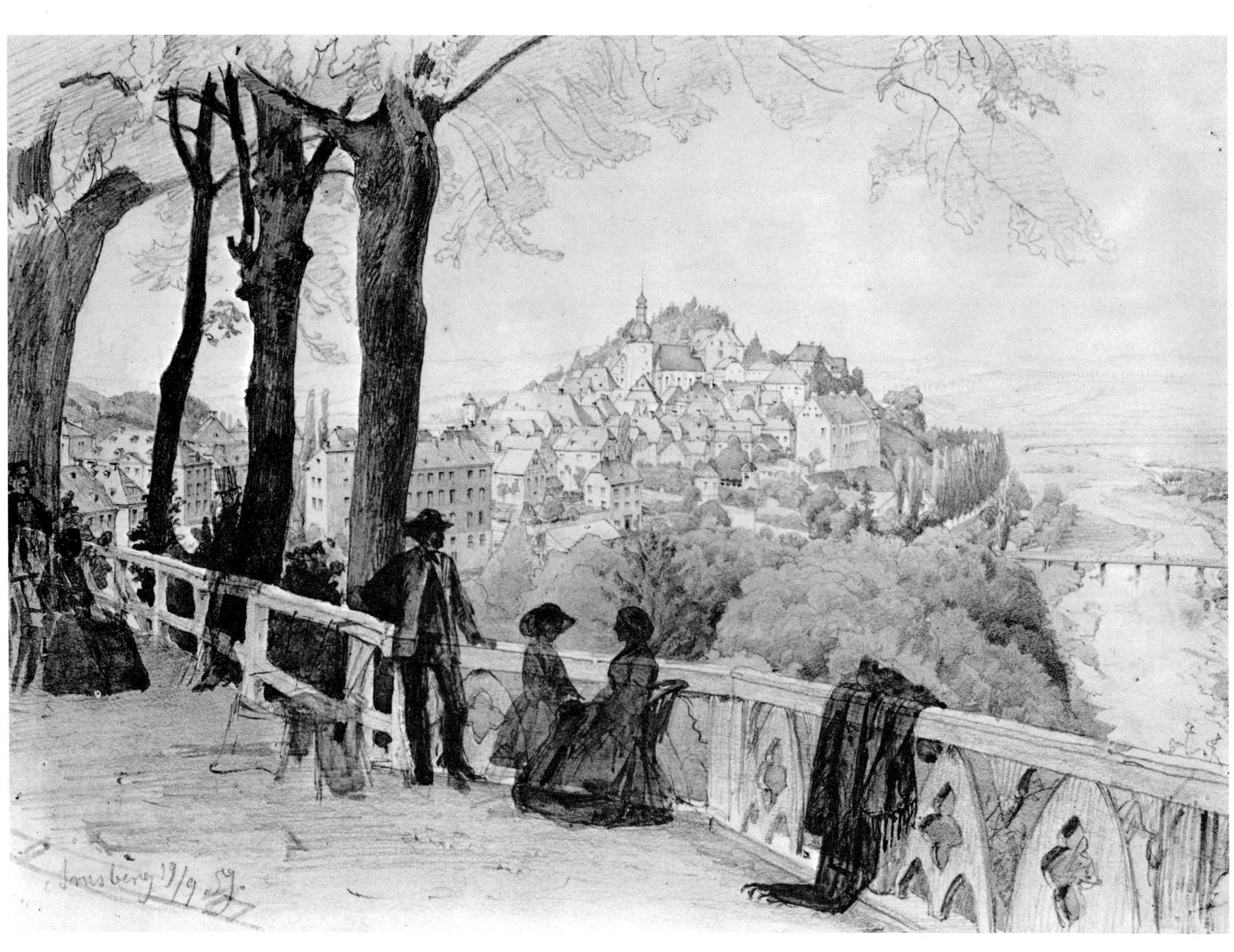

(33)

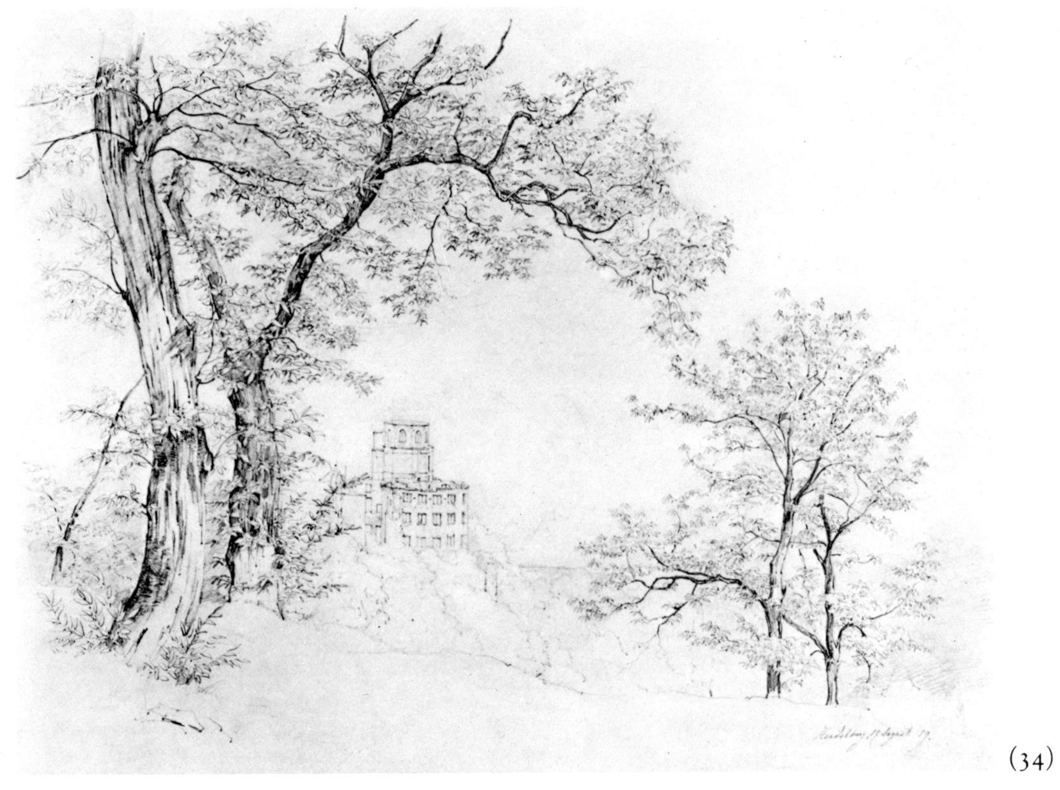
(34)

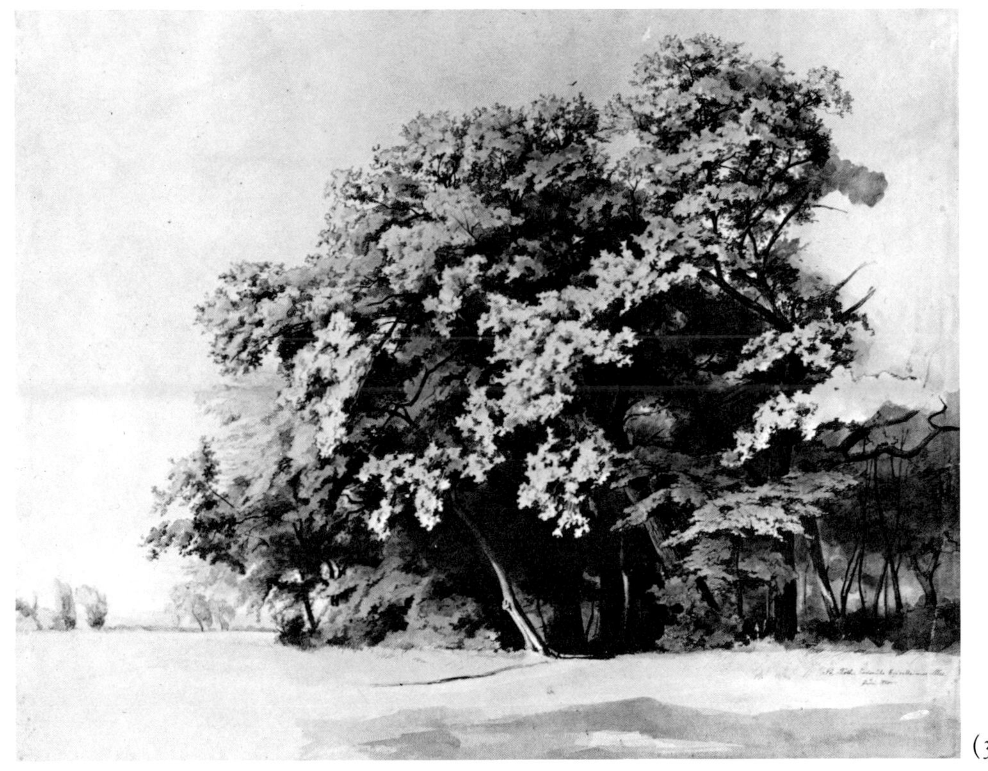
(35)

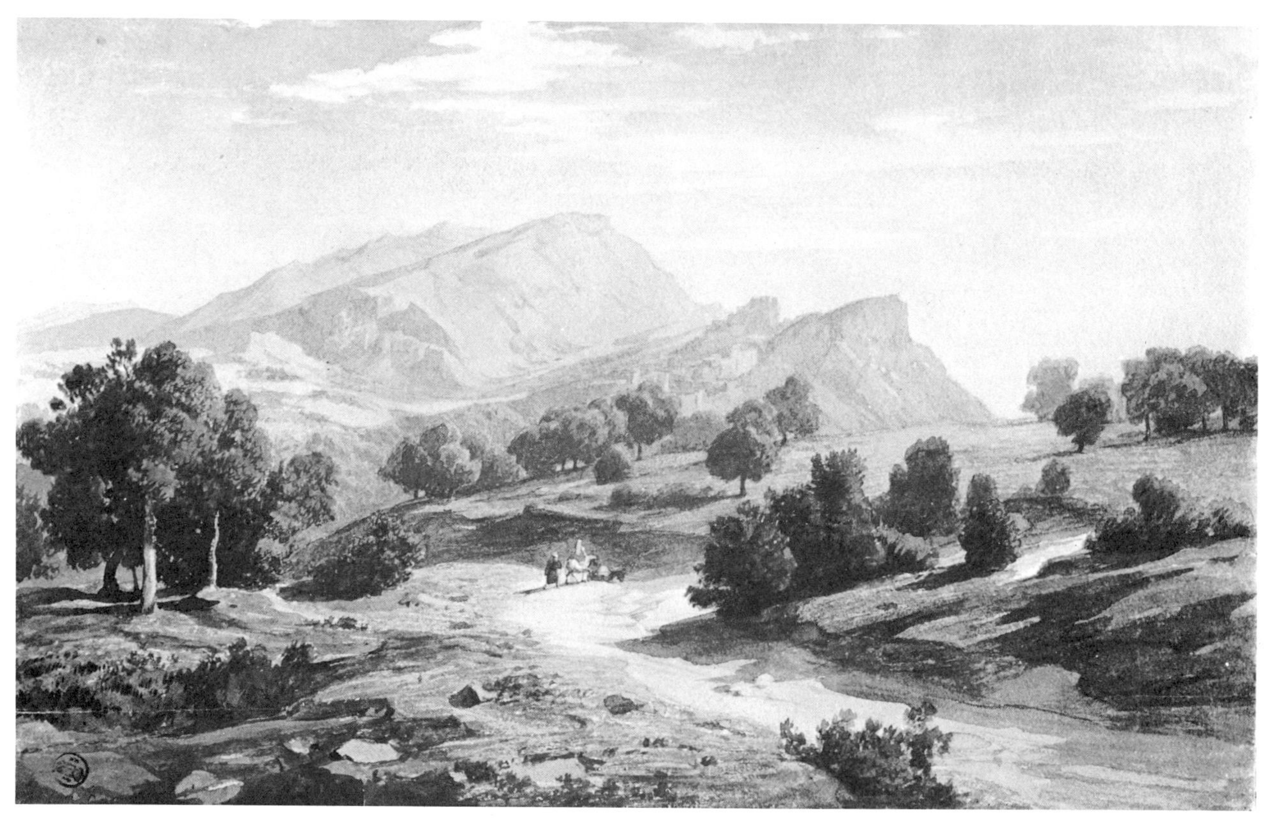

(37)

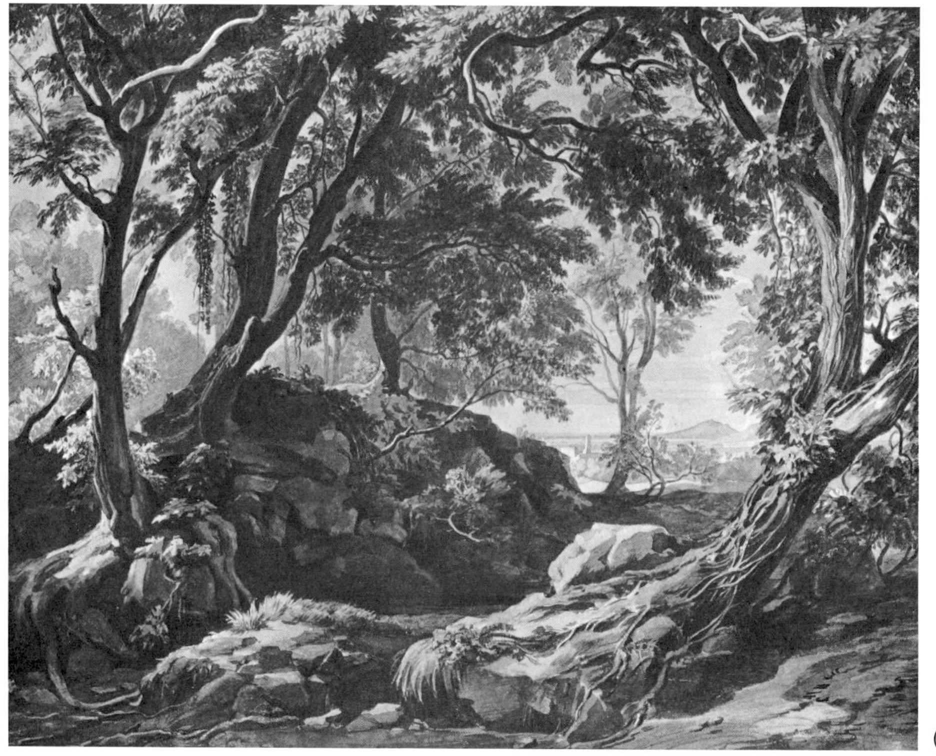

(38)

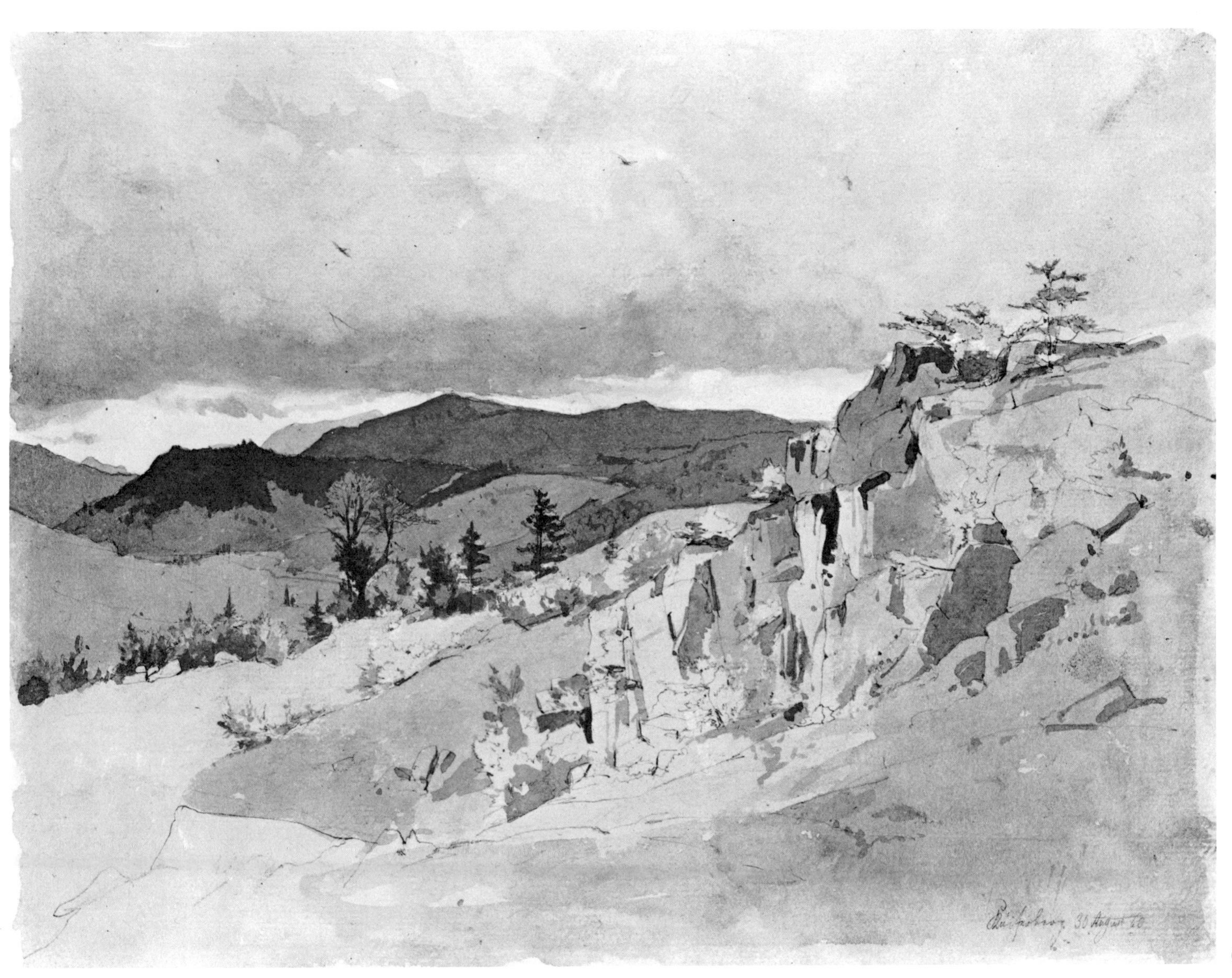

(36)

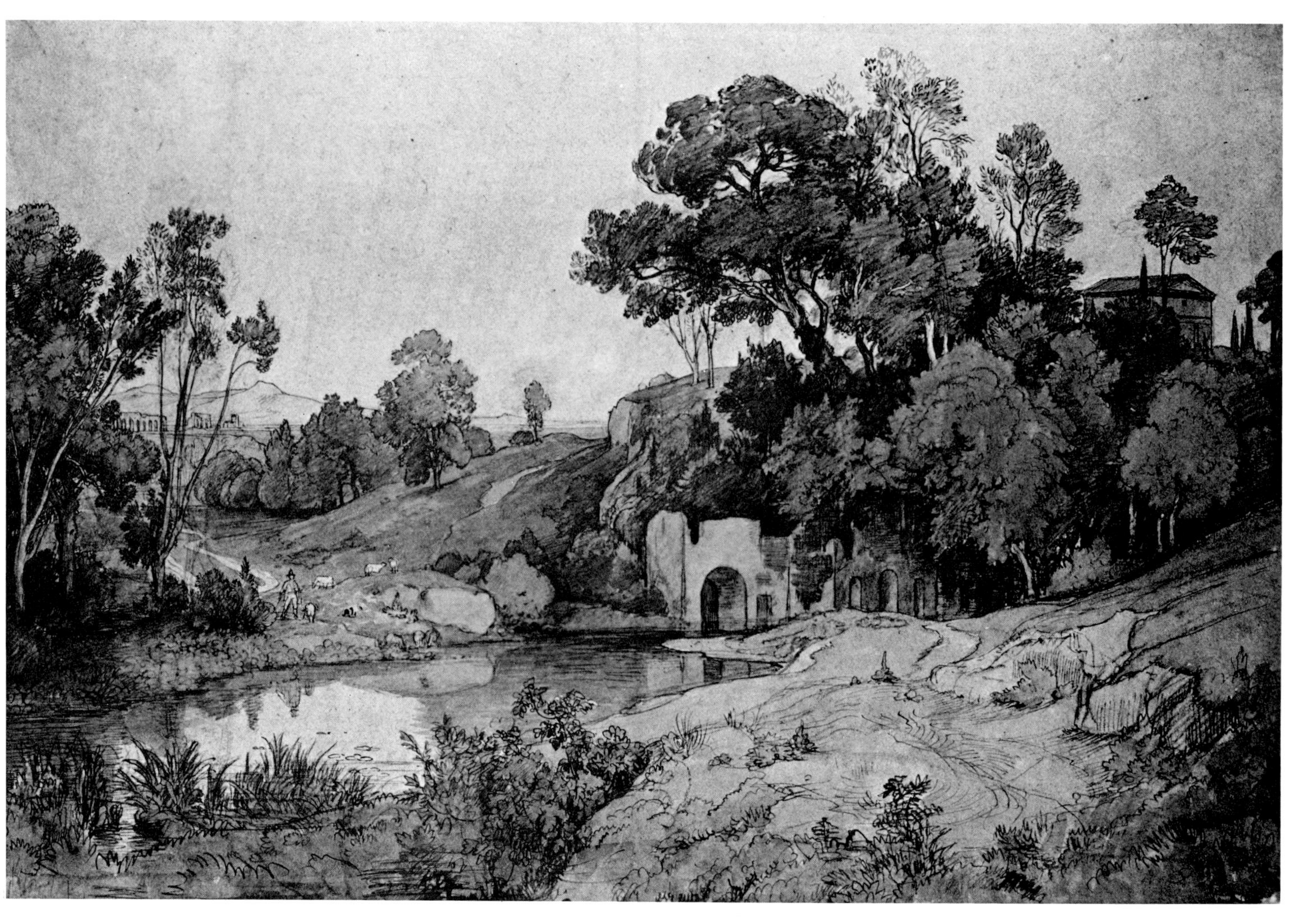
(39)

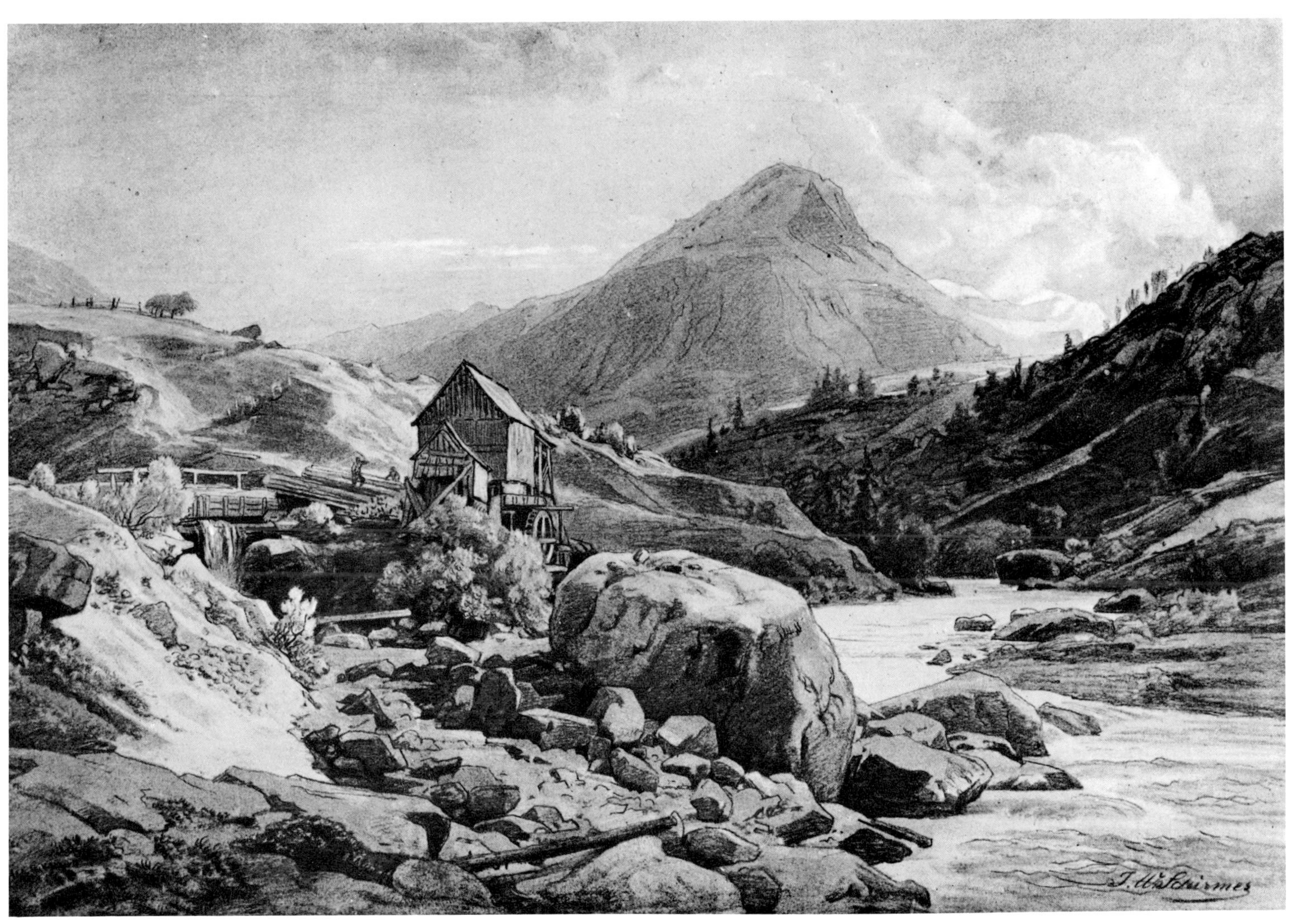

(40)

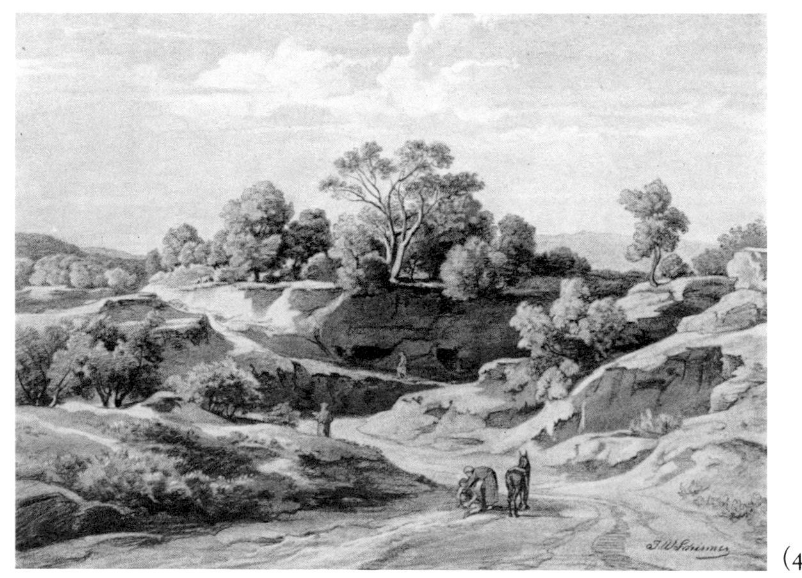

(41)

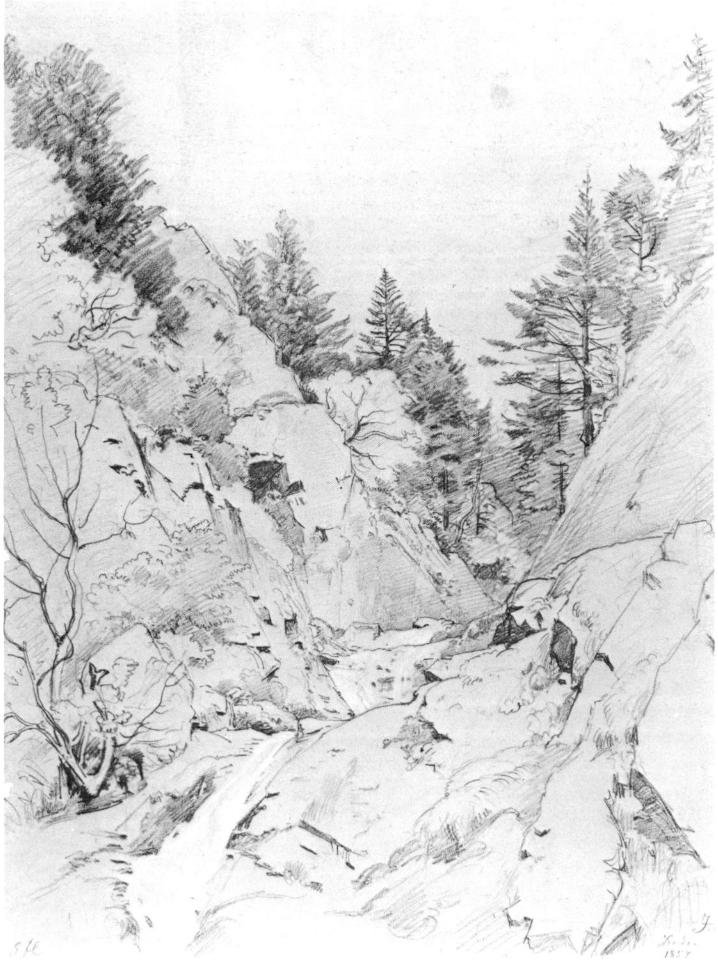

(43)

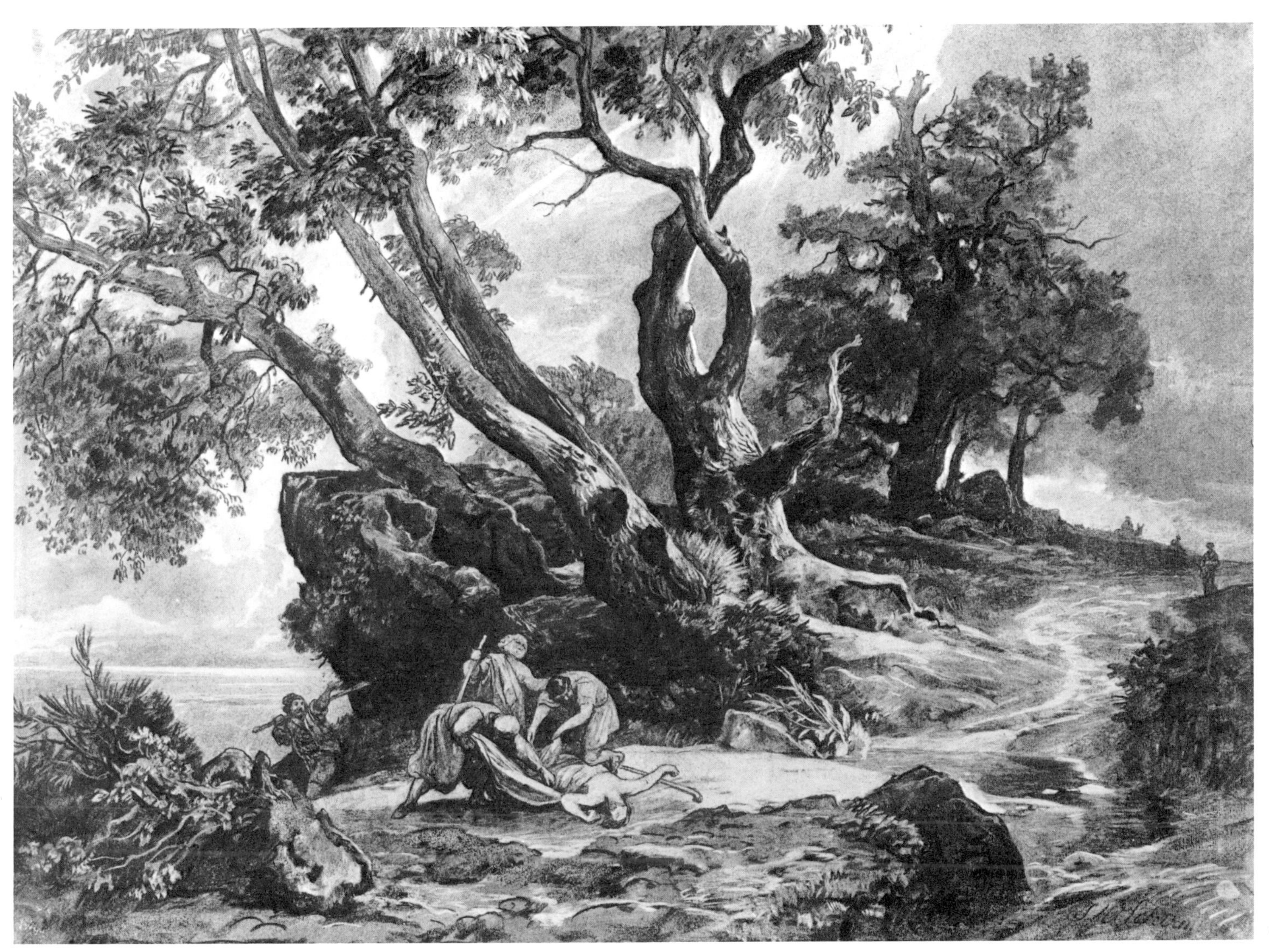
(42)

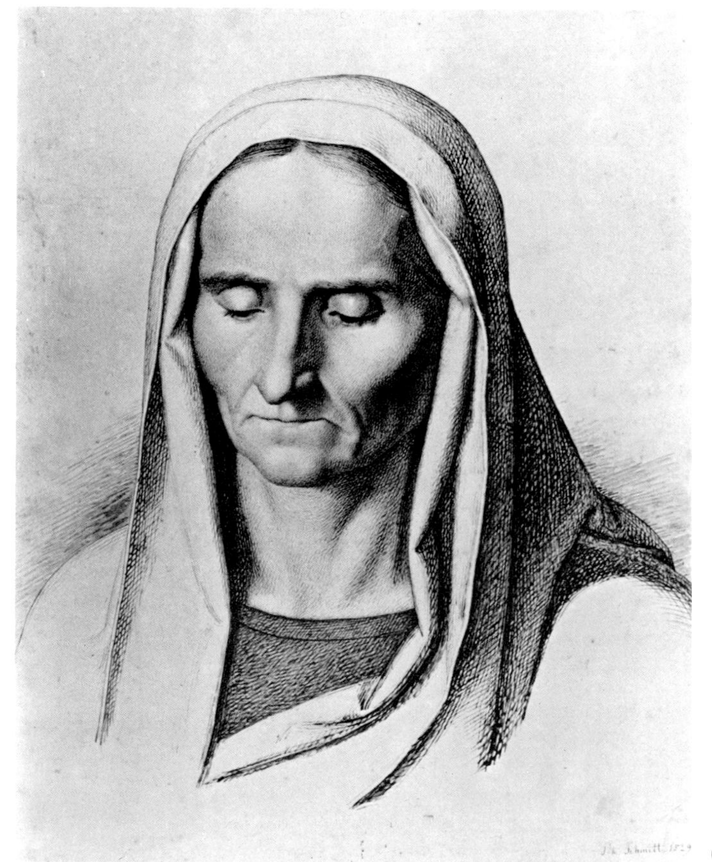

(44)

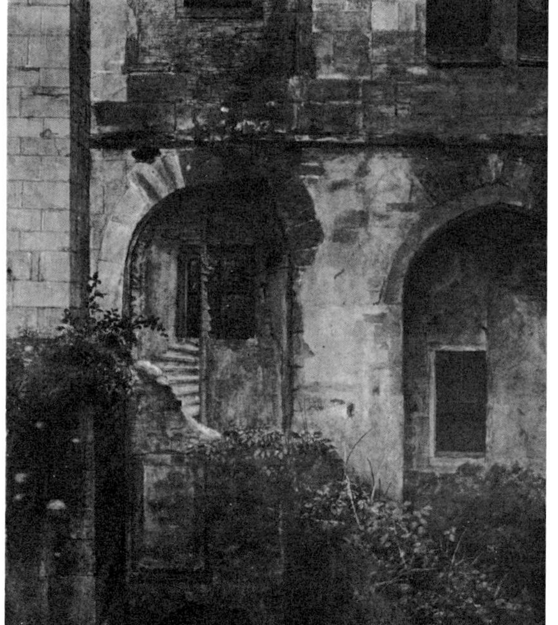

(45)

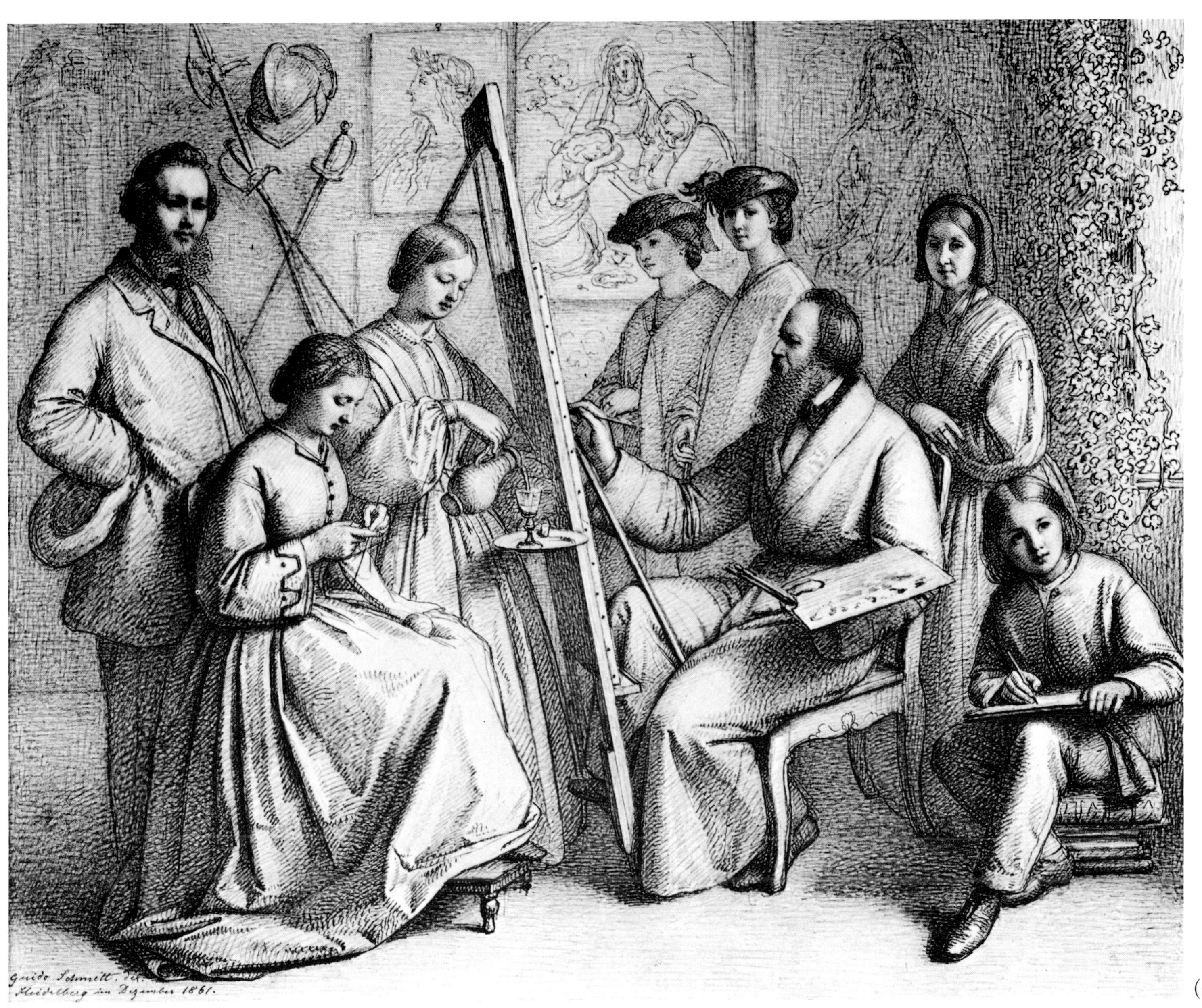

(46)

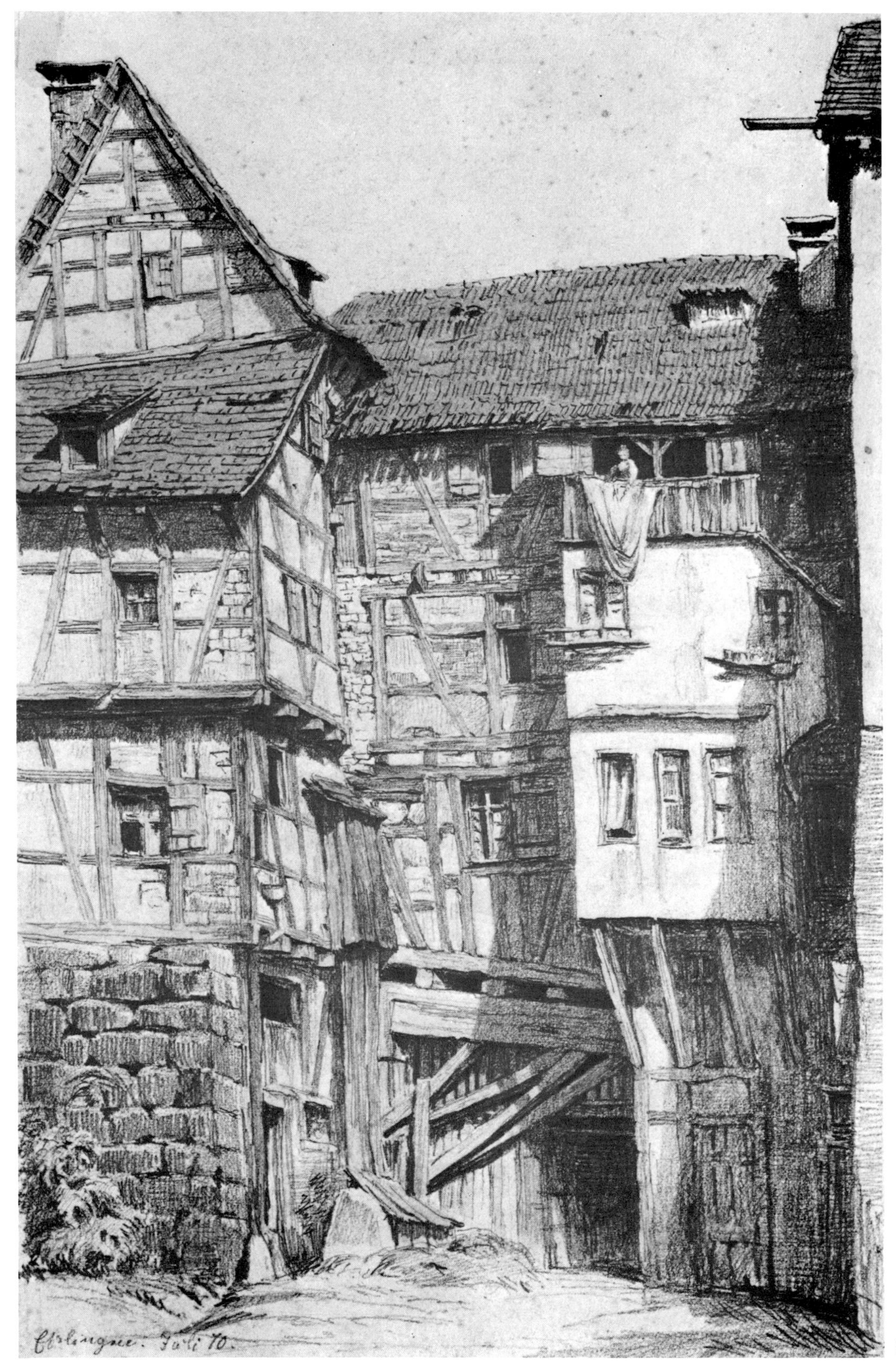

(47)

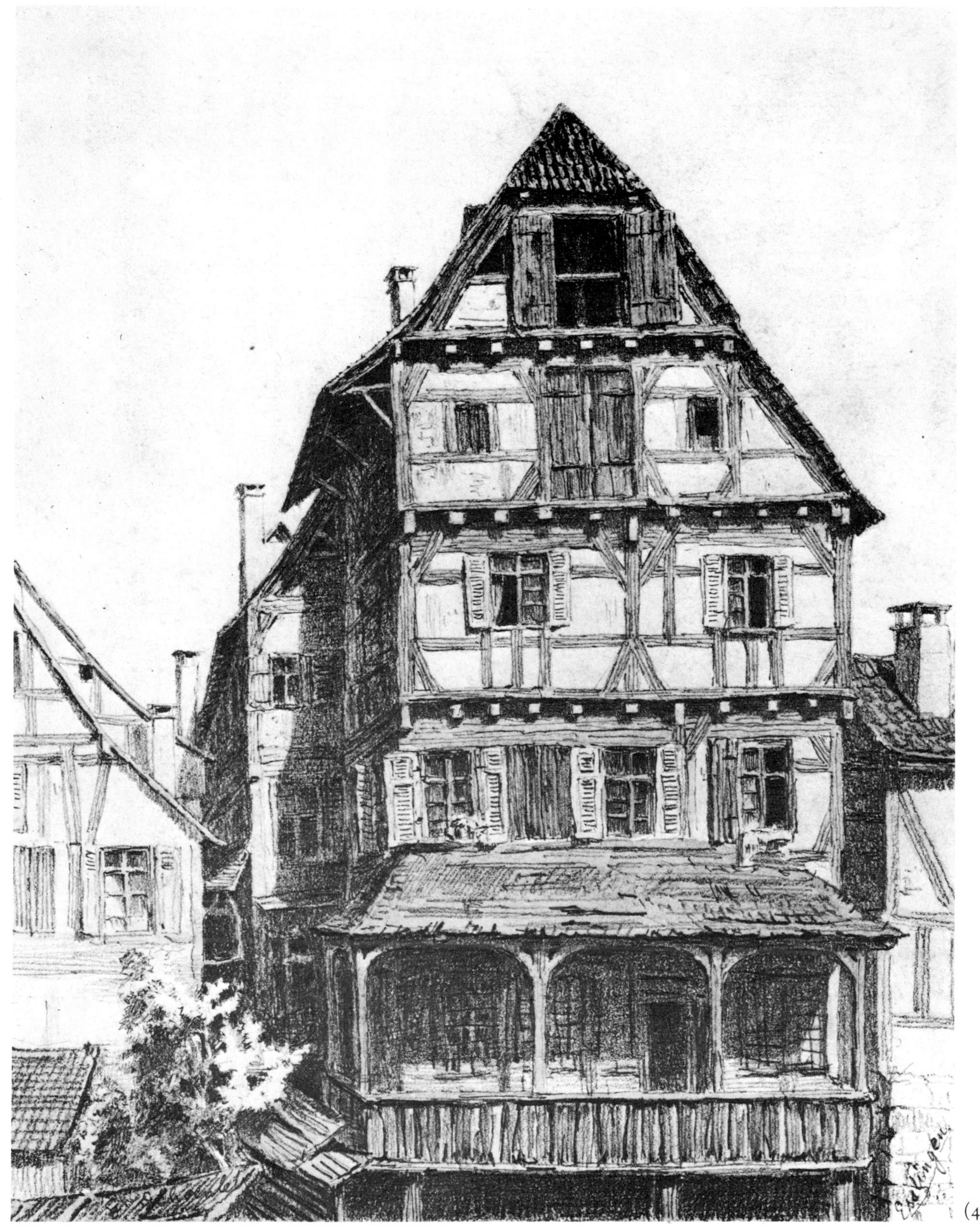

(48)

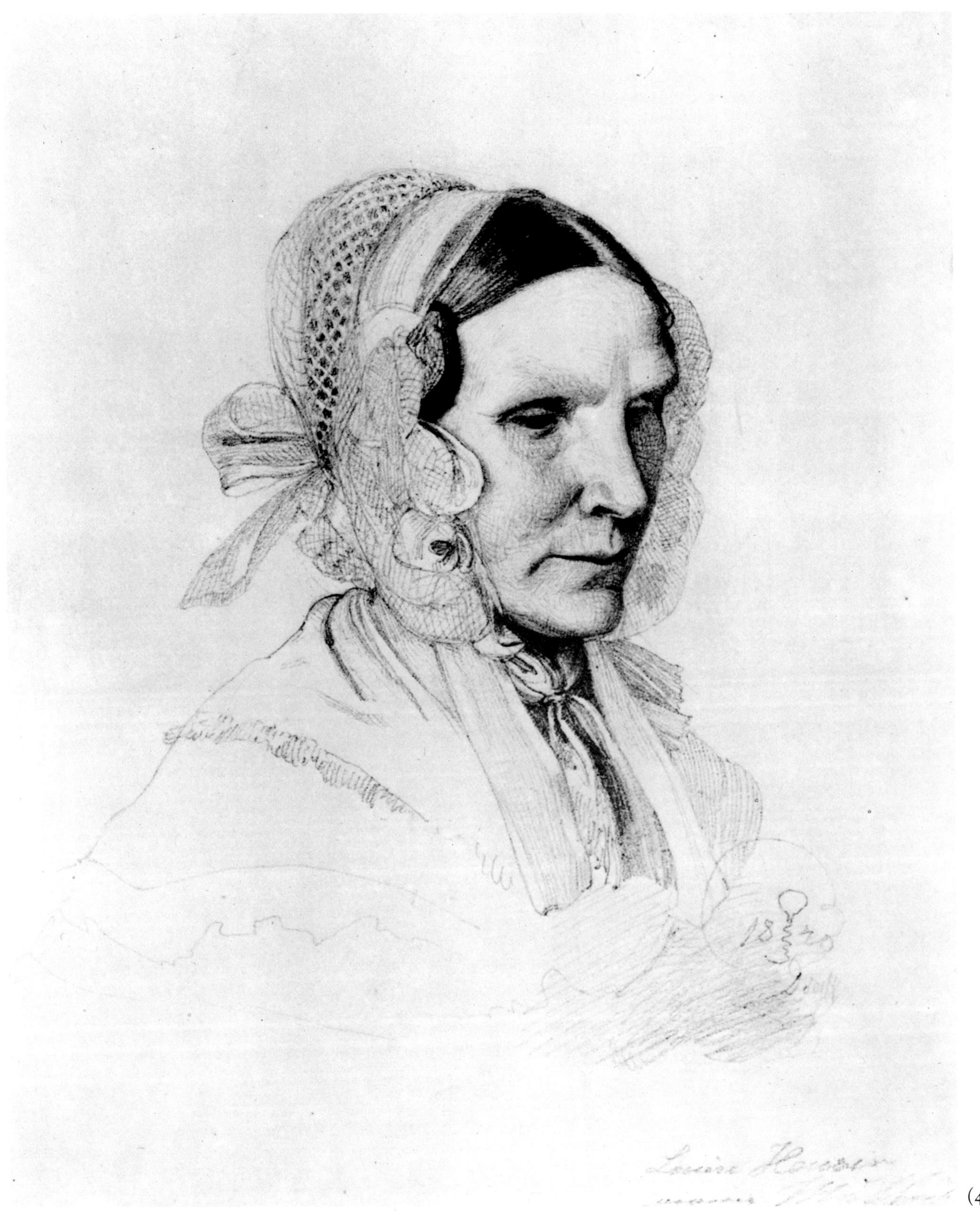

(49)

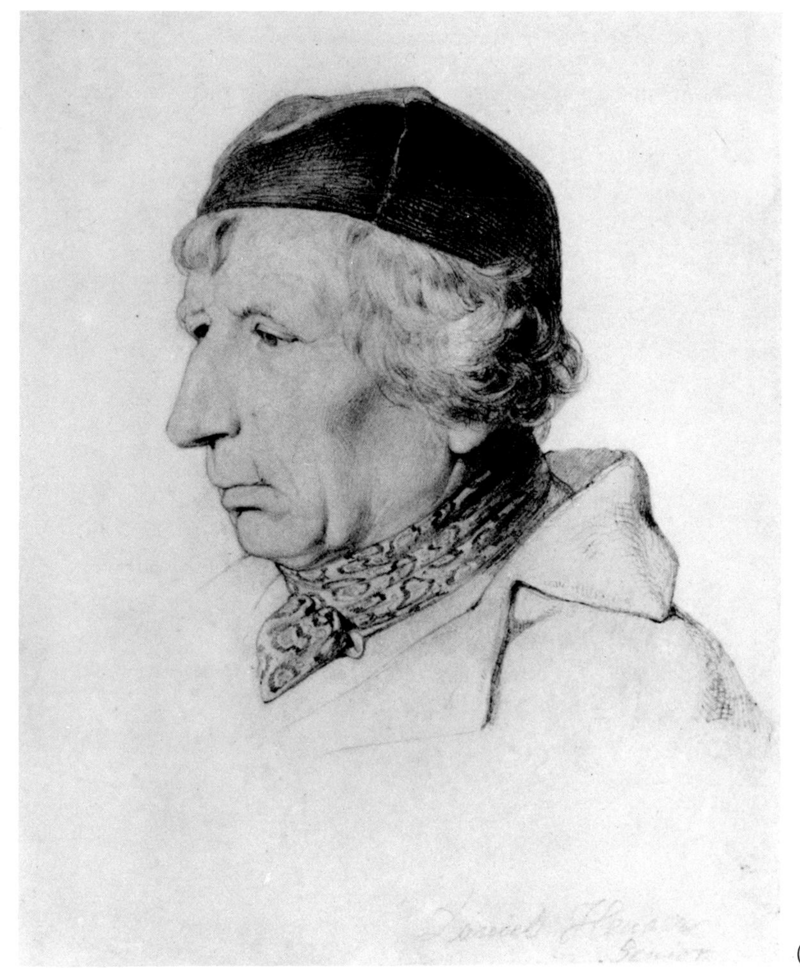

(50)

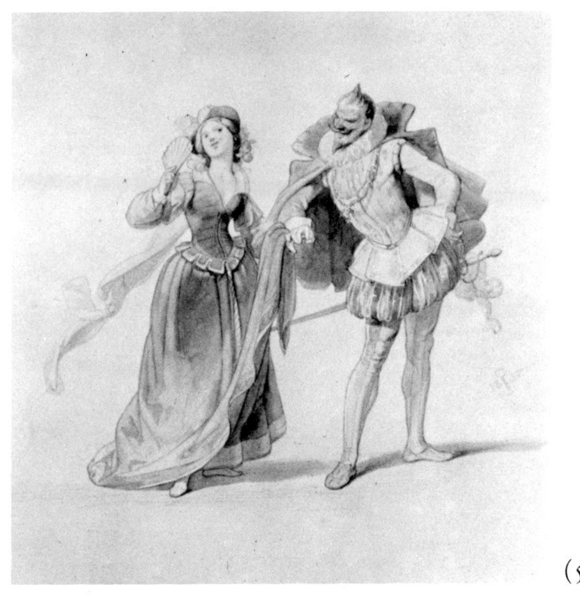

(51)

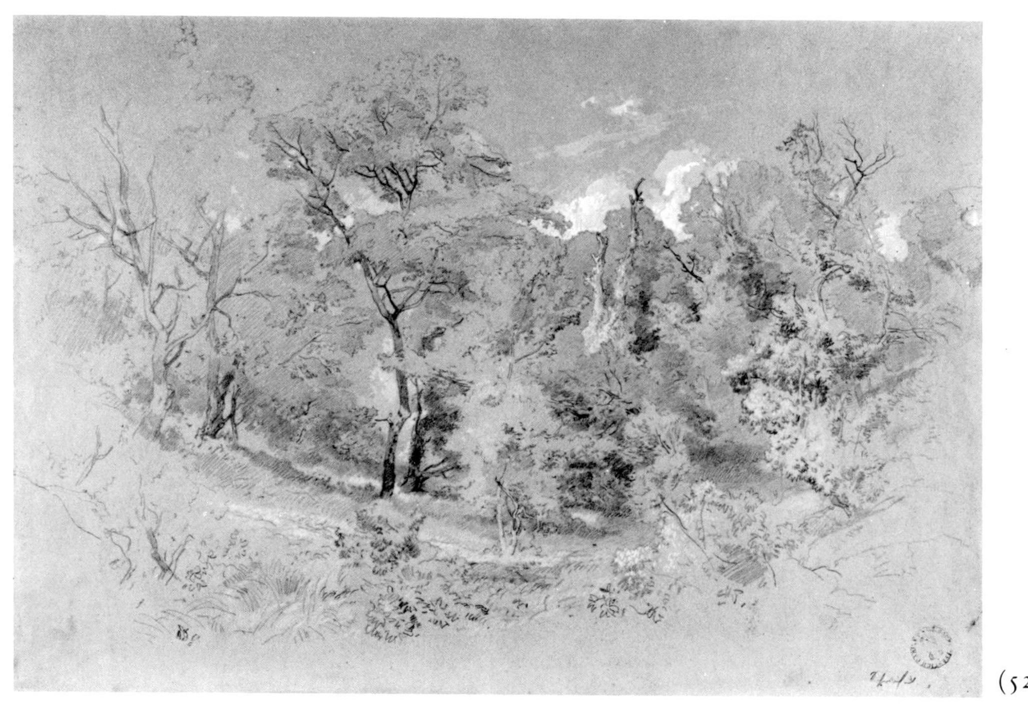

(52)

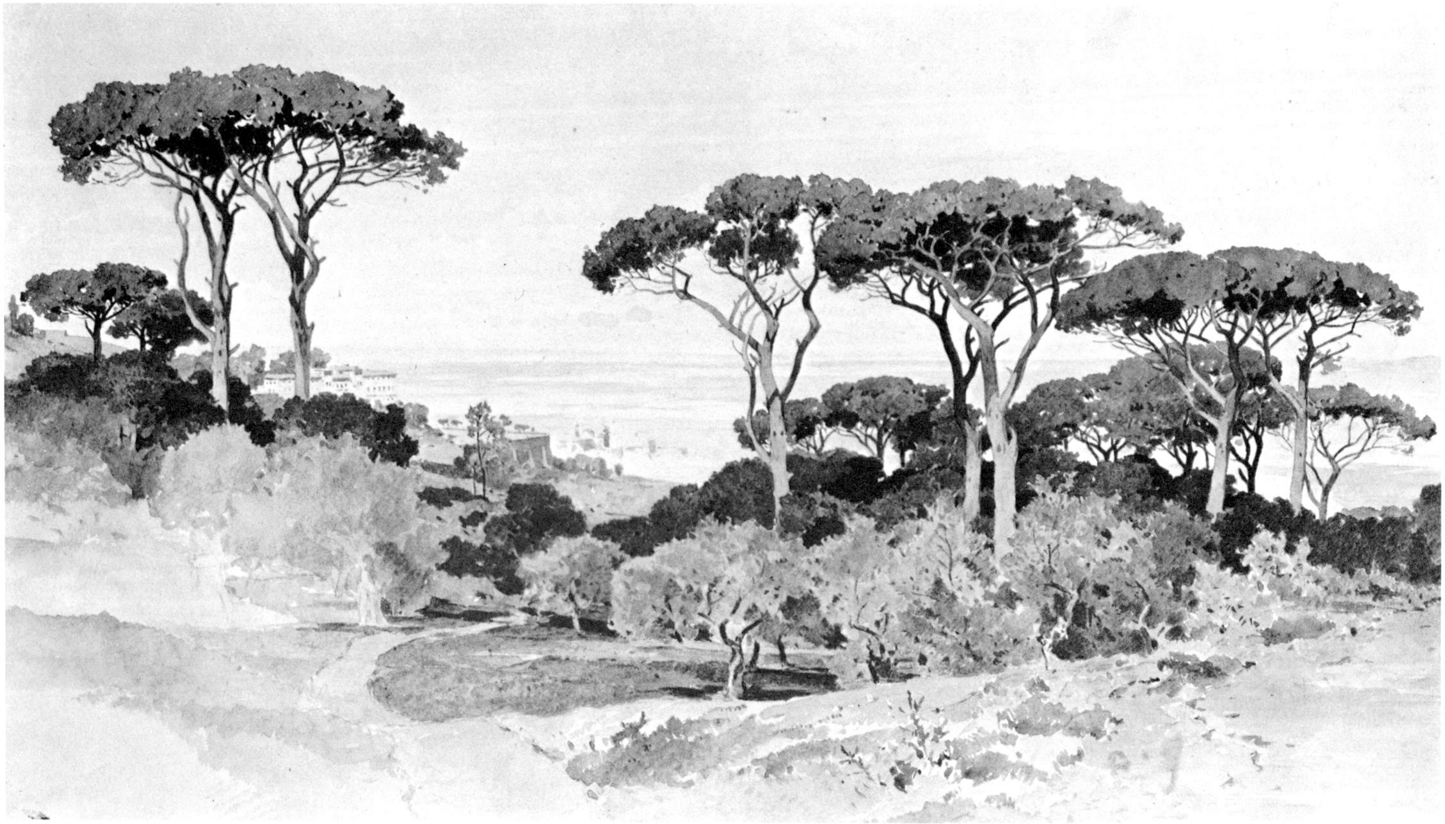

(53)

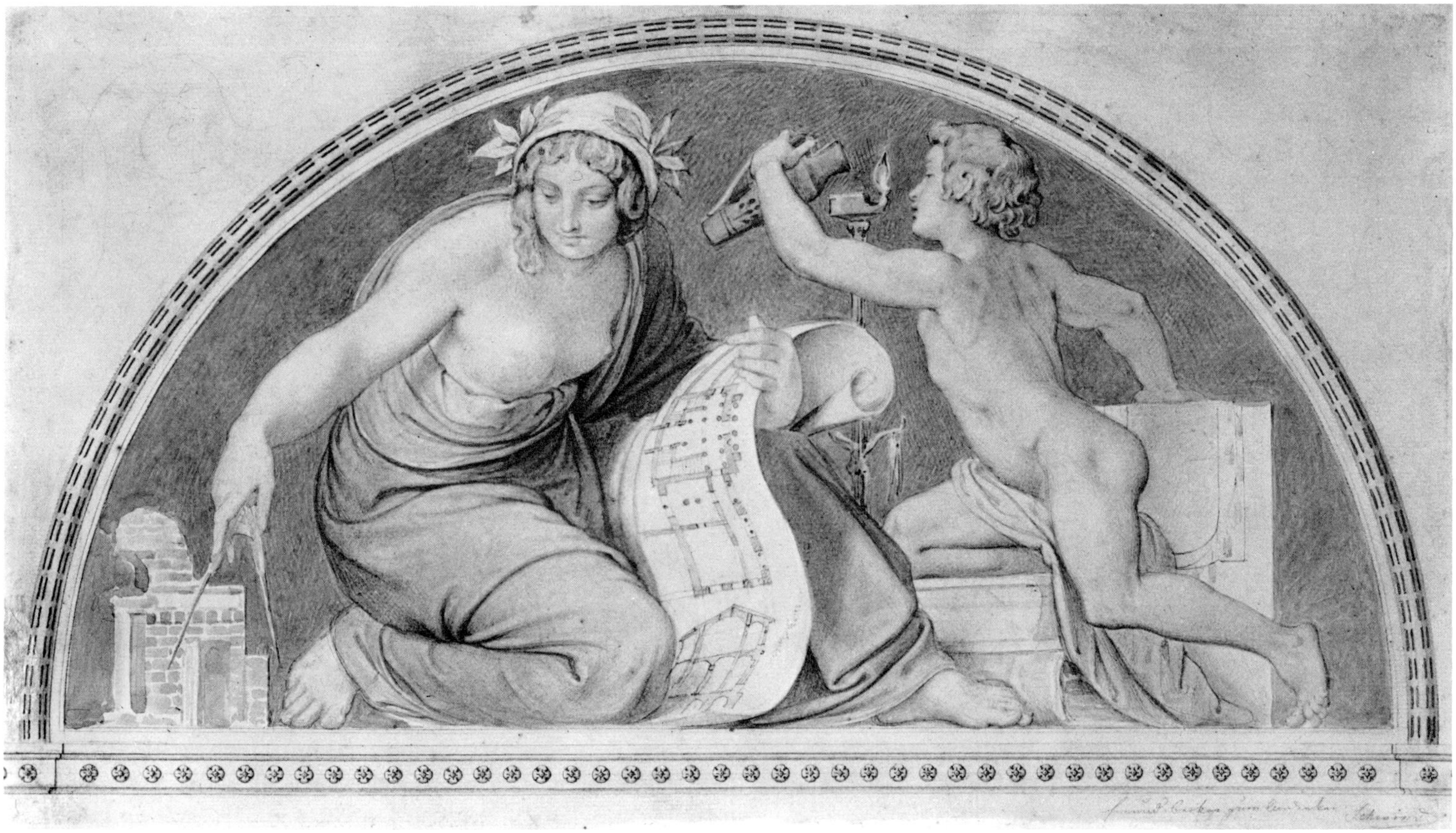

(54)

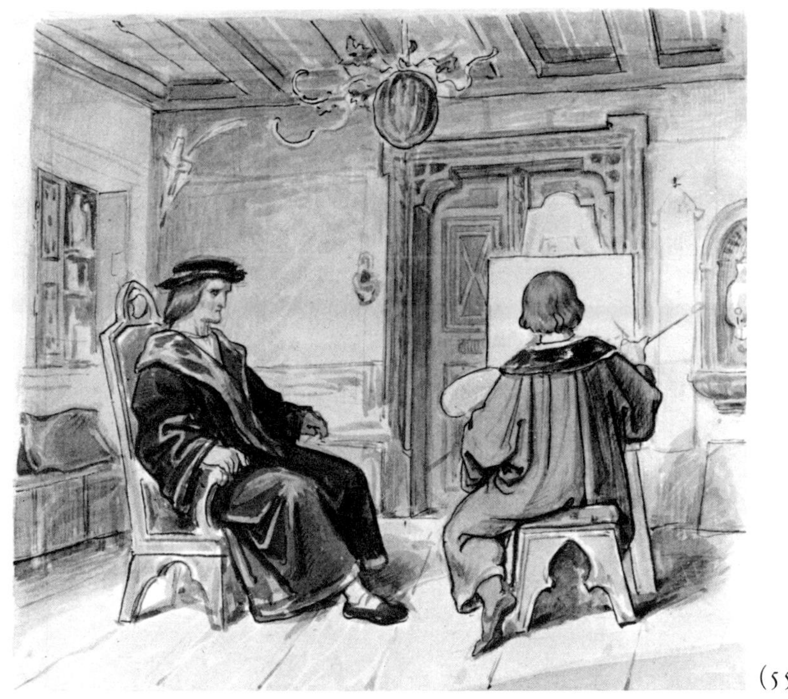

(55)

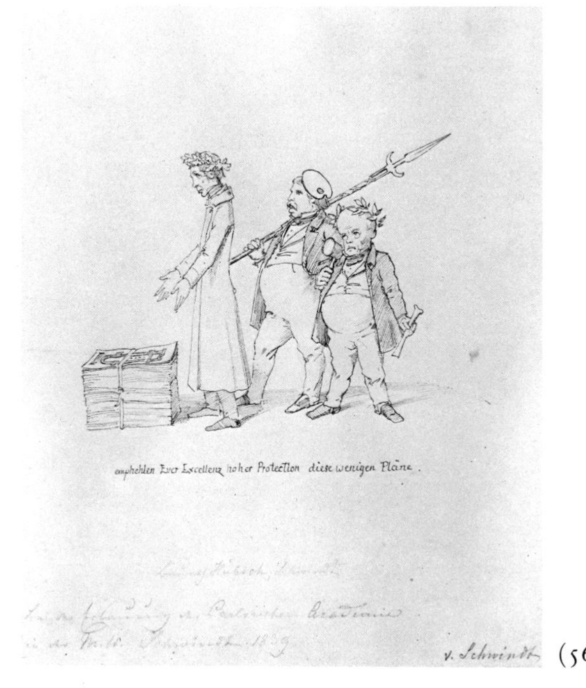
emphehlen Ever Excellenz hoher Protection diese wenigen Pläne.
v. Schwindt

(56)

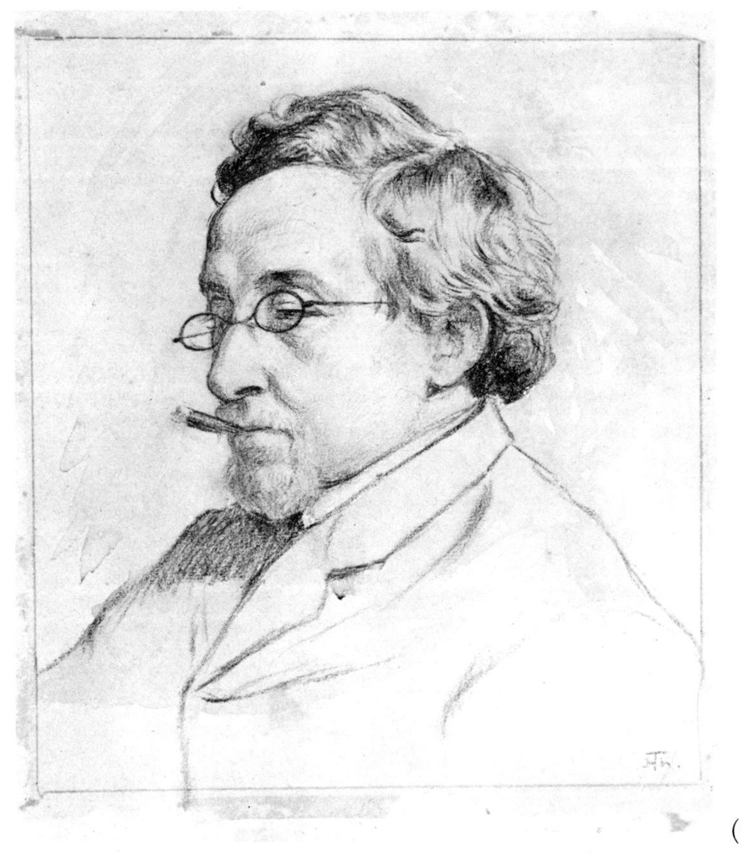

(57)

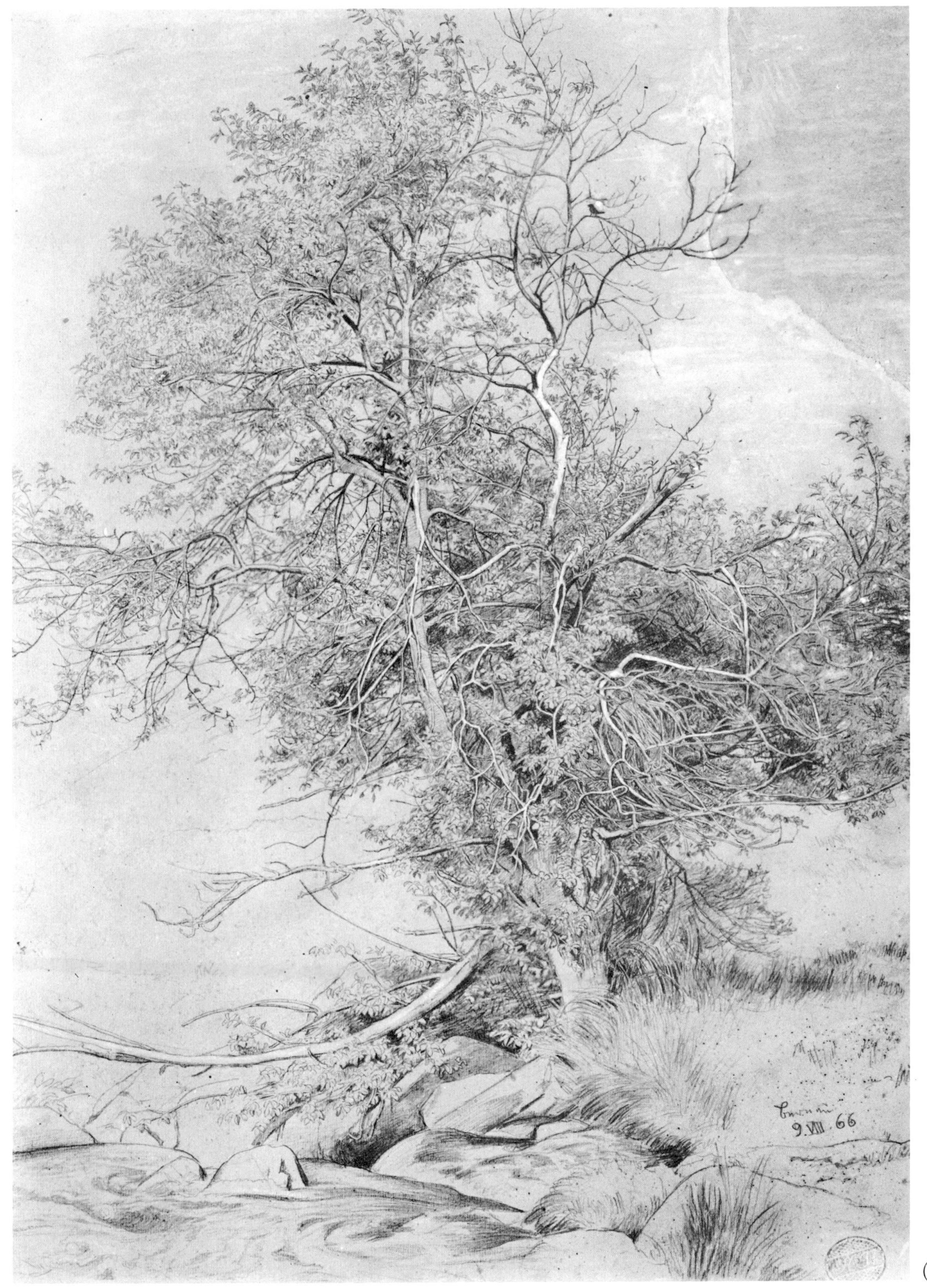

(58)

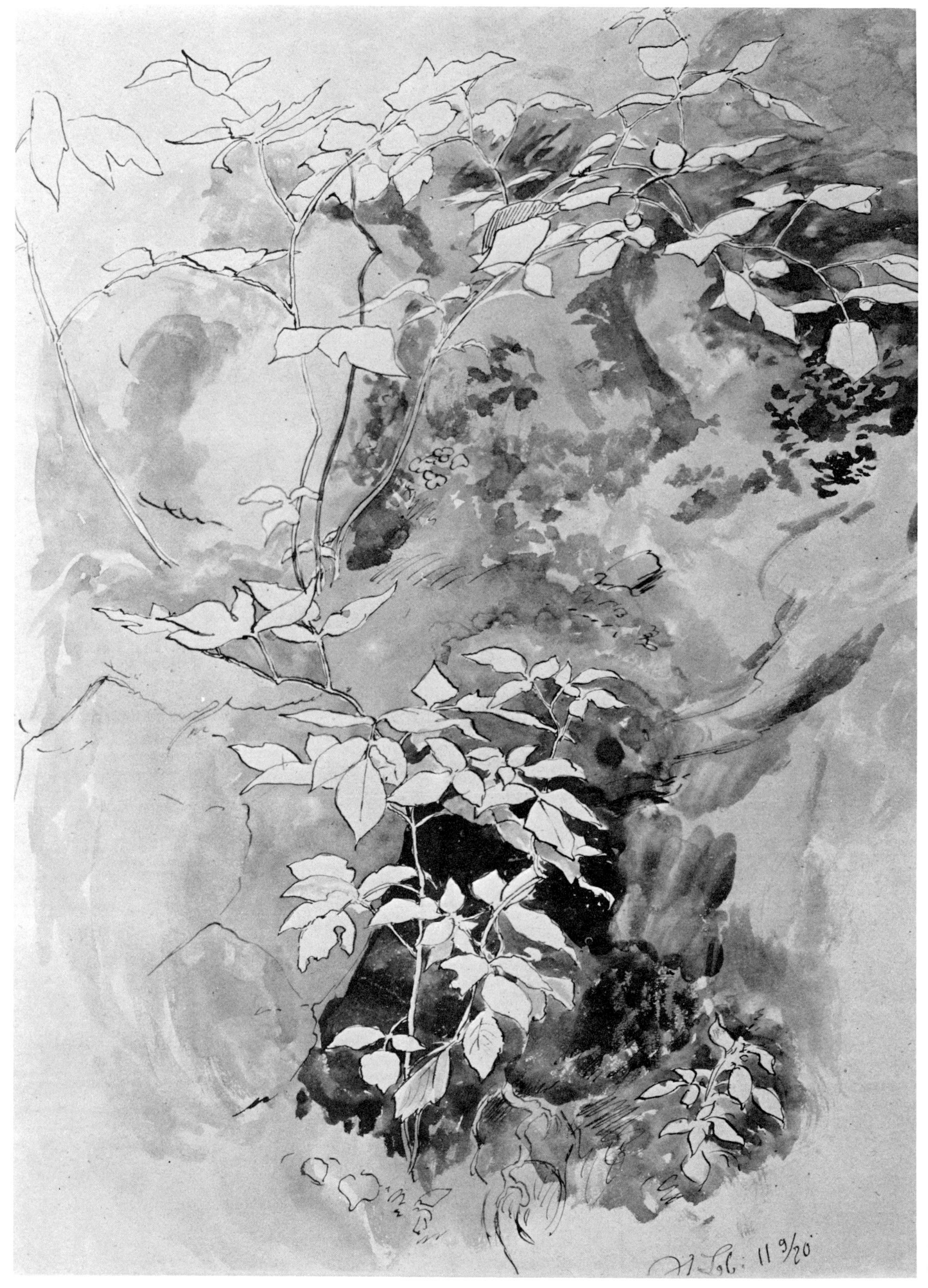

(59)

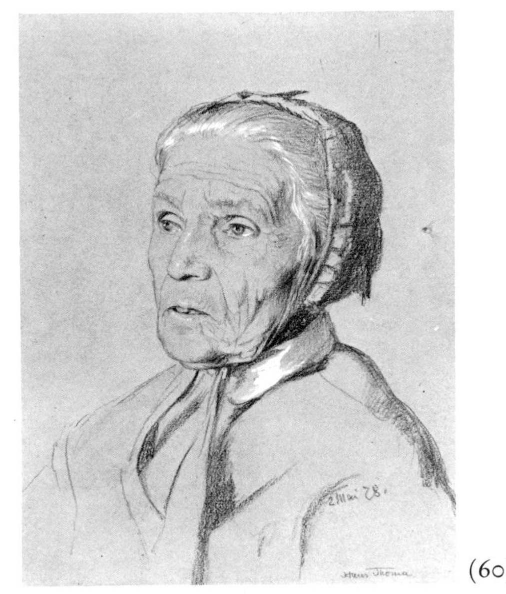

(60)

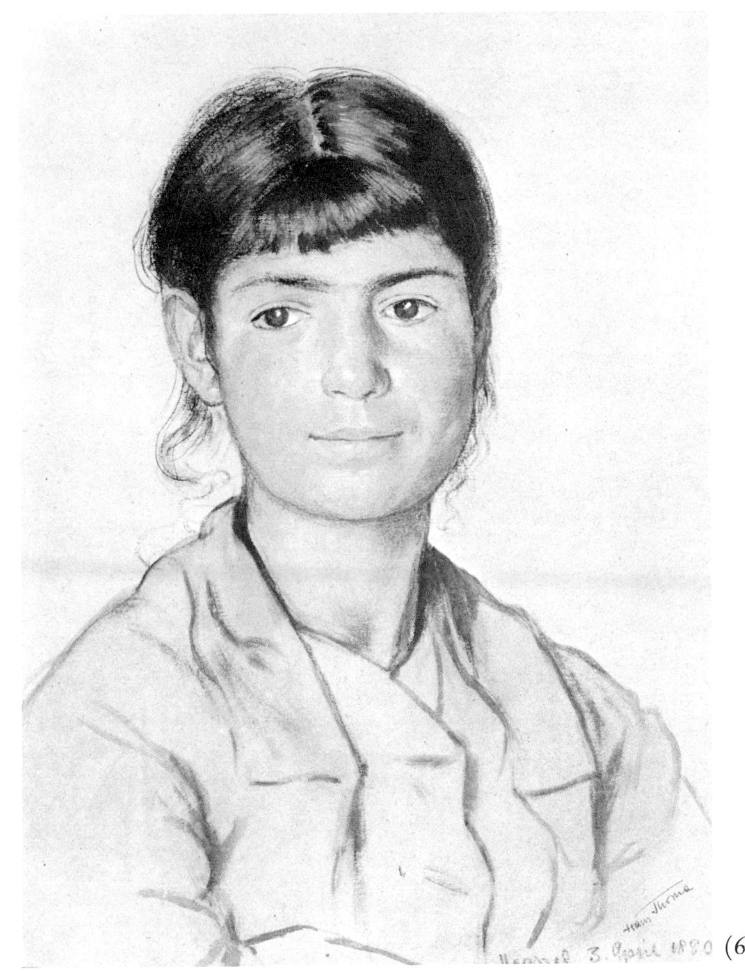

(61)

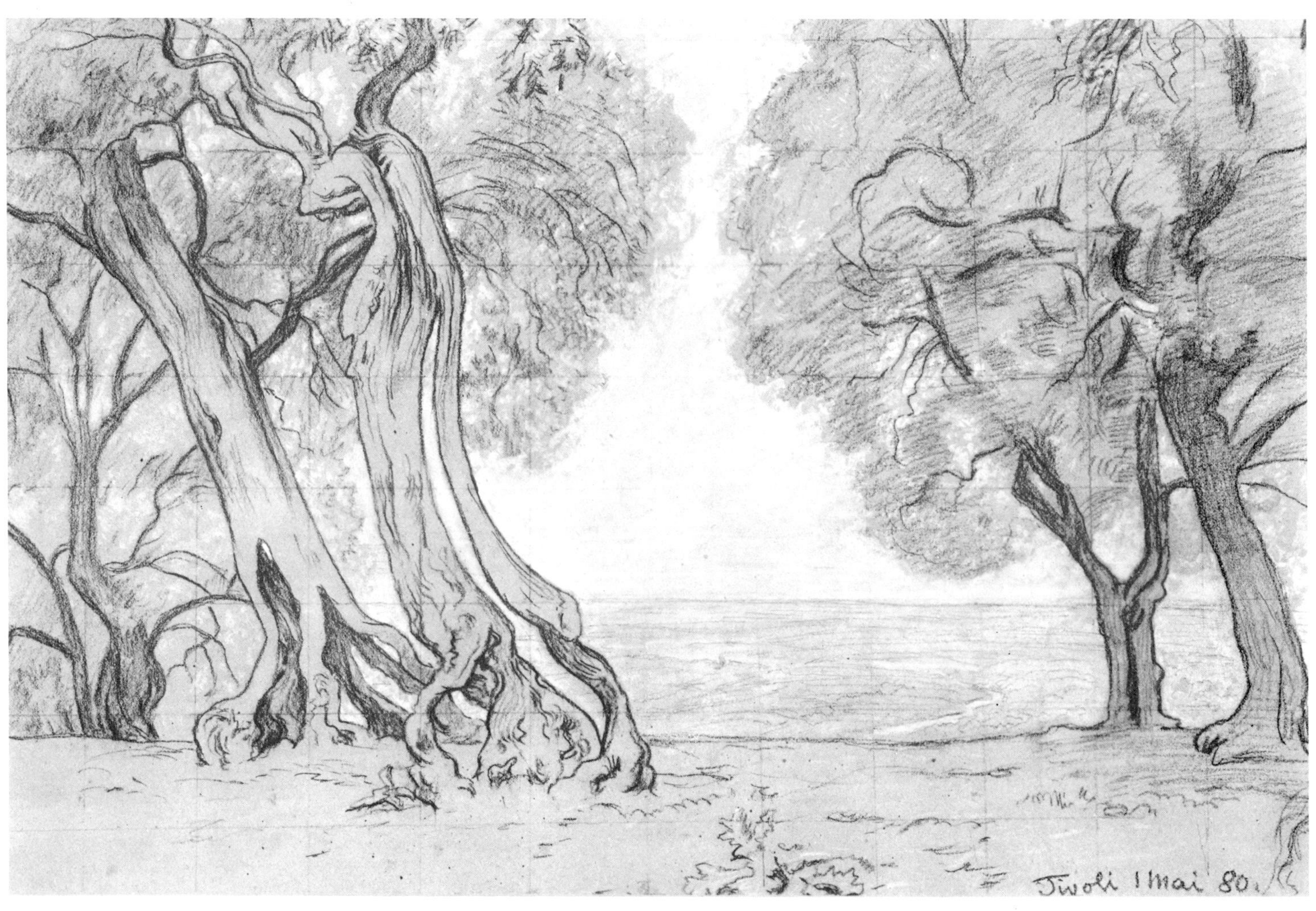

(62)

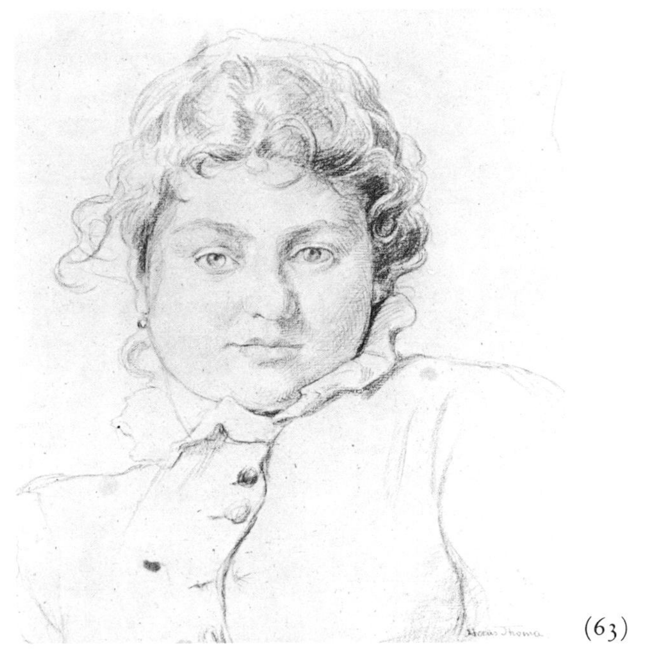

(63)

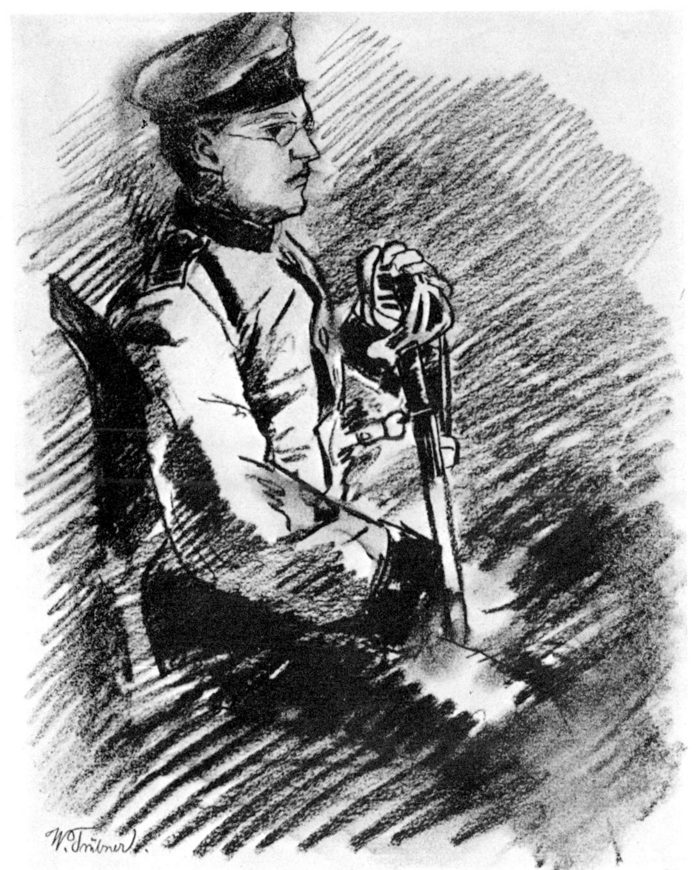

(64)

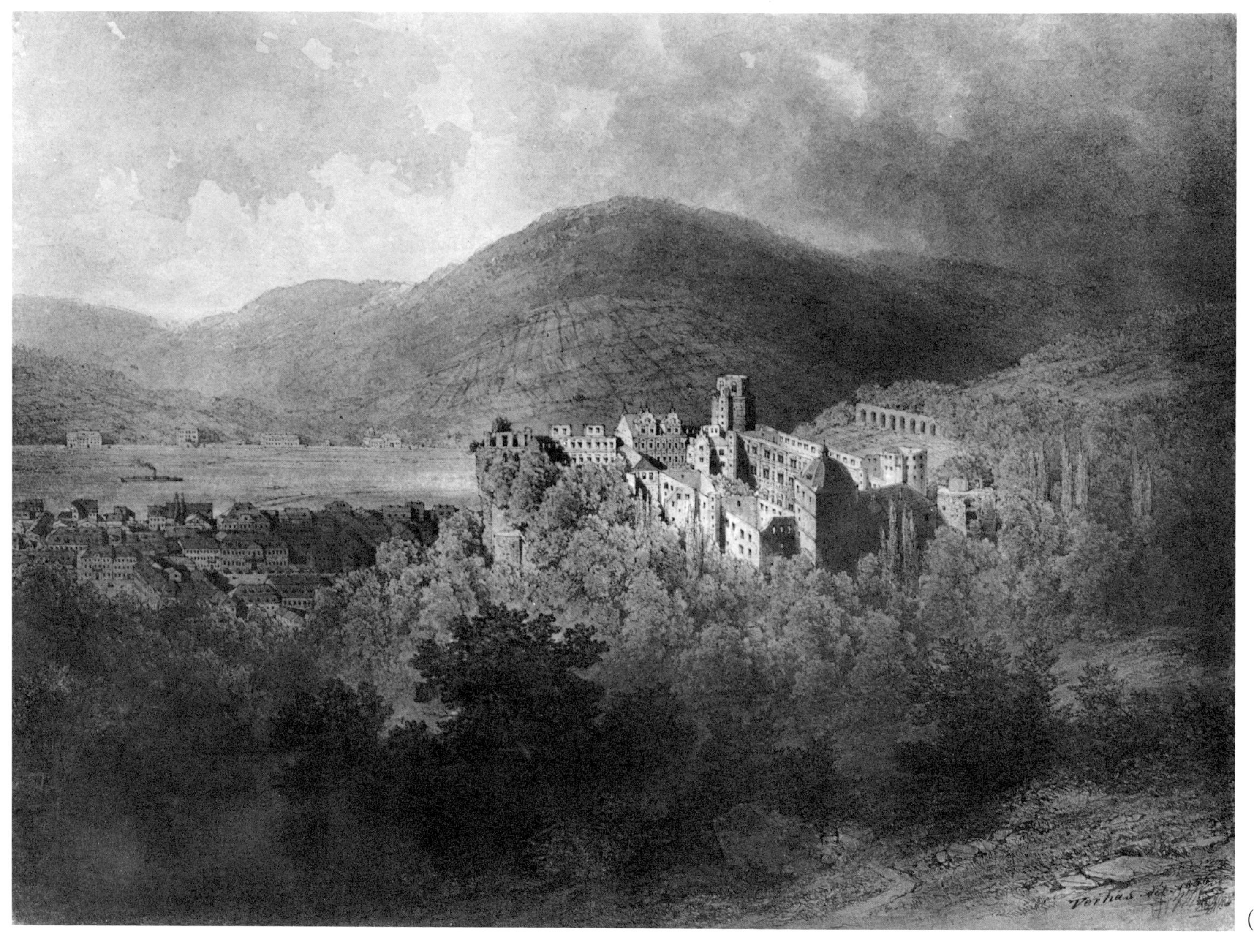

(65)

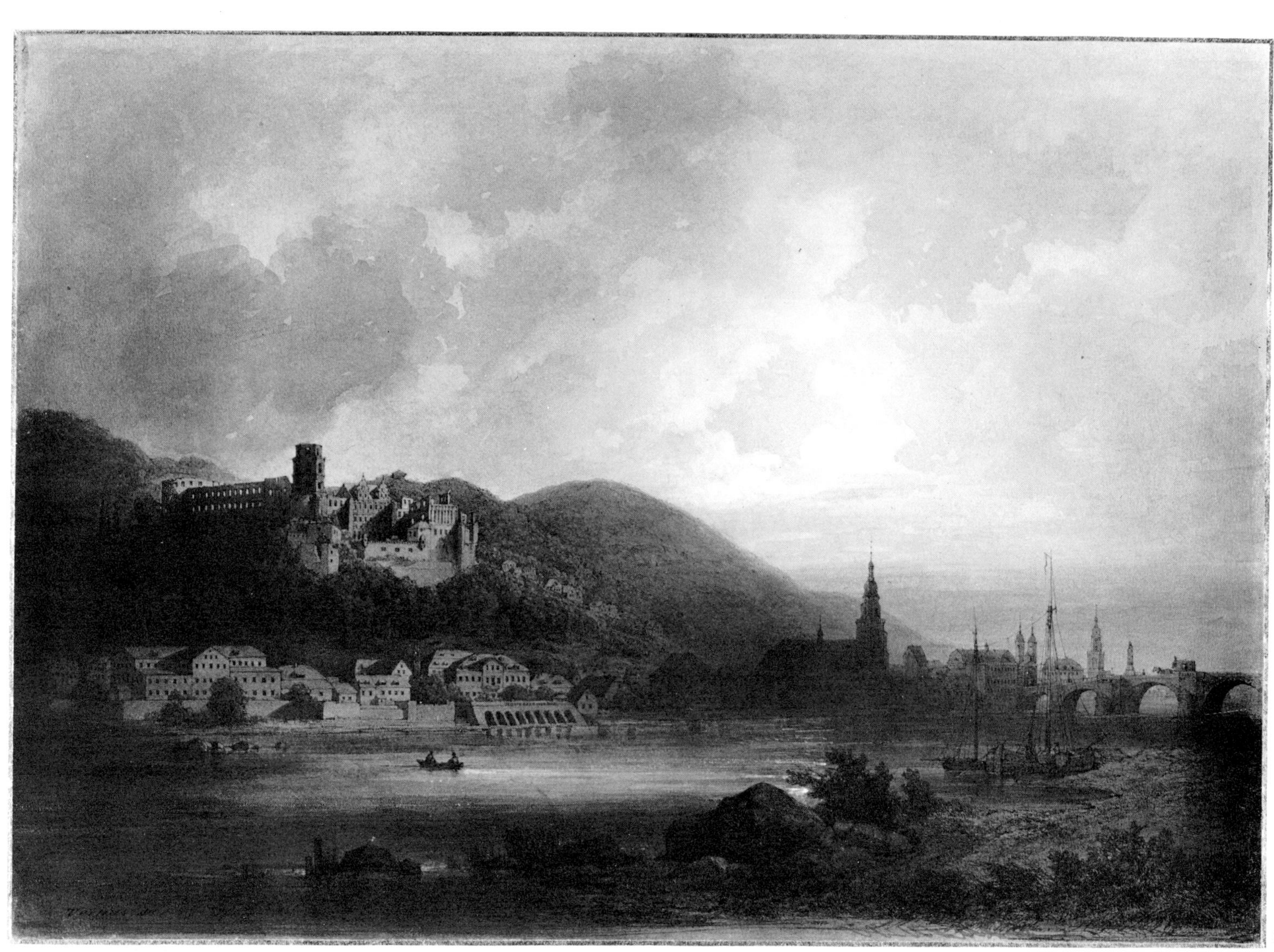

(66)

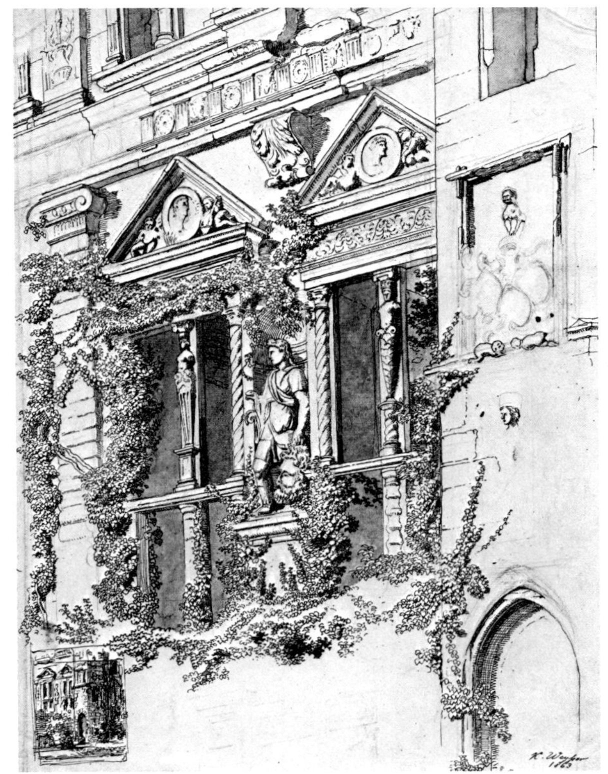

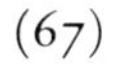

(67)

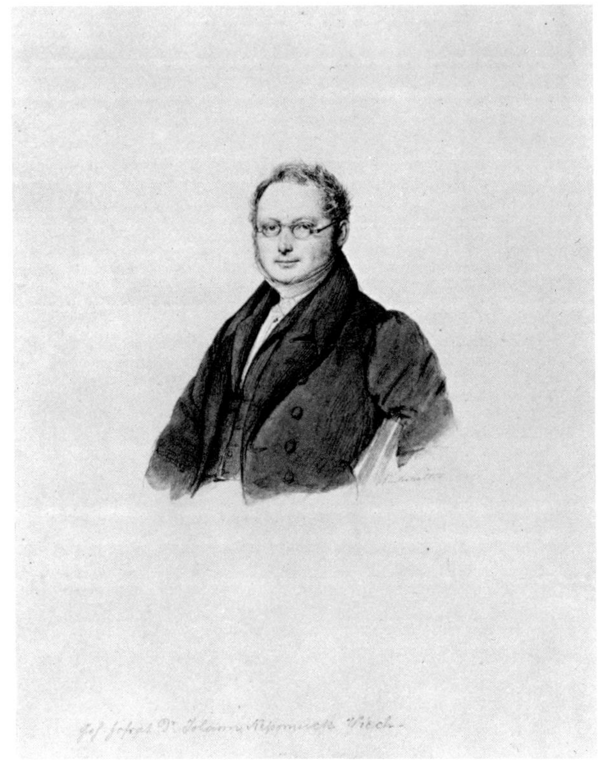

(68)

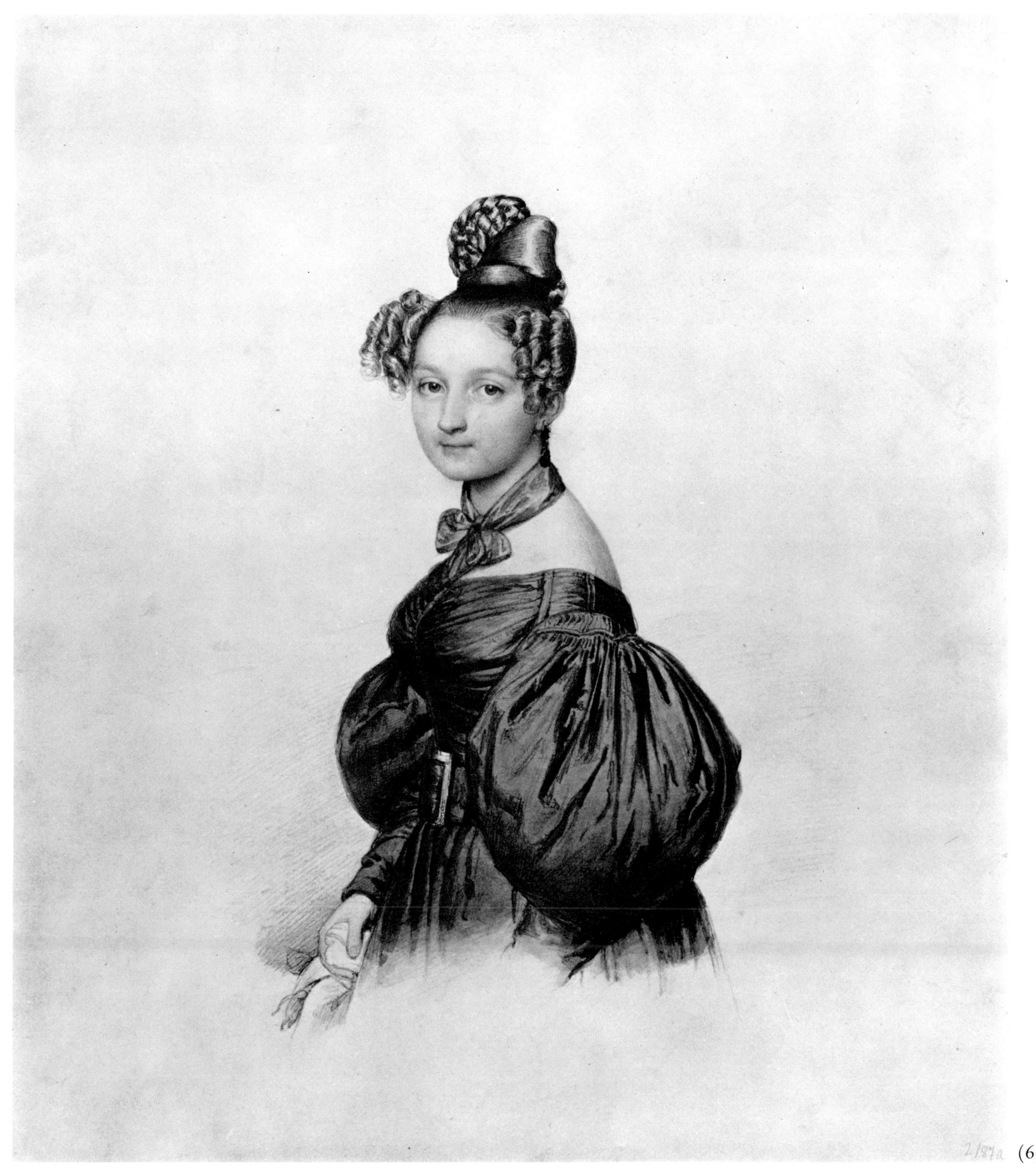

2/87a (69)

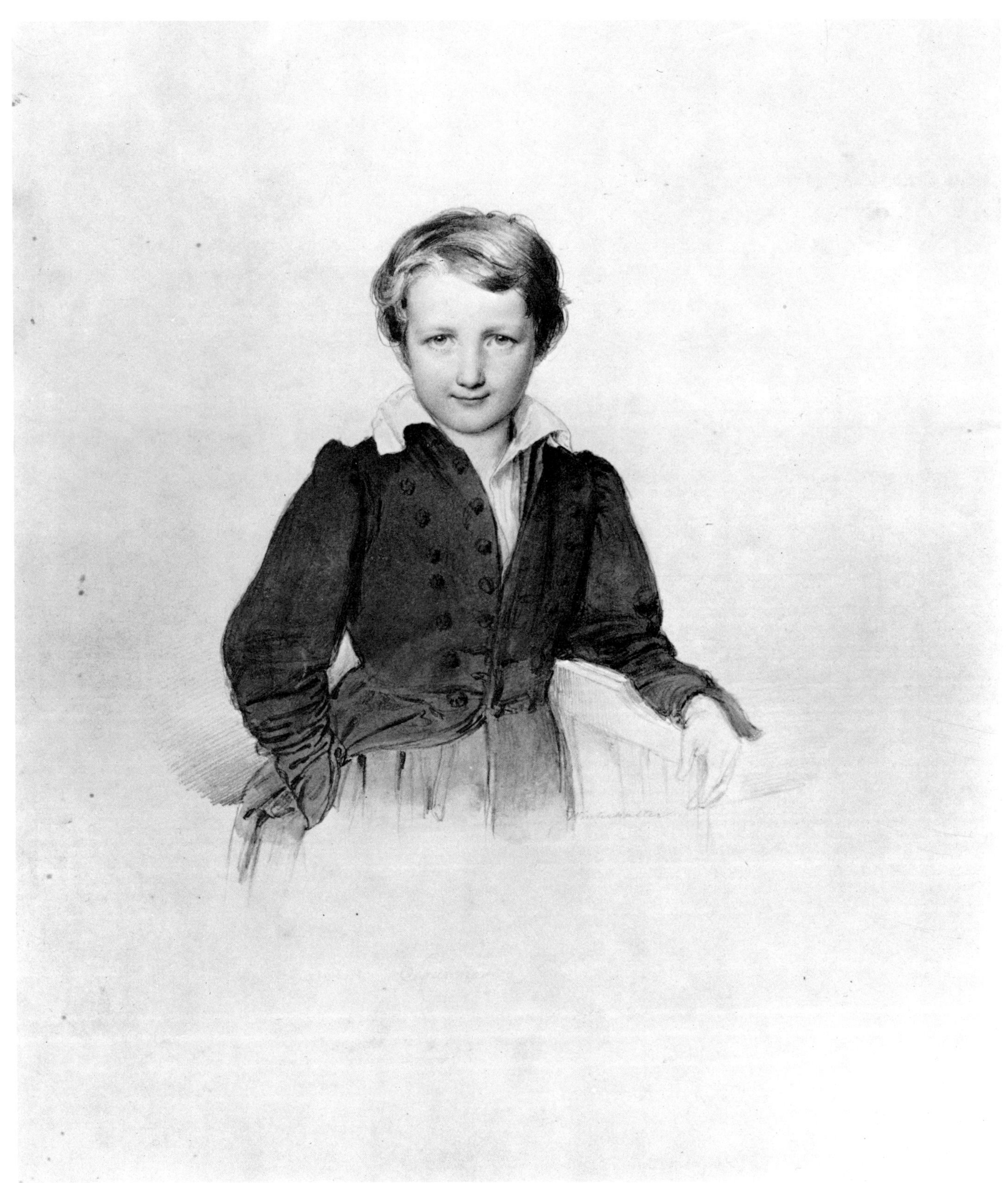

(70)

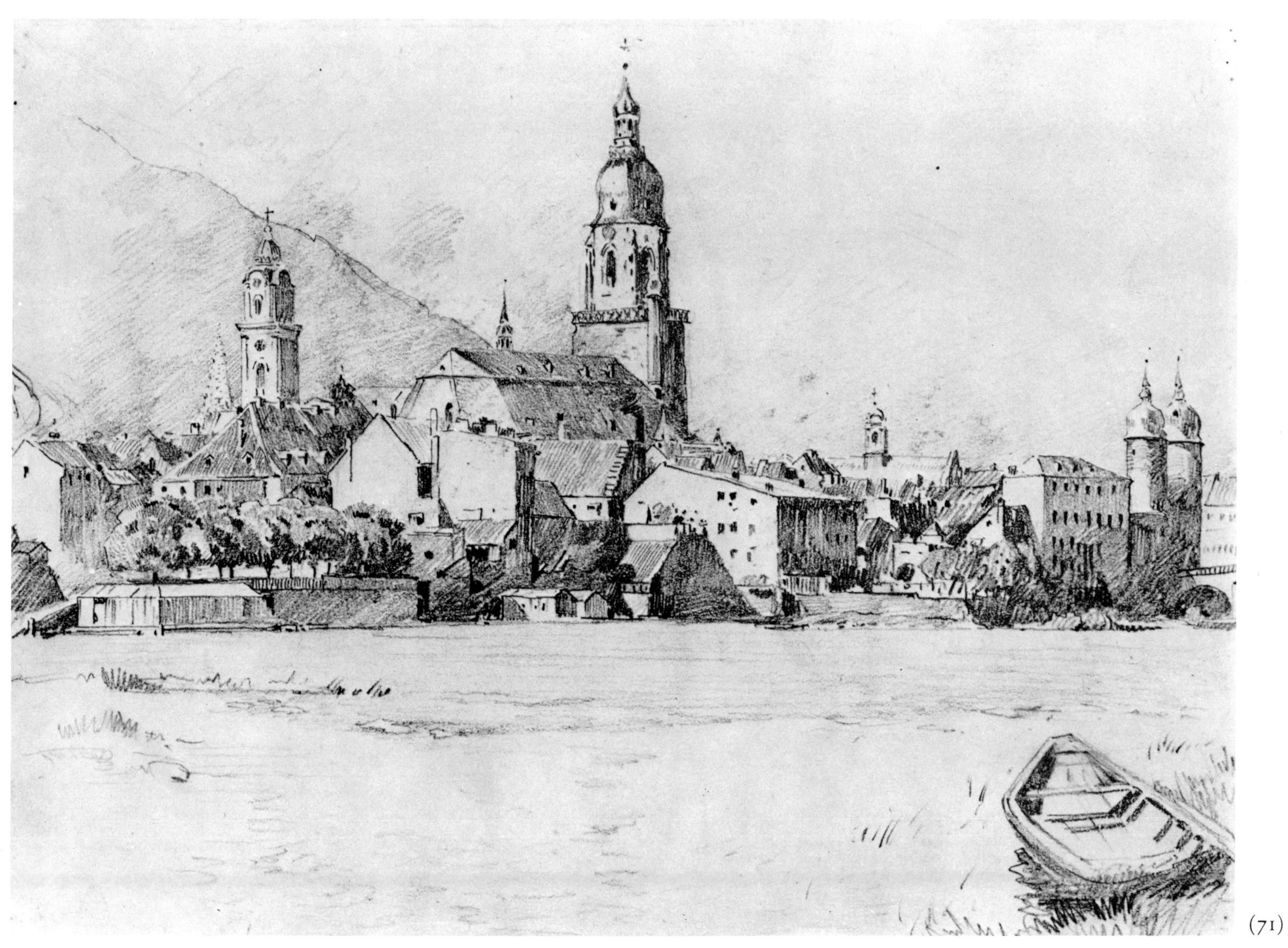

(71)

Index of Artists

Pages refer to biographies and entries.
Italicized pages denote illustrations.